SELLING
THE
WILD WEST

SELLING

THE

WILD WEST

Popular Western Fiction, 1860 to 1960

CHRISTINE BOLD

*Indiana
University
Press*

BLOOMINGTON AND INDIANAPOLIS

Manufactured in the United States of America

Library of Congress Cataloging-in-Publication Data
Bold, Christine, 1955–
    Selling the Wild West: popular western fiction,
1860 to 1960.
    Bibliography: p.
    Includes index.
    1. Western stories—History and criticism.
2. American fiction—West (U.S.)—History and
criticism. 3. Popular literature—United States—
History and criticism. 4. American fiction—19th
century—History and criticism. 5. American fiction—20th century—History and criticism. I. Title.
PS374.W4B65 1987   813'.0874'09   85-45581
ISBN 0-253-35151-0

1 2 3 4 5 90 89 88 87

To my mother

CONTENTS

Illustrations

Acknowledgments

I would like to thank the archival staff of the following institutions: the Rare Books and Manuscripts Division, the New York Public Library; the Manuscripts Division and Rare Books Department, the Library of Congress; the George Arents Research Library, the University of Syracuse; the Western History Research Center, the University of Wyoming; the Manuscripts Division, the Nebraska State Historical Society; and the Western History Department, Denver Public Library. I also thank Dr. Loren Grey for permission to quote from Zane Grey's diary, and Mrs. Walter Stokes for permission to quote from Owen Wister's correspondence and notebooks. A version of chapter one was first published in the *Journal of American Studies*, vol. 17, no. 1 (April 1983), pp. 29–46, and appears here by permission of the editors and Cambridge University Press. Part of chapter two appeared in *Western American Literature*, vol. 17, no. 2 (Summer 1982), pp. 117–35, and is reprinted here by permission of the Western Literature Association.

The preparation of this study was made possible by generous travel grants from the University of London Central Research Fund, the Scottish Education Department, and the Christie Bequest, University of Edinburgh.

I benefited greatly from the insights and encouragement of a number of scholars. In particular, I wish to thank Professor Stephen Fender, Professor Eric Mottram, Dr. Mick Gidley, and Jenni Calder for their rigorous reading of various drafts of this work. Michael Cleary, Jane Easton, Richard Etulain, Robert Gale, Loren Grey, Alden Norton, Tom Pilkington, Damarus Rowland, Henry Steeger, and Gary Topping were kind enough to furnish me with information about popular Western authors. Above all, I owe a debt of gratitude to Wesley Wark, who was always generous with his time and incisive in his comments on my many revisions. To him I give my warmest thanks.

Introduction

It is a nice irony that the authors who immortalized the Western hero transcending the boundaries of law and human fallibility themselves worked under all kinds of constraints. When mass publishing took off in America in the mid-nineteenth century, Western fiction became one of the most saleable genres and thus attracted huge numbers of writers. The large-scale production of popular literature made a few of these authors very rich and gave many a comfortable living, but it exerted on all a regimentation and standardization which directly affected the content of their fiction. However, some authors found a partial escape from these restrictions, through the form of their work. From time to time throughout the decades of the formulaic Western's popularity, certain authors implanted in their presentation of conventional plots signs of either their own authorial individuality, or their attempts to transcend the limitations of the genre, or their defiance of patterning. In every case, the form of the popular Western novel tells a more individual and unpredictable story than does its content.

Popular Western authors inherited their fictional materials from James Fenimore Cooper, who left them an emphatically dualistic model. In his *Leatherstocking Tales*, Cooper created a series of plots which dramatize the confrontation between wilderness and civilization, as well as the trials of the Western hero caught between these contending forces. He also underlined the oppositions enacted in the plot, by stressing counterpoint and division in his settings, his characters, and even his literary method. Thus, the setting is consistently made up of two adjacent, contrasting areas between which Natty Bumppo moves, such as the wilderness surrounding the lake dwelling in *The Deerslayer* (1841); and this composition is echoed in dramatic set pieces, like the final scene of *The Prairie* (1827), in which the dying Natty sits between one red and one white man. Certain characters also embody contrast: John Mohegan's speech and behavior in *The Pioneers* (1823) portray the war between savagery and civilization in his makeup, and Natty's costume, with its mixture of Indian finery and homespun, symbolizes his role as mediator. Finally, the author conjoins contrasting literary forms. As Henry Nash Smith and others have noted, when Cooper took up the new Western material he did not create a new literary form for it, but instead fitted the new images and themes, as far as they would go, into the traditional mold of the historical romance.[1] Thus, he maintained two plots and a double cast: the love story between a genteel heroine and an upper-class hero for the traditional romance, and the violent adventures of the ungenteel wilderness man for the frontier saga. This dualism, like the other formal details, emphasizes the theme of polarization: by conjoining the two sets of literary types, the author demonstrates their difference; and when he causes a character to stray into the sphere of the opposite literary form (as with Natty in his two love affairs) the point is the awkwardness of the match.

This, then, is the legacy which Cooper left to Western fiction: an emphasis on dualism in both content and form. In his own time, he was imitated by various minor writers. One example was Robert Montgomery Bird, who wrote a novel which copies closely Cooper's plot and cast, having both a wilderness figure to lead the adventurous action and an Eastern hero to participate in the love story. However, *Nick of the Woods* (1837) portrays the power of division more explosively than the *Leatherstocking Tales*: Bird's frontiersman is Nathan Slaughter, a Quaker and Indian-killer, in whom the competing forces of wilderness and civilization have created a savage, self-destructive schizophrenia.

From about 1860, imitations of Cooper's fiction appeared with such frequency and popularity that the pattern became established as a formula. From this point, although the oppositions in both content and form remained a crucial structuring principle, the dynamics of formularization also became important. Western authors began to juggle with convention and invention in the way described by John Cawelti.[2] In order to fulfill audience expectations, they adhered to the archetypal story pattern of the Western genre; at the same time, in order to provide a degree of excitement and suspense, they sometimes rang changes on details of setting, character, or plot, usually in response to the cultural climate. Thus, Cawelti demonstrates that the formulaic Western always concerns a clash between wilderness and civilization on the frontier; its cast is consistently arranged into the tripartite division of townspeople, savages, and the intermediate hero; and the major plot pattern has the hero resolving conflict between the townspeople and the villains, usually by participating in a sequence of capture, flight, and pursuit. Details of time, place, and character receive different emphases in different cultural milieux. For example, when the Western region came to be seen as an alternative to the industrialized East at the end of the nineteenth century, the fictional West changed from Cooper's untamed wilderness into a virile, healthy society. Later, when the actual West did not seem to be living up to its promise, the fictional scene became a symbolic, fantastical West in which heroic characters enforce traditional morality. Later still, as modern corporatism was seen to be erasing traditional values, popular fiction came to emphasize the elegiac quality of a West in which individualism has been destroyed by the powerful social forces of modern life. Cawelti's analysis shows that Cooper's plot of Western conflict is repeated over and over again in the nineteenth and twentieth centuries, though it is costumed slightly differently in different periods.

The cultural adjustments in the content of popular Westerns, which have been traced by Henry Nash Smith as well as Cawelti and both critics' followers, amount to a collective evolution of the genre by popular Western authors.[3] However, there is another, previously unexplored set of developments at work in the Western genre at a much more individual authorial level. What can be seen in the form of much Western fiction are innovations and variations which correspond to authors' individual reactions to their task, often to their positions within the publishing machine. Western authors were particularly affected by the rise of mass publishing in the United States, which began when technological inventions in printing and transportation came together with a vast literate audience, around 1860. In every phase of mass publishing, the Western has figured as the best-selling genre for a time; thus popular Western authors came in close contact with the characteristic principle of mass production—that profits come from large numbers of standardized goods.[4] All facets of commercial publishing firms were marked by this concentration on regimented uniformity: editors looked out for a successful literary formula, then supervised rapid repetitions of it until the readers showed that they had tired of that pattern; publishers packaged series of books and magazines in uniform covers which were instantly recognizable to consumers at newsstands and, later, supermarkets; distributors regularized prices, at low levels made possible by vast sales; and when advertisers became involved in the process, by paying for space in magazines, they sought guarantees that their appeals were reaching consistent numbers and types of readers. These various pressures ultimately devolved on the author, in the shape of either explicit or implicit demands that he produce reliable, formulaic fiction as efficiently as possible. All the authors who were successful commercially submitted to this marketplace dictum, but some of them managed to temper their conformity by developing variations of rhetoric or style in their presentation of their material. The resulting interplay between conventional patterns and individual initiatives constitutes the most dynamic element of the Western formula, changing as it does with different publishing innovations and different authors' reactions.

Chapter by chapter, this study examines some results of this authorial ingenuity throughout the decades. The first profitable mass literature in the United States was the Beadle dime novels, in 1860. Because enthusiasm for the West coincided with the technical innovations which made mass production and mass distribution possible, Westerns were the most numerous and most popular type of dime novel. Dime publishers could sell their novels at low prices because they used cheap materials and they regimented the production of their fiction, at first mainly in terms of its length and moral tone, but later in terms of its specific content, too. This commitment to standardization curtailed authors' range of artistic choices. The most interesting dime novelists are those who turned this limitation to their own advantage: Ned Buntline, Edward Ellis, Prentiss Ingraham, and Edward Wheeler managed to exploit their commercial status as servants of the marketplace to mark their fairly mechanical stories with their own authorial personalities.

In the twentieth century, pulp magazines took over from dime novels as the main commercial vehicle for Western fiction. These publications were produced under much the same system as dime novels, but they made their commercialism more blatant in their format: pulp magazines incorporated some advertising, and they regularly featured negotiations between editors and readers regarding fictional content. Pulp authors found that the paraphernalia of commercial publishing encroached increasingly on their work. Chapter one looks at the rhetoric developed by some dime novelists and the ways in which authorial strategies were eroded in the writings of pulp authors, as publishing demands became increasingly stringent.

At almost the same time as pulp magazines began, there came into being another type of magazine, called "slick" because it was made of good quality, coated paper. These publications featured genre fiction which was similar to that in the pulps, but they were more sophisticated in their presentation and their marketing techniques. With a profusion of colorful illustrations, slicks were much more expensive to produce than pulps, but they kept their prices down by attracting a great deal of advertising revenue. Advertisers wanted proof that they were paying for exposure to the right kind of audience and so, from the late 1920s, many slick publishers developed market surveys. All this meant that, while slick magazines did not feature the blatant sales appeals of the pulps, they were heavily involved in the economics of the marketplace. Chapter three looks at three major writers of popular Westerns—Zane Grey, Max Brand, and Ernest Haycox—who published in both the pulps and the slicks. The chapter considers to what extent and in what ways the commercial environment established by these magazines is echoed in these authors' narratives.

The last major publishing event which is relevant here is the "paperback revolution" which, in America, took off in 1939 with Robert de Graff's Pocket Books. In many ways, mass-market paperbacks are reminiscent of dime novels: they are complete novels, bound in paper and pocket-sized, with illustrated covers featuring the series insignia, sold at low prices. But in the economics of modern paperback publishing, the ante has been raised considerably. Twentieth-century America has a much larger population—thus many more potential consumers—than in the nineteenth century, there are a vastly increased number of sales outlets, and merchandising techniques have become much more aggressive. Chapter four looks at three Western authors who wrote at the time of the "paperback revolution" and can be seen to respond to the repetitiveness of mass production. Alan Le May had only average success commercially, but he identified and exploited the formulaic mechanism central to the successful reduplication of the popular Western. Jack Schaefer deliberately turned away from commercial practices and created fine works which develop out of the Western formula but defy incorporation into the system of reproduction. Louis L'Amour was the only one of the three to become heavily involved in paperback "originals"; he has immersed himself in commercialism so successfully that he writes marketplace strategies into his Western novels.

There was one important moment in the development of the popular Western when historical circumstances affected the fictional form even more than commercial dictates. This occurred around the turn of the twentieth century, when the closing of the frontier was a widely discussed event throughout America. Two artists in particular—Owen Wister and Frederic Remington—carried their responses to the end of the frontier into popular fiction. They used the same kinds of characters, adventures, and settings as the formulists and, again, a struggle is perceptible in their presentation of this material. However, the terms of this friction are different from that in the dimes and pulps. What drove Wister and Remington was a desire to create, in stylized fiction, an alternative to the pattern of Western history. They struggled to present the Western archetypes in ways which would protect their own versions of the West from the changes happening on the real frontier. Chapter two explores the effects of this interplay on the details of Wister's and Remington's literary and visual works.

Finally, at what might be seen as another historic moment, all these limited attempts to undercut the conformity of commercial writing rose to the surface. In the 1960s, a very vocal segment of the American population began to rebel against the systematization and standardization of modern life. Many authors echoed this social movement by demonstrating their own disenchantment with conventional patterning in literature. Some of these authors chose the conventions of the Western as the butt of their rebellion, parodying a formula which they considered a major representative of illusory American traditions. These authors were, of course, a far cry from the popular formulists who constitute the main subject of this study. Nevertheless, the focus of their parodic fiction is the same tension between convention and invention which is hinted at by commercial writers over the years. Chapter five examines the ways in which some anti-Western novelists—particularly E. L. Doctorow, James Leo Herlihy, and Robert Ward—expose the problems which remain submerged and fragmentary in conventional Western fiction.

These, then, are the authors and concerns on which this study concentrates. It is not a survey of the publishing industry or of Western authors: I have included only those details of publishing history which seem immediately relevant to the context in which commercial authors worked; and there are many popular Western writers, like Mayne Reid, Eugene Manlove Rhodes, and Luke Short, who would be important additions to those considered here. Nor does this work deal with the film industry. From about the mid-1920s, best-selling Western authors regularly had novels adapted for cinema, and many of those whom I discuss from this later period were involved in filmmaking in concrete ways: Grey ran his own motion picture business for a short time; Brand, Le May and L'Amour wrote a number of scripts for Hollywood; and Haycox attended the filming of some of his novels. However, most of the changes which I chart in these authors' fiction bear no clear relation to the demands of the film industry. Story conferences in film studios concentrate on novels' plots and characters, the very features which change relatively little in Westerns over the hundred years.[5] The authors' different writing styles, in which I see the most important shifts, are not translated into the screen versions of their novels; on the other hand, they do seem to respond directly to the authors' attitudes toward communicating with their audiences through language. Of course, in general terms, the film industry must have had similar effects on the author to the publishing industry. When Max Brand's work, for example, was sucked into the "committee method" of film production in the 1930s and the editorial systems of the pulp magazines in the same period, the author was encountering two different instances of the same demand for formula.[6]

However numerous the causes, what I have found repeatedly in the writings of the best-selling authors under discussion is evidence of a tension between formula and individual initiatives. This tension is important because it reaffirms the conflict which is central to the Western theme. In early literature about adventures in the West, it is clear that a conflict between nature and culture is played out both in the plot and in the narrative technique. Thus, in the Leatherstocking cycle, the content describes the battle between wilderness and civilization on the frontier, while the form demonstrates the friction between Western material and Eastern conventions for expressing it. In the post-1860 Westerns, the plots become increasingly mechanical and convey less and less sense of any genuine battle. However, if the characters no longer act out dramatic struggles in these fictions, the authors still do. The ways in which these Westerns are narrated show that their authors are involved in a conflict analogous to that between nature and culture. The writers oppose the effects of civilization or culture in one of two ways. Less commercial writers, like Wister and Remington, are clearly concerned to arrest the domestication of the wild West. They resist the advance of civilization which they relate in their plots by creating their own, alternative patterns for the development of the West, in the form of their novels. When the commercial machine intervenes heavily between the authors and their material, in dime, pulp, and paperback productions, the formulists become less concerned with the survival of the wild West than with the fate of their own individualism.[7] Like the Western hero, they react against the imposition of restraining conventions, though in a very different way: they rebel fruitlessly and to a limited extent against the constrictions of formula, by tinkering with their presentation of their narratives.

Both authorial procedures mean that a version of the nature-culture debate is demonstrated in all these popular Westerns, though some express it more directly and more vividly than others. When authors become involved in popular and commercial writing, they do deal in imitation and systematization, and they produce the predictable plots which have been seen as almost subliterary in their lack of creativity. However, some authors also enter into an interplay with the conditions of their production and the materials of their fiction, and this dialogue is translated into their articulation of the adventure stories. When each author strives to create some individual variation within the formulaic outline, he creates a friction which represents the most significant drama in the Western. This friction is the main subject of this book.

SELLING
THE
WILD WEST

ONE

The Voice of the Fiction Factory in Dime and Pulp Westerns

> I define a hack as a man who refuses as a matter of principle to improve the production apparatus. . . .
>
> Walter Benjamin[1]

Writers of dime and pulp Westerns were always hacks, in Walter Benjamin's terms, because, from the beginning of the dime novel in 1860 to the end of the pulp magazine around 1950, they consistently subscribed to the conditions of labor in the "fiction factories." In producing mass literature, authors entered into a network of commercial relationships which included publishers, wholesale and retail distributors, advertisers, and, of course, readers. Each of these groups regarded the fictional product in a rather different way. Distributors considered it simply as merchandise whose unit price determined their own percentile payment, and when advertisers became involved in cheap literature, they saw it only as a vehicle for their messages to consumers. The attitudes of publishers and readers were somewhat more complex, since they varied through time with changes in marketplace conditions: in their search for profits, publishers at first concentrated on wooing the largest possible audience, but later turned their attention to advertisers also; and readers functioned mainly as buyers of the publications, but came to be encouraged to sell and contribute to them as well.

While all the participants in this evolving network impinged on the writers' role to some degree, the authors' most direct relationship was with the publishers. Hacks were hired by dime novel and, later, pulp magazine firms to churn out formulaic Westerns to their employers' stipulations. This they did without protest. Not only did they comply with publishers' directives by producing thousands of almost mechanically repetitive tales, variations on a single successful formula, but they even pointed out the advantages of regimented production, like its possible financial rewards. They contributed to a system of mass production which left them no room for the usual authorial decisions or opportunities for original creation.

Yet some dime novelists managed to invent a new kind of creativity out of their position of limited autonomy. They did this not by protesting against commercial conditions, but by exploiting the one authorial function left to them: the actual writing of the stories. While conforming to the frontier adventure formula, early dime novelists also created a storytelling voice to talk to the reader about the process of composition and the commercial contract. Later, as the marketing strategies of dime and pulp publishing became more complex, the authorial rhetoric diminished: the direct address by the narrator was blocked by the publishers. By that time, however, the business of the marketplace had become an inextricable part of the formulaic action.

Given the restrictions of their authorial task, the hacks' most significant accomplishment was managing to write into their Westerns their reactions to the publishing machine. Before discussing their individual commentaries, however, this chapter must consider the publishing system to which they were a response, then the formulaic fiction in which they were embedded. Finally, it will examine the strategies by which the most prolific Western authors articulated in their novels their own commercial status.

PUBLISHING CONDITIONS

The first dime novel house was run by the Beadles, from 1860 to 1898. Their primary marketing strategy was neither to concentrate on a specific content, nor to target a particular audience, but to standardize the packaging of their fiction.[2] This meant that, while their authors were part of a systematic production line, they were free to construct their own audience image and the details of their fiction.

Beadle dime novels were all adventure fiction, but they were a mixture of reprinted classics and original stories, and they covered a wide range of genres, the main one being the Western. As well as handling many different types of fiction, the publishers also, initially at least, directed their products at a wide range of the population: they advertised their books in the nationally influential *New York Tribune*; some of their publications were reviewed (favorably) in the highbrow *North American Review*; and they succeeded in reaching a huge audience which was heterogeneous in age, class, and geographical location.[3] Only toward the end of the firm's life did Beadle and Adams begin to cultivate a specific readership—boys.

The Beadles' major innovation, which distinguished them from the other firms that could claim to have invented the cheap weekly novel, was their establishment of a uniform series of complete, predominantly

American novels with a standardized packaging and price. Beadle's Dime Novels began in June 1860 with *Malaeska: The Indian Wife of the White Hunter* by Mrs. Ann S. Stephens. There was nothing new about the content, since the story was reprinted from an 1830s story-paper and the authoress was already widely popular; with this first dime novel, the firm's risk lay wholly in the format and price. Beadle and Adams marshalled all their fiction into series of pamphlets, each costing 10¢ or 5¢ and each having a distinctive cover design, made up of head matter, price, title, and increasingly sensational illustration. Since the major outlet for the dime novel was the newsstand, the recognizable format served as the firm's major selling point: the cover not only attracted buyers but also demonstrated visually that the product—the fiction—was reliable, consistent, yet exciting.

Beadle and Adams had regimented procedures for dealing with authors too. They had fixed payment rates and manuscript lengths: for a 35,000-word novel, all but the most famous authors were paid $75–$150 and for 70,000 words, $150–$300.[4] Once the publishers bought a manuscript, they acquired full rights over it and could present it according to their own system, with whatever embellishments they pleased. The case of Edward Wheeler shows that the firm could override an author's individuality for the sake of the standardization of their product. Wheeler was an author in the Beadle stable who wrote thirty-three issues of the very successful Deadwood Dick stories. When he died in 1885, the publishers kept his death an absolute secret, even from their regular authors, and coached other writers to continue the series with ninety-seven more "Deadwood Dick, Jr." stories, all with the byline "Edward Wheeler."[5] Both Wheeler and the substitute authors (some of whom have never been identified) were treated by the publishers as adjuncts to the successful product.

However, on the surviving evidence, it seems that the firm did not exert its control over its writers at the most detailed level. Certainly, the authors must have been strongly influenced by the atmosphere of commercial caution and conservatism within which they wrote, but, apparently, they were not given specific orders about what they should put in their fiction. Toward the end of the firm's life, to save money on woodcuts, authors were sometimes requested to concoct stories to suit preexistent illustrations. Generally, however, Orville J. Victor, the chief editor, enforced imperatives which were more moral than literary: the first two Beadle instructions to authors were, "We prohibit all things offensive to good taste in expression and incident" and "We prohibit subjects or characters that carry an immoral taint."[6] Also, it is certain that Beadle's first big success, *Seth Jones; or, The Captives of the Frontier* (1860) by Edward Ellis, came into the office unbidden, and the publishers contributed to its popularity by their sprightly advertising campaign, not

by any work on the story itself.[7] Finally, one Beadle author, Gilbert
Patten, records in his autobiography that he modelled his work on ex-
isting dime novels, but he does not mention the firm ever supplying him
with plot details or outlines.[8] The impression is that Beadle and Adams
were always most stringent in regimenting the presentation of the novels,
but supplied only general instructions on their content.

The principle of systematization penetrated much more deeply into
the relationships between publisher, editor, author, and audience in the
firm of Street and Smith. This was the longest-living pulp fiction firm.
It entered the dime novel field late, in 1889, but immediately became
Beadle's strongest competitor and survived into the 1950s as a publisher
of pulp magazines.

In their dime publishing, Street and Smith aimed much more exclusively than Beadle and Adams at a juvenile audience, as can be seen by
their novels' content, presentation, and advertising gimmicks. Their
Western fiction concentrates on the adventures of adolescents, whose
interests and morality are tailored to a young readership. Competition
with other cheap periodicals on the newsstands stimulated ever more
garish covers, depicting in full color boys and girls in heroic poses. Competition, too, accounted for a new sales strategy. Fiction was no longer
the only product sold by these publishers: Street and Smith started to
offer money and novelties to boys who read their publications and persuaded others to do likewise. They also incorporated a small amount of
advertising for trick gadgets and patent medicine. Yet, despite this de-
liberate tailoring, the publishers had no precise understanding of, or
control over, their readership. This is clear in a complaint by Smith in
1898, when he wrote to one of his authors to inform him of a failed
series. He said plaintively, "I do not think that the quality of the manuscripts is so much at fault as the character of the library itself, though
it is very difficult always to know just what the boys want."[9] Street and
Smith did try to clarify their picture of their audience by inviting readers
to write to their magazine editors about the quality of the publications,
but they did not use methodical market research and ultimately they
tapped audience response by trial and error and instinct.

Street and Smith were also more specific than the Beadles in their
requirements concerning content. They limited their editors' decision-
making powers and treated their authors quite dictatorially, too.[10] For
example, just when Street and Smith began producing dime fiction, one
writer in their stable created a detective, Nick Carter, who became popular immediately. The publishers wanted that author for another series,
so they assigned the writing of Nick Carter stories to Frederic Marma-
duke Van Rensselaer Dey. After several issues, Dey decided to have Nick
marry. When the publishers vetoed the idea, he smuggled the installment
past the copyreader. However, the printer's devil in the linotype room

read the episode while setting it, and he rushed off to the publishers, who made Dey rewrite the installment.[11]

A letter survives from 1896 which proves that the publishers' contribution to the fiction could be very detailed indeed. In that year, one of the firm's most successful series, Tip Top Weekly, began. Gilbert Patten was chosen to write the stories, under the house pseudonym, "Burt L. Standish," but the letter to Patten from Ormond Smith shows how small a hand the author had in creating either characters, plots, or scenes. Smith described his plans:

> the idea being to issue a library containing a series of stories covering this class of incident, in all of which will appear one prominent character surrounded by suitable satellites. It would be an advantage to the series to have introduced the Dutchman, the Negro, the Irishman, and any other dialect that you are familiar with. . . . It is important that the main character in the series should have a catchy name. . . . The essential idea of this series is to interest young readers in the career of a young man at a boarding school, preferably a military or a naval academy. . . . After the first twelve numbers, the hero is obliged to leave the academy, or takes it upon himself to leave. It is essential that he should come into a considerable amount of money at this period. When he leaves the academy he takes with him one of the professor's servants, a chum. In fact any of the characters you have introduced and made prominent in the story. A little love element would also not be amiss, though this is not particularly important.
>
> When the hero is once projected on his travels there is an infinite variety of incident to choose from. In the Island School Series, published by one of our London connections, you will find scenes of foreign travel, with color. This material you are at liberty to use freely, with our hero as the central character, of course, and up-to-date dialogue.
>
> After we run through twenty or thirty numbers of this, we would bring the hero back and have him go to college—say, Yale University; thence we could take him on his travels again to the South Seas or anywhere.
>
> If you can do the opening stories of school life, you will be able to do them all as we shall assist you in the matter of local color for the stories of travel.
>
> This letter will, of course, be held as confidential.[12]

One of the few inventions left to Patten was that of the "catchy name" Smith requested for "our hero"—the famous Frank Merriwell. Throughout the twenty years Patten wrote the Merriwell stories, the publishers continued to advise on details. Occasionally, Patten won an argument, such as one on a question of style; more often Street and Smith prevailed, as when they obliged him to introduce a younger half-brother when Frank outgrew his college days.[13] After Patten retired, the publishers instructed other writers in the production of Merriwell stories, molding from the contributions of many authors a uniform series, all under the byline "Burt L. Standish."

In his autobiography, one of these writers, William Wallace Cook, left an unusually full picture of authorship under Street and Smith. Cook wrote for Street and Smith, off and on, from 1893 to 1928. The tale is one of repeated quick-change artistry. At one moment, he would be required to write as "Stella Edwards" about *Bessie, the Beautiful Blind Girl*; halfway through the composition of that tale, he would be told to switch to an installment for a new detective library. In his autobiography, Cook transcribes some of the correspondence which he received from the publishers. This shows how they dissected his stories, approving certain incidents, discarding others, reminding him of formulaic requirements such as the inclusion of technological novelties or the one wedding which should occur at the opening of the story. Very often, Cook would be supplied with title, plot, and synopsis. The author, like the pen names and the series, belonged to the publishers; he was only one element in the material which they shaped for the market.

The evidence shows Street and Smith's general policy to have been the attempted targeting of a particular audience and the repeated interference with authorial decisions. This firm's supervision of production was clearly more demanding and specific than Beadle and Adams's. To be an author of their stories was to be a rather minor member of a collaboration, someone who followed orders in the very writing of the fiction.

Dime publishers themselves continually worked under a number of commercial pressures, which in turn conditioned their demands on authors. For instance, printers and paper suppliers demanded regular payment for their services, the monopoly distributors insisted on uniform prices, and the audience, unpredictable in terms of its specific tastes, always expected a steady diet of sensational reading. From time to time, additional regulatory pressures were imposed on publishers, underlining the tenuousness of their position. One example is afforded by the fate of Frank Tousey. Tousey began publishing dime novels in 1878, and by the twentieth century he was Street and Smith's biggest competitor in the dime novel field. Tousey fell afoul of the postmaster general. Any periodical publication depended on favorable postal rates for its profitable distribution to subscribers. The privilege of second-class mailing was controlled by the postmaster general, and his regulations concerned both the format and the content of periodicals. He ruled that publications must be issued regularly to a list of subscribers and must avoid obscene or inflammatory matter. Tousey first suffered in 1883, when sixty-six issues of his Wide Awake Library, all dealing with outlaws such as Jesse James, were banned by the postmaster general as incitement to murder. The scrutiny continued through the turn of the century, and under this pressure all the dime novel publishers subdued their content by about 1904. Next, however, the post office began to question the format of these novels, doubting their eligibility as magazines. From 1907 until 1913, Tousey juggled with his novels, adding short stories, news items, editorial pages, and advertisements. He even cut up the main story into disjointed sections, to make it look like a serial. Infuriating his audience more and more, he struggled to comply with postal regulations, but he repeatedly lost his mailing privilege and, increasingly, his public.[14] He could outmaneuver rival publishing houses, but not the nation's bureaucracy. This story illustrates how publishers, like writers, had to twist form and content to demands from above; authors were only the last stage in a line of directly exerted pressure.

Partly because of the postal restrictions, pulp magazines took over from dime novels after the First World War, bringing with them a new format and different editorial methods. These magazines were miscellanies of short and long fiction with various features like quizzes, letters pages, and factual articles. They contained more material than dime novels, they appeared weekly or monthly and they cost 10¢ or 15¢. Pulps had been invented in 1896, when Frank Munsey had the "economical notion" that people would pay for sensational stories, printed closely together on cheap pulpwood paper without illustrations.[15] At the beginning of the twentieth century, many publishers—Street and Smith included—followed his profitable example; but it was only after 1919, when pulps began to specialize, that they reached the height of their popularity. Street and Smith were first with that innovation, turning their New Buffalo Bill Weekly (itself a reprint series out of Buffalo Bill Stories) into the all-Western *Western Story Magazine*.

Pulp publishers cultivated advertising revenue more assiduously than the later dime publishers. In doing so, they experienced a new commercial pressure, which affected their relationship with their audience. Pulp magazines never included a huge number or a lavish display of advertisements, partly because the pulpwood paper format did not attract manufacturers in large numbers and partly because an overabundance of advertisements would have raised the shipping costs for the publishers. Nevertheless, they valued advertising enough to publish copy without charge until coupon returns proved to the advertisers that their magazines were effective vehicles.[16] One of the advertisers' main concerns was that their notices should be seen by readers likely to buy their products. Ensuring that the right kind of copy was put before the right kind of reader was mainly the task of the advertising agencies, which used their experience and, sometimes, market research to identify the reading and buying habits of different segments of the population.[17] But many pulp publishers also became caught up in the attempt to prove their product's worth by identifying their audience. Occasionally a pulp publisher conducted his own market surveys: one such was mounted by Popular Publications, who found that their typical reader was a young, married man in a manual job who had limited resources and lived in an industrial town; however, at least one of Popular's editors considered that this information "did practically nothing useful for the firm."[18] It was more usual for pulp publishers and editors to try to gauge and manipulate audience response directly, through the letters pages and editorial columns of the magazines. These overtures affected the content substantially, and they will be discussed in detail in a later section which considers the development of the magazines' literary form. Suffice it here to say that publishers did manage to characterize and systematize their audience's responses to a large extent.

The concentration of editorial ingenuity on audience and advertisers may well account for the relative slackening in the supervision of authors. Pulp publishers did establish a uniform payment rate—of 2¢ and, later, 1¢ per word—for the run of pulp contributors and they regulated manuscript lengths at either 5,000 words for a story, 30,000 words for a novelette, or 60,000 words for a serial. Moreover, it was not unknown for pulp publishers and editors to provide ideas for their authors: one *Wild West Weekly* contributor has said that the magazine's earliest heroes were concocted in outline by the editor; and an artist for Popular Publications has described the publisher, editor, and himself hashing out an idea for an illustration, to which an author had to fit a story.[19] Nevertheless, publishers and editors did not supply authors with detailed scenarios. Frank Gruber, a pulp writer who sold stories to Street and Smith, Popular Publications, and Standard Magazines in the 1930s, described his experience of editorial policy:

> No editor has ever given me a plot or the smallest hint of an idea. No editor has ever contributed anything to any of my writing. . . . Oh, they've criticized me and at times made me rewrite things, and I did it. But. . . I do not believe that one single editor has ever contributed anything to the craft or skill of any single writer at any time.[20]

That description has been corroborated recently by Henry Steeger, who began Popular Publications in 1930, and Alden Norton, editor of many of Popular's Western magazines. They insist that, in the Western field, the author had almost complete autonomy. While his stories would be subject to copy editing, there existed no dictation of character or collaboration on events, such as prevailed in Street and Smith at the time of the dime novel.[21] Norton further confirms that the editor had complete freedom from the publisher in selecting the material for his magazine.

This return to relative authorial freedom did not indicate any influx of experimentation, as the stories themselves attest: they are sensationalized versions of dime novels and just as homogeneous and convention-ridden as the earlier fiction. The relaxation of editorial control was merely a sign that the conventions of cheap fiction were now so firmly entrenched that their production needed only perfunctory surveillance. Indeed, Harold Hersey, another pulp Western editor and publisher, has said that he could give his authors carte blanche, precisely because they had trained themselves to despise "that inspiration and individuality in self-expression which are so precious to the serious artist and so utterly worthless to the quantity writer."[22]

The pulp magazine died as a popular form around 1950, although short-lived resurrections, like *Zane Grey's Western Magazine*, occurred in the early 1970s; there was even a new, all-fiction Western magazine launched as recently as 1978. Competition from television is usually cited as the main cause of the pulps' demise. However, Daisy Bacon, who was an editor at Street and Smith and whose magazines (*Romantic Range, Detective Story*, and *Love Story*) collapsed about 1949, blamed the methods of production. She said that the new ranks of management in the pulp houses gave all their attention to production techniques and none to the magazines' writers and readers:

> Changes were designed for easy running company management and to eliminate all the risks that are associated with printing words on paper. . . .
>
> Mention any of these magazine publishers, and it will be said: "It was too bad, but they just couldn't buck television." I believe, however, that if surveys were made it would be found that the real trouble was that the magazines couldn't buck their *publishers*! These people—business managers, sales managers, financial analysts and whatever—were perhaps good in their own line of work, but they were not publishers nor likely candidates ever to be. They took the magazines off course into alien and uncharted waters and in the process they killed the goose that laid the golden egg.[23]

It would seem that the goal which inspired Beadle and Adams's first dime novel series—the desire to create a profitable publishing machine— was also the main cause of the pulp magazine's death.

In terms of the dime and pulp authors' experience, the most important thread running through all the publishers' methods is their attempt to flood the market quickly and cheaply with as many saleable novels as possible. In order to do this, publishers and editors systematized production increasingly. From 1860, Beadle and Adams channeled their authors' contributions into uniform packages. When Street and Smith won the market around 1889, they supervised their writers much more closely than Beadle, taking over more and more authorial decisions. After the First World War, by which time the formula was well established, pulp editors switched their most intense surveillance from authors to audience. The authors who entered the dime and pulp system always worked according to general rules of imitation and reproduction. To greater and lesser degrees, they also had to negotiate with their publishers over details of plot, characterization and scene, while the publishers, in turn, might be busy negotiating with both the overseeing authorities and the audience. The result was that, throughout the life of the genre, the actual writing of the fiction was conditioned on all sides by accumulating levels of constraint.

THE WESTERN FORMULA

The fictional formulas at the center of these commercial negotiations certainly seem marked by the general constraint and conformity of mass production. Dime and pulp novelists inherited their character and plot materials from James Fenimore Cooper, but where he dealt with social conflict and historical inevitability, they concentrated primarily on ritualistic adventure. The result was that, for almost a century, the majority of dime and pulp writers treated the Leatherstocking model in the same fashion: they attempted to imitate it in such a way that the tension between East and West was erased.

The repetitions built into the search for easy entertainment are perhaps best illustrated by the dime and pulp characterization of the Western hero. Each dime novel house I have mentioned—Beadle and Adams, Street and Smith, and Frank Tousey—produced at least one fictional hero who gained a cult readership in his time and whose name remains today a byword for the melodramatic Westerner. The model behind these heroes is clearly Leatherstocking. However, Cooper's portrait emphasizes the irresolvable conflict between East and West in the frontier hero and his unfitness for the romantic role; the dime novelists copy the outlines of Cooper's figure, but they water down the opposition between culture and nature in the heroic character. A detailed consideration of the Western characters created by some prolific dime novelists over the years shows how one author after another tries out strategies for creating a Western hero without confronting the problem of conflicting Eastern and Western values. Ultimately, all of them come up with the same solution: they present a hero who turns out to be an Easterner or, at least, has a large amount of Eastern gloss. However, the various ways in which the different authors arrive at this final balance are instructive of the constraints which standardized publishing methods could put on fictional content.

Edward S. Ellis produced the paradigmatic Western dime novel and Beadle and Co.'s first bestseller when he wrote *Seth Jones; or, The Captives of the Frontier* (Beadle's Dime Novels, no. 8, June 1860). The novel stays close to Fenimore Cooper's Leatherstocking tales in plot, characters, and setting. In the forests of western New York State, the Mohawks capture a settler's daughter. Seth Jones, a garrulous, avuncular and, on one occasion, violent frontiersman, goes to Ina's rescue, accompanied by her father, her Eastern lover, and an Indian-fighter who is bent on revenge for the massacre of his family. After various chases, escapes, and rescues, the party arrives safely at a settlement, where Seth reveals that he is not really an uncultured frontiersman. He is Eugene Morton, an Eastern gentleman and the fiancé of Ina's aunt Mary, who has disguised himself for his foray into the backwoods. The novel ends with a triple wedding, involving Morton and Mary, Ina and her lover, and a couple of comic villagers.

Obviously, the cast and the plot owe much to both the Leatherstocking cycle and *Nick of the Woods*. But Ellis circumvents the major source of tension in Cooper and Bird: the frontiersman's opposing tendencies toward savagery and civilization. While Cooper stresses this dilemma in his theme, characterization and narrative technique, Ellis resolves it artificially, by means of disguise. He only pretends to bring the savage hunter and the genteel Easterner together in one person: because Seth's physical metamorphosis near the end is unbelievable, there is no true sense that Seth Jones and Eugene Morton are one person. Moreover, as one character realizes, the two types are not fused at all:

I am puzzled to know who [Seth] is. It seems to me that he is only playing a part. Several times in conversing with him, he has used language such as none but a scholar and polished gentleman would use. At others and most of the time, he uses that ungainly mode of expression, which, in itself, is laughable.[24]

Ellis never repeated that character device—reverting, thereafter, to the partnership of Eastern love hero and Western frontiersman—but its presence in his first novel is symptomatic of the lack of genuine conflict in his work. From Cooper, he retained only the action of attack, captivity, and pursuit. He repeated that pattern of action almost exactly, with very similar casts, in the hundreds of dime novels which he wrote between 1860 and 1874. (For example, in his earliest novels, his only villains are red men. When, later, he occasionally introduced white villains, he disguised them heavily as Indians for most of the story.) Thus, his plots constitute purely ritualized conflicts with set moves and predictable endings. In introducing this plot and the disguised Western hero, Ellis created the axis around which subsequent Western dime novels revolve.

Ned Buntline's Western tales are generally more sensational and more complicated versions of Ellis's, but they bring one innovation to the Western scene, by introducing Buffalo Bill as the main hero. Buntline discovered William Cody in Nebraska in 1869 and decided to make him a star. He first used him as the hero of a novel in *Buffalo Bill, the King of Border Men!* which appeared in Street and Smith's *New York Weekly* in installments from December 1869 to March 1870. The story begins in Kansas, where the Southern villain, M'Kandlas, murders Mr. Cody, father of William and his twin sisters. The son vows revenge and he next appears several years later, when he takes part in the Civil War alongside Wild Bill Hickok. They scout for the Republican army, lead forays against the Sioux in the Black Hills, and arrest outlaws who are ravaging the Kansas-Missouri border. In the course of this action, Buffalo Bill pursues the villains who attacked his father and rescues various female members of his family from captivity. At the end, he participates in a triple wedding by marrying the daughter of an Eastern banker.

When Buntline put the native Westerner into the heroic role previously reserved for an Eastern gentleman, he did not break sharply with the other conventions of the romantic hero. For example, one important characteristic of the love hero is his avoidance of the gory; the Western frontiersman, older and coarser than the Easterner, always executes the bloodiest killings. Buntline still supplies the uncouth frontiersman in Wild Bill Hickok, who talks in frontier dialect, executes the villains, and dies at the end of the book. But by fitting Buffalo Bill into that conventional pattern, the author produces some awkward episodes. Buffalo Bill is strongly motivated by revenge—against M'Kandlas for murdering his father and against Dave Tutt for the abduction of his sister—and, as a skillful Western plainsman, he pursues them vigorously. Yet Wild Bill Hickok enacts the most dramatic individual confrontations and eventually kills both these men. Buffalo Bill can look somewhat superfluous in his chases after villains who, the reader knows, have already died at the hands of Wild Bill. When Buffalo Bill hears that his partner has beaten him to M'Kandlas, as well as Tutt, he begins a tortuous self-justification:

> Mate, I loved you before better than I loved my own life—I don't know how I can love you more. But if I ever have a chance to *die* for you, I'll laugh while I'm going. I should like to have given old Jake his dose, but it came just as good from your hand. He knew you and me were one.

Finally, however, he bursts out, "Thunder, Bill—you don't leave nothin' for me to do!"[25]

Buntline never seems quite at ease with his Western hero. In a later tale, Buffalo Bill leads Texas Jack, a scout, and Eugene Overton, an Eastern tenderfoot, to the rescue of two female emigrants who are held in Indian captivity. Bill disagrees with Texas Jack repeatedly over the interpretation of tracks and smoke signals and, although Bill is Jack's "boss" and evident leader, again and again Jack's plainscraft proves to be superior. Even Buntline, prime publicist for the new Western hero, could create only a transitional figure, a hero who exists somewhere between the Eastern love hero and the avuncular frontiersman, but is not yet surely placed. The hero's fluctuations suggest the dime author's hesitancy about making any changes to a successful formula.

Buntline and Cody fell out in 1873, and in 1879 Prentiss Ingraham took over as Buffalo Bill's "official" author by writing a play for him. In Ingraham's hands, Buffalo Bill loses his ambiguous status. He becomes "the hero of heroes" who is superior in plainscraft to all the frontiersmen around him, who can execute villains and who yet remains attractive to women. Ingraham manages to bring together the civilized and the savage in his hero by creating an exotic exterior for his violent plainsman. His Buffalo Bill is a much more flamboyant figure than Buntline's. He wears elaborate dress, fitted out with finely wrought ornamentation, and he is described as beautiful and even feminine. This is true of all Ingraham's Western heroes (other regulars are Wild Bill Hickok and Buck Taylor, "a cowboy dandy"). It is as if their Westernness is offset by the luxury of their dress and the beauty of their features, which imply a degree of civilized culture. These physical details carry special weight in Ingraham, because his fantastically complicated plots depend heavily on visual effects, like mysterious disguises and elaborate symbols in the form of tattoos, cryptograms and sign language. Ingraham created a hero who straddles categories which Ellis, and others, kept discrete, but he did not introduce any new material to the dime novel: his plots still revolve around captivities and rescues, and his heroes are composites of frontiersmen and gentlemen, though the emphasis is now more on their frontier qualities.

Edward Wheeler brought about perhaps the greatest shift in emphasis in the dime novel. He returned to the Eastern hero who operates in the West under a disguise, but the disguise involves a moral ambiguity which was the mark peculiar to Wheeler's fiction. He began Beadle's Half Dime Library with *Deadwood Dick, the Prince of the Road; or, The Black Rider of the Black Hills* in 1877. In the first installment, Ned Harris comes to Dakota from the East, where he has been ruined financially by the criminal activities of the Fillmores. He becomes a road agent, leading a double life—as Ned Harris living with his sister Anita in a secluded valley and as Deadwood Dick, the outlaw in black costume and mask who terrorizes the Black Hills with his violent gang. Various friends and enemies come West, most of them in disguise and all of them, it turns out, related to each other in some way. In the West already are various miners, outlaws, and ruffians who participate in the plot. There is also Calamity Jane, who has been seduced in the past and now leads a man's life, often helping Deadwood Dick out of danger. When all these characters come together, there are duels, captures, rescues, and escapes that finally culminate in the weddings of various Eastern lovers and the hanging of the Fillmores by Deadwood Dick and his gang. At the end, Dick proposes first to an Eastern woman, then to Calamity Jane, making marriage the condition by which he will return to his law-abiding life as Ned Harris.

Both women reject him and he leaves to roam the hills, living off the proceeds from his gold mine and vowing to continue his career of outlawry.

Within this huge cast, disguise operates more intricately than in Ellis. It is not unusual to find Calamity Jane (the name itself a disguise) dressed up as Deadwood Dick dressed up as an old man, or to have two false Deadwood Dicks, the real one being disguised as a female fortune-teller, all in the same episode. Often, there are discrepancies in a character's physique when he changes his disguise. Thus, the "large and knotted" hands of Deadwood Dick metamorphose into fingers which "were as white and soft as any girl's" when he is in the guise of Ned Harris.[26] This is an authorial mistake, of course, but the point is that these two figures are not genuinely conceived as one character. Like Ellis, Wheeler uses disguise as an artifice for reconciling the Eastern and Western characteristics of the hero.

But the disguise which this hero dons for most of the series is that of an outlaw. By taking such a type as his hero, Wheeler disregards the moral categories which hold sway in earlier dime novels. None of his major characters, indeed, fits neatly into the dime novel mold of heroism or villainy, since they all vacillate between moral extremes. Dick has been an honest victim who becomes an outlaw, tries to recant, returns to outlawry and eventually reforms, becoming a type of detective who roots out and punishes evil. His first wife, Leone, enters as an innocent captive, but when Dick rescues another woman, Edith, from captivity, Leone becomes jealous and rebels against Dick, inciting his gang to mutiny. She repents, is reunited with her husband and kills Edith, who is now insane. Nine episodes later, however, Leone has degenerated to drunkenness and adultery, and Deadwood Dick is seeking to kill her. In this book, she dies. Accompanying this new immorality is an increase in violence and sensationalism. For example, when the Eastern heroine is rescued from Indian captivity in the first story of the series, she is no mere blushing victim, but a woman in bondage, stripped to the waist, tied to a post, and bleeding from whip marks.

This flamboyant and immoral hero, who, strangely enough, was intended for a juvenile audience, was the last major Western figure to appear under the Beadle and Adams imprint. He was also one of the main characters to be imitated by later publishing houses. His earliest imitator was even more violent, though he was morally sound. This was Diamond Dick, who first appeared in Street and Smith's *New York Weekly* in 1878, with his ten-year-old son, Bertie, both dressed in exotic Mexican costumes and both battling with incredibly vicious women. Soon Bertie took over the center of the stage from his father, the symbolic handover being stressed as if to emphasize the shift to the juvenile market. The series title changed to Diamond Dick, Jr. and lasted in that form until

1911. Around the turn of the century (when the postmaster general was banning Tousey's Jesse James novels), the hero became a tamer figure, substituting a neat ranger suit for his theatrical Mexican costume in 1904. At this point, the dime novels' flirtation with sensationalism ended. In the long run, the emphasis on juvenility and the series format, not the note of immorality, left the lasting mark.

Around the turn of the century another important development occurred: multiple authorship of series became the rule. For example, the Diamond Dick series was written by four men, all under the byline "W. B. Lawson." Dime novel enthusiasts have identified which episodes were written by each man, but changes in characterization and costume do not seem to correspond to changes in authorship.[27] It seems as if some editorial overseer must have dictated alterations in emphasis, according to time and fashion. In the twentieth century, therefore, formulas belonged more to the publishers than to individual authors.

The most successful twentieth-century dime series were moralistic adventure stories about clean-cut boys. The most popular Western version of this formula was Wild West Weekly, which Frank Tousey began in 1902. This series returned to and outdid the moral rectitude of the older Beadle and Adams novels, while it adopted the format of the Deadwood Dick stories and the juvenile emphasis of the Diamond Dick, Jr. weekly. The central figure is a fifteen-year-old boy who is a younger, more law-abiding version of Deadwood Dick. Like his predecessor, he is an Easterner who is named after his Western environment: as a baby, he was the sole survivor of an emigrant wagon train and named Young Wild West "because it was in a very wild part of the West where I was found and I was so young."[28] He gathers around him a group which is much more domesticated than Dick's gang. It is made up of an older scout and his wife, a Western boy and his fiancée, a Negro and a Chinese cook, and Arietta, Wild's Western sweetheart whom he saves from Indian captivity in the first installment of the series. Like Dick, too, Wild wins a gold mine and various properties, and so he finances the group's activities as they move all over the West punishing criminals, fighting Indians, and saving various females from captivity by Indians, outlaws, and Eastern criminals. There is none of Wheeler's sensationalism: not only is there little interest in flamboyant disguise, but a general atmosphere of chasteness surrounds all the adventures. The air of refinement and the domesticity are quite reminiscent of Owen Wister's fiction. If the nineteenth-century dime novel derives from Fenimore Cooper, by way of Edward Ellis, the typical twentieth-century dime series bears, in addition, the impress of the genteel Wister.

Two years after Wild West Weekly began, Street and Smith brought out a very close imitation, which presented the disguised hero and his Western environment in their tamest and most modern form yet. The series was at first called Young Rough Rider Weekly, though later, in response to poor sales, its covers and titles were remodelled to resemble Wild West Weekly more closely and at that time the series heading was changed to Rough Rider Weekly. The cast is a group of Eastern boys, led by Ted Strong, who initially come to Dakota to work on the ranch which one of them has inherited. In time, they extend their activities, roaming all over the Western states to act as semiofficial law-enforcers. Changes were made in the cast, too, in an attempt to emulate Wild West: the main heroine changes from the Eastern Louise Rossiter to the Western Stella, and Bud, who appears in the first number of the series as a young cowboy, metamorphoses in 1906 into an older, avuncular plainsman who corresponds to the scout in Wild West.

The costume which these Easterners adopt is not a flamboyant disguise, but a mark of their status as law officers. It is "a neatly-fitting khaki uniform such as those worn by the Rough Riders during the Spanish-American War."[29] The dress links Ted not to a wild frontiersman but to Roosevelt, who was beginning his second term as president when the series began. There are other references of this order: Ted, who has been a sergeant in the United States Volunteers at San Juan Hill, disproves his tenderfoot status in the West by beating a ruffian who could easily be a caricature of the Mingusville bully whom Roosevelt vanquished; Ted is also part owner of two ranches in the Dakotas and one in Texas. Some reflections smack more of Wister than Roosevelt. Talking of the cowboy, the author delivers a statement which could have been lifted straight from Wister's diary: "Men like Bud are plentiful enough in the far West, where civilization and the fashion plates have not brought everyone down to the dead level of the commonplace in manner and appearance."[30] Both influences become more overt toward the end of the series. *King of the Wild West's Bronco Ball Tossers; or, Stella Bluffs the Umpire* (4 May 1907) has a late-night Virginia reel copied directly from the midnight antics of the cowboys in *The Virginian* and the spectacle of the story (a baseball match) climaxes with a band playing Roosevelt's theme tune, "There'll be a hot time in the old town tonight."

The whole setting is imbued with modern, Eastern associations: although the central captivity-and-rescue ritual survives, it is hedged round with battles to do with commerce, property, and even sport, rather than life-and-death struggles with Indians. (In fact, none of these boys ever kills anyone.) Ted is awarded the title "King of the Wild West" not for winning a gun battle or for arresting an outlaw gang, but for beating various speculators in a race for land in the Black Hills. In *Ted Strong, King of the Wild West; or, Winning a Town by a Ride* (1905), the government throws an Indian reservation open to settlers, and Ted is commissioned by a group of cattlemen to win the townsite beside the railroad, which he duly does. In this setting, a question of money distinguishes the conventional types of the genteel Eastern hero (Ted) and the more violent Western companion (Bud). While Ted is invited west by the group to lead them and becomes rich independently by winning various properties, Bud is hired by the group as foreman of the ranch and paid a salary. Generally, these boys are very conscious of property rights and financial gain, and their adventures involve new railroad and motor car technology, government policy, and corporate banking methods. Especially toward the end of the series, competitions from rifle marksmanship to baseball abound. With all these novelties in the scene, the West in this series is not very wild, and that may have been why Rough Rider lasted only three years, whereas Wild West survived unchanged for twenty-five.

If twentieth-century dime fiction restates familiar characters and scenarios from nineteenth-century dimes in more modern terms, rather than adding genuinely new material to the form, pulp magazines are even less inventive. The magazine *Wild West* is typical. When Tousey failed in 1927, Street and Smith bought Wild West Weekly from him and turned it into a pulp. For the first few years, it always carried a story in which the scene—a ranch inhabited by a leader and his satellites—harks back to Rough Rider, and the characters are those of Wild West Weekly matured into young men. Billy West, the hero, has a history identical to Wild's, down to his christening, and his adventures are of the same type, but slightly more violent. Because pulp magazines are miscellanies, their contents are diffuse and they were written by a whole range of authors. Generally, though, they reuse character types and plots from the twentieth-century dime novel, only dispensing with the juvenile emphasis and adding some violence and sex to the action.

A brief review of the fiction shows that it moves beyond its earliest format very little and never changes in abrupt ways. Some of its development is circular: early and late, the dime hero is an Easterner who dresses up to go west, where he leads a group of people, all less skilled and less cultured than him, to the rescue of a female captive and in battles against various enemies. Sometimes a change reflects a national development: for example, the heroic function expands with the advancing frontier. Seth Jones saves Ina from the wilderness without trying to eradicate all its dangers, saying of the Indians, "for all I detest his whole cowardly race, I don't believe in killing them, except when they've done you some injury or are trying to" (*Seth Jones*, p. 110); the twentieth-century version of Buffalo Bill believes that the only good Indian is a dead one; and Ted Strong not only rescues captured women, but destroys raucous towns, expunges Mormon polygamy, and generally works to remove the wildness from the West. The pattern of the hero's development holds true for all the major characters, settings, and plots in this fiction. Characters change only their outward forms through time, adopting different habits as society's mores changed; the setting moves to different geographical locations as the country filled up with settlers, but is always a Western area which is wild in some way; and the plot always consists of heroic battles against the forces of savagery.

The methods by which dime and pulp authors sustain this repetitive model over the hundred years accord well with one of John Cawelti's theories. He contends that formulaic art is analogous to certain kinds of game or play which have to do with role playing and the artificial resolution of conflict.[31] Working within restricting conditions, dime and pulp authors try to imitate Cooper's Western adventures while circumventing his emphasis on irresolvable conflict. Repeatedly they manage this balancing act by employing pretenses and artifices often associated with games. The preponderance of disguise in the Beadle novels—in the character transformations in Ellis and Wheeler or in the elaborate costumes of Ingraham—points to this element of play. While Wild West and Rough Rider eschew such exoticism, they simply make the connection between dime fiction and games more overt, with their many sporting contests in shooting, horse racing, and baseball. Whatever the subtle variations in the formula, these authors' handling of character, plot and setting attests vividly to the homogenizing effects of mass production.

THE AUTHORIAL VOICE

Even if dime novelists were held to a predetermined set of Western images and events, as the evidence of the publishing methods and the fictional formulas suggests, each still had the responsibility of putting together the narratives assigned to him. This meant that each author functioned as an individual, if only at the level of construction rather than genuine creation, and each had to find his own means of accommodating his work to the publishing machine. Authors left two kinds of records of their reactions as individual writers to the commercial system: their comments on their careers in interviews and autobiographies and, in more complex form, their authorial voices in the fiction itself.

The extent to which the apparatus of the "fiction factory" bit into the authors' consciousnesses comes through clearly in their evaluations of their own writing. The statements which survive contain only enthusiasm for the dime and pulp business. Authors came to absorb the values of commercial publishing more and more, increasingly conflating commercial standards and literary judgments.

The Beadle authors frankly recognized the financial motive behind their work: Prentiss Ingraham, for example, declared that, "I write for a living and not for glory."[32] Some went further, praising dime fiction as superior writing precisely because it gave such financial rewards. Frederick Whittaker justified his trade against widespread criticisms in the 1880s:

> The only men, as a class, in America today, who are able to live by pure literary labor, are the writers of what you call "dime novels," that is to say, of books written for the largest possible market in this country. . . . Had Poe lived in these days he would have been a writer of dime novels; for his prose stories have all the qualities which are required in a good "dime." Had he done so, he might have ended his days in comfort, instead of dying in misery, for good dime work pays well.[33]

Later, dime novelists began to describe their work in language associated with manufacturing, and thus characterized writing not only as a job done for money, but as an industrial occupation. This attitude surfaced occasionally late in the nineteenth century, as when T. C. Harbaugh, a Beadle and Adams author, said, "The building of a dime novel is something of which the reading public knows little. . . . All authors do not build their stories alike."[34] But the sense of writing as one of the technological processes involved in cheap publishing flowered fully only in the twentieth century. The most detailed evidence of this was given by William Wallace Cook. As a writer for Street and Smith—a firm which prided itself on its modern automation—he was an enthusiast of new technology. The title of his autobiography reflects his belief that his literary creation was part of the mechanics of modern life: *The Fiction Factory: Being the Experience of a Writer who, for Twenty-two Years, has Kept a Story-Mill Grinding Successfully*. . . . Despite the romances which he wrote, his conception of writing was not Romantic at all. He believed that the writer fitted easily into a market society:

> A writer is neither better nor worse than any other man who happens to be in trade. He is a manufacturer. After gathering his raw product, he puts it through the mill of his imagination, retorts from the mass the personal equation, refines it with a sufficient amount of common sense and runs it into bars—of bullion, let us say. If the product is good it passes at face value and becomes a medium of exchange.[35]

In his nondime writings, Cook bears witness both to how completely the hack could adopt the principles of mass production and to the mental hoops this involved. In his own eyes, his magnum opus was a handbook, *Plotto: A New Method of Plot Suggestion for Writers of Creative Fiction* (1928), in which he advocates production line techniques to budding authors. He explains that fiction is a mechanical artifact:

> There is, of course, a mechanical structure underlying every properly constructed story . . . the plot, in itself, is purely mechanical. . . . Plausibility is attained when fine discrimination, true judgment and a facility with words

so cover the necessary mechanism that it does not intrude at any point upon the completed work and therein lies the art of the story teller.[36]

To make this clearer, he describes theme, plot, and characterization as interlocking with each other in the same way as "an interlocking directorate" in a corporate business organization. Following these principles, he concocts a pseudoscientific system whereby, from a basic formula of "Conflict" and a range of numbered clauses, the writer can construct an infinite number of unique stories. This mechanistic plan suits not only fiction but life itself: Cook suggests that the "plottoist" use the Masterplots both to "fight for your reader's attention and interest" and to alleviate personal difficulties. "If you are in pecuniary distress, meditate upon Conflicts 941 and 942; . . . if you have committed a wrong and are troubled by conscience, walk with the protagonist of Conflict 918a."[37] Cook was so enthusiastic about the method of writing he had learned during his years in the Street and Smith stable that he made it a gospel for success in modern life.

However, his wholehearted subscription to the apparatus of mass publishing made his identity as an individual author problematic. Cook's autobiography is a paean to Street and Smith, yet in it he deals in concepts—like the artistic quality of his fiction and his authorial identity—which these publishers, by their methods of production, had either decreed irrelevant or erased altogether. The very fact that he wrote the autobiography contradicted his status as a Street and Smith hack. In his account, he uses a pseudonym for himself (John Milton Edwards) and the firm (Harte and Perkins), and he refers to himself in the third person only. The schism in his thinking comes out most clearly when he relates a conversation between himself and an editor, about his desire to write a book which would not be a dime novel:

> "Write it," advised the noted one, "but not under your own name."
>
> Edwards fell silent. What was there in the work he had done which made it impossible to put "John Milton Edwards" on the title page of his most ambitious effort? Were the nickel novels and the popular paperbacks to rise in judgment against him? He could not think so then, and he does not think so now.[38]

The noted editor advised him to write a book of his experiences as an author; this is the book, and it is, after all, written under a pseudonym. Cook seems not to recognize the paradox of his description; his work had been appearing under numerous Street and Smith pseudonyms for twenty years, and he no longer had a clear idea of his own authorial identity.

The final stage of the hack's identification with his commercial function was enacted by the pulp author. He considered that the system of production alone classified both fiction and author. This attitude is illustrated by D. B. Newton, a contemporary author of Westerns, who wrote pulp stories in the 1940s. Newton faced poverty in 1949, when pulp magazines began to vanish. A few years later, however, the paperback revolution launched a profusion of pocket-sized Westerns. The ex–pulp writers began to make money from paperback novels, both by writing new work for them and by reprinting magazine stories in book form. Newton says, "we all at once discovered we were what many of us had secretly always wanted to be—novelists, instead of mere pulp-paper hacks. It was a good feeling."[39] They were not writing different stories: it was the manner of publishing which had changed, not the matter at all. So completely had the authors absorbed the publishers' marketplace definitions, that the change was sufficient to transform their role as writers, at least in their own eyes.

These comments show that the hack writer's relationship to the publishing machine went beyond producing fictions to order for money. Where the Beadle author was enthusiastic about the system because it gave him a living, his Street and Smith successor saw in it truths about how to write and how to live. By the time of the pulp magazine, authors were judging their literary achievements purely according to the formal categories of commercial publishing. The force of Benjamin's definition shows up here: these writers did not just comply with certain working conditions; they made them over into a set of values for regulating both their art and their lives.

No other dime or pulp writer left as complete an account as Cook of his reactions to the marketplace and the commercial contract. This may have been partly because the nineteenth-century dime novelist had more leeway in the editorial system than his twentieth-century counterpart, and thus more opportunity to insert his responses to the publishing machine into the fiction itself. Early dime novelists spend much time in their repetitive tales of captivity, chase, and rescue on the frontier talking to the reader about the process of composition and hinting at their own positions as authors. They develop a storytelling voice which brings the marketplace into the fiction by making the business of writing to order part of the formulaic action. In the earliest dime novels, the voice which discusses the writing process clearly belongs to the narrator, but later it is attributed to the characters, who take over the mock dialogue with the audience. Finally, in the turn-of-the-century dime series and in pulp magazines generally, the discussion is usurped by the publishers, who block authorial strategies by talking to the audience directly themselves. This development is documented in the details of the fiction and it is tantamount to a running commentary by the individual author on his place in the production line.

In the first period, the play made with the notion of writing within

conventions and contracts is best illustrated by the four main authors of
Westerns in the Beadle and Adams stable, whose fiction I have already
described: Ned Buntline, Edward Ellis, Prentiss Ingraham, and Edward
Wheeler. Of the four, only Buntline wrote professionally before his dime
novel work, and he was the most famous of them, as much for his adventures as for his writing. The others—Ellis, a schoolteacher, Ingraham,
a former army officer who knew various real-life Western heroes, and
Wheeler, about whom little is known except that he was never in the
West—all began writing careers as dime novelists. They all produced
that kind of fiction exclusively for many years and were among Beadle's
most prolific authors. Therefore, they were likely candidates for being
influenced by their professional environment. The four began writing
in the order in which they are listed, although there is some overlapping
in the chronology of their publications. Read in this order, they represent
a momentum which carries the dime novel from sub-Cooper romance,
with the usual programmatic structures, to a more highly structured
kind of writing in which the rituals owe more to the conventions of
commercial production than to those of literary genre.

However escapist Ned Buntline's stories may seem, his reader is rarely
allowed to immerse himself completely in the illusion of the fictional
adventures. The author repeatedly interrupts the action to remind his
audience of his presence as narrator and the conditions under which he
works. He reveals his idea of an author's role when he describes a ship-
wrecked company listening to a narrator: "Most of both crew and passengers were of a class of men who needed something to interest their
minds—books were too tame, and it was only when the personality and
action of the story-teller excited the attention that they could keep from
falling into despondency."[40] Certainly Buntline supplies much autobio-
graphical information in the course of his own melodramatic frontier
tales. He talks about his experiences in the Florida war, he mentions his
divorce, and he stresses the sacrifices he makes in his private life to fulfill
this public work: he tells the reader that "this story has been written on
a bed of sickness, amid pain and suffering, with a fevered brow and a
nervous hand,"[41] or, at greater length, during a poignant moment, he
complains:

> I would linger o'er this scene, for *I* had an angel mother once, who blessed
> *me* thus, when she gave me to my country's cause!—alas! the green turf lays
> heavy o'er her now—but I cannot. On, like unresisting Time, my pen must
> travel—for the journey is yet long before it.[42]

Buntline becomes one of the most vivid figures in his tales; few of his
stereotyped characters appear as regularly or with as much biographical
detail.

The reader is never allowed to forget that these stories are told by an author working with formal narrative devices. Buntline concentrates on chapter divisions especially, often pausing for an aside like "but of that another chapter will speak; this one must close to give us a chance to look elsewhere" (*The White Wizard*, p. 5). Sometimes he explains his technique in some detail:

> This chapter, which has been strictly historical, has been given to the reader, more to show the strength, skill, and cunning of the so-called savages in that war, than because it had a direct connection with other of our characters than Chikika and his braves.
>
> With this explanation, I will now return to those whom, I presume, the reader feels the most interested in. [*The White Wizard*, p. 24]

Chapter headings act as signposts, indicating the stages of the action: "The Plot Drawing to a Knot," "The Hour Approaches," "A General Clearing up of Mystery."[43] These titles reappear frequently, giving the impression that the tales are organized according to a standard format.

Buntline also reminds the reader that there are marketplace conditions at work. He evaluates the text in financial terms: "Excuse a momentary digression—the chapter wouldn't be worth an old-fashioned cent without it" (*Saul Sabberday*, p. 10). He also alludes to the commercial contract, saying "I hope you feel as if you had got your money's worth. It is my private opinion that you have" (*The White Wizard*, p. 32). The rhetoric shows Buntline acting as editor as well as author within his texts. At the same time, he was an actual editor, constantly reviving and abandoning his magazine *Ned Buntline's Own*. He finds room in his fiction to reflect on both these roles, introducing a peripheral character simply to have him lament the editor's lot:

> The poor editor shook his head sorrowfully, and murmured: ". . . If I could find a rich and happy editor, I would make my fortune by exhibiting him at sixpence a peep! A happy editor! Barnum would hunt the world over, if he heard of one, but what he'd have him! Get out with your woolly horses, your Joyce Heath's, nigger-baby-shows and codfish mermaids! Just show me a *live*, rich, happy editor or tell me that one ever lived!" [*The White Wizard*, p. 32]

It is notable that, much as Buntline circumvents his stories in these examples to talk to the reader about himself and the conventions which condition his narration, he never admits that the stories themselves are influenced by literary convention or market forces. He presents his tales as accurate historical records (more accurate, he claims, than those by professional historians), often supported by scholarly-looking footnotes. In a typical Buffalo Bill tale ("The Wildest and Truest Story I Ever Wrote"), the author insists that this is "a story founded entirely on fact, with real characters for its actors."[44] In *Buffalo Bill's Last Victory* (1883), in which "every scene [is] true to nature," he points out that Buffalo Bill "carried that long range rifle—a gift from the author of this story."[45]

Yet, without ever acknowledging the fictionality of his tales, he makes it clear, in time, that formalized devices are central to his characters' existence, as well as to his own delivery. The new emphasis begins when Buntline changed from story-paper fiction (much of which was reprinted in dime format) to dime novels proper. The later works mark a lessening of the author's ebullient presence and a new interest in signs, codes, and signals. In *Buffalo Bill's Last Victory*, again, much is made of tracks, smoke signals, speaking papers (the Indian name for letters), and a codified Western vocabulary—an Easterner complains, "Keep the trail warm? Why don't you talk English that a fellow can understand. What do you mean by it?" (p. 129). The more Buntline moved into dime fiction, the more attention he paid to these sign systems and the less to self-reflection. He switches his attention from the author to the characters, but characters as conventional symbols, not complex people. He emphasizes increasingly their function as two-dimensional, representative types. An early dime novel, *Red Ralph, The River Rover; or, The Brother's Revenge* (1870), hardly pauses to acknowledge the author, but makes much material out of a comic Negro who is used as the new, living signpost: he is carved with anchors, his forehead is cut with a cross, letters are pinned to his breast, and finally he is scalded white. Buntline had found a new set of conventions to protect his story from tameness.

Edward Ellis continues the practice of direct address and he brings his characters into it, using their voices to build up his dialogue with the audience. While never referring to his private life, Ellis discusses his narrative technique even more than Buntline. Indeed, he goes further, pretending to anticipate his readers' response and fashion his storytelling to that. During his tales of frontiersmen and Indians, he constantly gestures toward the audience, with interjections such as "with the reader's permission," "as perhaps the reader has surmised," and—revealing the community character Ellis ascribed to his readership—"if our readers be any judge of Indian warfare, no doubt they have agreed that the action . . . was curious, to say the least."[46] At one point, he includes a parody of his own procedure. In a story of the Revolution, a British captain addresses a crowd, trying to persuade it to join his camp. To improve his effect on the audience, he has an assistant:

> Honyost Schuyler stood by the elbow of Butler, and performed the office of *anticipator*, so acceptable at all times to a public speaker. He looked in the face of the auditors, and, if he detected the premonitions of a smile, he instantly sprang into the air, clapped his hands, and burst into his boisterous haw! haw! haw! which always proved infectious.[47]

It is common for Ellis's characters to voice concerns that can equally be ascribed to the author. In his authorial voice, Ellis is consistently willing to confess the fictionality of his tales, both in preface and in the body of his work (though he also footnotes any authentic events). Characters seem to realize that they are participating in conventional action: in *The Mystic Canoe* (1865), Father Jonois "had no doubt the whole plot was already revealed, and the part he was to play was to be eminently that of rescuer."[48] Some characters appear as aware as the author of the need to balance repetition and surprise. Ellis reassures the reader directly that the element of surprise will remain: "the *insult* to the Indian was so great that he contemplated a far sweeter compensation than death itself. Whatever that might be, time would be sure to develop it, and that, too, at the moment when least expected."[49] Characters emphasize that too great complacency about the predictability of events must be prevented, else there be no story to tell:

> "Oh, we are so rejoiced that someone has followed us here," said the lady devoutly. "Juliette was in despair, and I was almost; but I told her that Heaven would not forsake us, and it has not. I am so glad we are going to be rescued."
>
> "Don't be too sart'in of that," replied Nick Whiffles; "that's the business that brought me and Oregon Sol, and Marinyo here; but the thing ain't done yet, and may be it won't be done."[50]

One comic tenderfoot even considers writing the same kind of stories as Ellis, with his fellow actors as the characters. He soliloquizes on Old Zip, a frontiersman who is guiding him through the wilderness:

> I wonder if he can't be turned to account? In all the Indian stories and novels that I have read, there is always a sharp-witted hunter that can't talk good English, but knows more than all the Indians together. Now, I wonder if old Zip can't fill that role? If he can, I'll embalm him in a stunning story that will take down the Leatherstocking novels altogether.[51]

At times, characters outrightly acknowledge their inclusion in a book. When the comic Dutchman in *Oonomoo, the Huron* (1862) wants to recapitulate the preceding tale, *The Hunter's Cabin*, he says to his Indian companion, "don't t'ink dey will get her there, 'cause dey tried it once— dat time, you remember, when we was all in de HUNTER'S CABIN in de woods."[52] The typography shows Vanderbum to be considering himself both in a building and "in" a story. This sense of a character looking at himself as a figure in a book is conveyed most elaborately in *Nathan Todd; or, The Fate of the Sioux Captive* (1861). The old frontiersman, Bill Biddon, says, "I spect Jarsey has got me in some thar books or newspapers down thar. I'd kinder like to see how Bill Biddon would look in a book, and see some thar picters of 'im. Jarsey told me he was goin' to do it, and I s'pose the feller has."[53] This passage can point the reader toward an earlier novel, *Bill Biddon, Trapper* (1860), which has a fictional narrator nicknamed "Jarsey" and includes Biddon in its cast. It can also be read as an oblique acknowledgment of Biddon's appearance in the present tale: Ellis signs his authorial preface "New Jersey 1860" and the novel is fronted by a "picter" of Biddon himself.

Of course, first and foremost all these comments by characters pertain to the action within the tale and not to the conventions of the story itself. But Ellis encourages the reader to understand double meanings in his language by peppering his writing with puns. Some are simple—Haverland, the settler in *Seth Jones*, is referred to as "Mr. Have-Your-Land" (p. 7)—while others contribute to the process whereby characters both enact and discuss the plot. When Seth is following an Indian trail, his companion tells him that dawn is near. Seth responds, "I'm glad of it, for we want some light on this subject" (p. 128). Ellis thus comes close to equating trail and book, an identification which he later makes overt: "Those signs, invisible in the deep labyrinths of the woods to common eyes, were as plain to him as the printed pages of the book to the scholar."[54]

Ellis was not an intellectual or a modernist, but, when he created figures who recognize that they are participating in a series of conventional plots and who admit that they appear in books, he produced unusually self-reflexive texts. By conducting a dialogue with the audience in his own voice and in that of his characters, he acknowledges that a contract exists between character and reader. Thus, he took the dime novel the first step toward incorporating marketplace rules into its content.

Prentiss Ingraham played not with words, but with the visual and the concrete, following on from the later Buntline, with a profusion of signs, masks, codes, costumes, and documents, which he shaped into a more elaborate sign language. In a different way from Ellis, he made his stories reflect their marketplace function.

He began his association with Bill Cody by writing a play for him, and in his stories he continues to talk from the stance of a ringmaster or stage manager. He calls on the reader particularly at changes in time or place, treating his readership as some kind of theatre audience: "To this place I would have the reader accompany me to see and not be seen"; "an individual whom the reader would have recognized, had it been light enough."[55] It is significant that when a character describes himself as "author" the vocabulary has less to do with words or plots than with counterfeit images. In *The Cowboy Clan; or, The Tigress of Texas* (1891), an outlaw explains to his gang how he managed to tell Buck Taylor a convincing lie about the location of their hideout. He reminds his companions, "You know the boys called me the *author* because I could write sketches and poems and read them to them in camp?" He repeats the story he told Taylor, commenting, "You see my talent as an author here came in well to aid me in lying—see? . . . I wish you could see the maps I drew, the hieroglyphics and directions I wrote out, with countersigns and a lot of other stuff. I played my part well."[56] It is as if the written document is being made into something less verbal, more visual and diagrammatic. Whereas Ellis compares the creating or following of a trail to the writing or reading of a book, in Ingraham the simile works in the opposite direction. In a story full of characters pursuing each others' trails, the author says, "I will now beg my readers to follow my ink-trail."[57]

If the author and reader are working with codes, so are the characters. For example, in *Buffalo Bill's Redskin Ruse; or, Texas Jack's Death-Shot* (1895), characters spend much time translating secret messages, "Reading Signs" on trails, and constructing "talking papers" or maps. The centerpiece of the spectacle is an exercise in decipherment. Buffalo Bill and two soldiers find a mysterious corpse, and they try ponderously to read its identity from clues left on the body:

> "See here," [Bill] suddenly cried, and he drew from the small finger of [the corpse's] left hand a ring.
> Washing it off in the brook near, a heavy gold seal was revealed.
> A design was engraved on the seal.
> It was a red stone, and in it was cut a hand grasping a knife, and in a semi-circle beneath were the words in French:
> "*Le jour viendra.*"
> "The day will come!" said the colonel, translating the French, and he added sadly:
> "The day has come, did come for him, poor fellow.
> "But what do you make out of it, Cody?"
> "I do not know, sir.
> "But look! this tells a story."
> The scout pointed to the skull, and in the very center of it was a small, round hole.[58]

The scene continues in this vein for some time, and succeeding chapters return to it repeatedly. It is reminiscent of the examination of Asa Bush's corpse in Cooper's *The Prairie*, but here the sign-reading is more elaborate and more crucial to the plot, and it exemplifies how codified romantic formulas become in the dime novel. The development in the contents parallels the writer's position nicely: characters spend more time working with codes when their author is subject to a set of rigid conventions. Ingraham worked within a system which bound him to certain formulas and his stories were published in the usual dime format which amounts to a visual code, with covers always carrying the same diagrammatic arrangement of emblems which signify publisher, series, and type of story.

In other dime novels, Ingraham created a more obvious parallel with the publishing world. He changed the central motif from the code to the game: while he still stressed disguise, the operation of rules, and the need for decoding, he also emphasized competition. He did this most obviously when he introduced another Western hero, Buck Taylor. Buck always projects himself as a competitor, qualifying for Ranger service by winning a fistfight and challenging a traitor to a duel with the words, "there is a game I wish you to play with me and see if you will win." In the same story, Buck thinks up a "little game" to trap some Mexican outlaws. He arranges that he and Captain McNally stage a fight, a "mimic tragedy," in the Raiders' sight, so that he can pretend to join them as a disaffected Ranger. "Sly as was the Raider Chief, Buck Taylor had thus far shown him that he could give him odds and beat him, where it was a game of life and death."[59] To enhance the effect of his playacting, he makes a death-defying leap over a wide gorge in his flight from the Rangers to the outlaws. The recurrent contests echo the continual market competition in which Beadle and Adams, Ingraham's employers, were engaged. Later Street and Smith dime novels followed Ingraham's lead: when the competition grew even fiercer, the heroes became more exhibitionist and the fictional action became even more clearly analogous to a game.[60]

Another Beadle author, Edward Wheeler, developed the practices of Ellis and Ingraham, to take the contents of the dime novel the final step from historical romance to declared competitor in the publishing battle. In his work, the characters take over all the authorial functions: they invent their own stories, they acknowledge the conventions of their existence, and they recognize, finally, that these conventions derive directly from the commercial contract.

Wheeler makes his presence as author felt in conventional ways. He talks to the reader, signposts chapters and pretends to authenticity. But whereas Buntline or Ingraham asks the reader to follow his peripatetic lead, Wheeler encounters each new scene or character from the perspective of the audience: "As we enter and work our way toward the center of the apartment, our attention is attracted by [etc.] . . . We will listen"; "We will force our way up through the surging crowd, 'taking notes' as we proceed"; and, most obviously in contrast to Ingraham, "As we approach nearer, we are able, by the aid of the flood of wierd [sic] moonlight, to define this spectacle, and make it out to be the body of a man, hung by the neck."[61] Whereas Ingraham can see in the dark that which the reader cannot, Wheeler is no more powerful than his audience. His fiction illustrates the diminution of the author's power, just around the time when authors were losing more of their autonomy in the publishing hierarchy.

The characters themselves orchestrate revelations and reunions, from the *Unknown* in *Corduroy Charlie* (1879), knower of everyone's secrets, to Deadwood Dick in *Deadwood Dick as Detective* (1879), who adopts the deific stance:

> Fear not that man, for in your hour of need Deadwood Dick is on deck. When you least dream of it, he is lurking near, watching for your welfare, with a brother's care, and removing such obstacles as will be apt to trip you and throw you into the power of enemies.[62]

As the series progresses, Dick approaches the authorial role more overtly. In *Deadwood Dick's Dream; or, The Rivals of the Road* (1881), he first dreams, then enacts, the action of the novel. As well as projecting the action, he comments on it as he leaves the scene at the end of the tale, "going happy in the knowledge that I leave behind as a momento of this little campaign a clearer and more honest record for the famous name of Deadwood Dick."[63] Other characters show a similar autonomy: Buffalo Ben discovers his identity from the tattoo of his name on his own arm, and at one stage Leone confronts the incredibility in her own makeup, preempting an author's acknowledgment or a reader's incredulity:

> I have wronged deeply, and should be sorry, perhaps; but I ain't. I scarcely can credit the change in me during a few weeks, myself, but such change there is, that I would not go back to the tame, retired life for all the world. No, no!—not for Deadwood Dick, or the whole world![64]

The characters finally extend their gaze beyond the limits of their own story or their own series, to comment on activities in the publishing world. While the Deadwood Dick series was in full flight, Street and Smith brought out a close imitator, in Diamond Dick, who first appeared on 8 April 1878. The Deadwood Dick issue for 14 May 1878 involves three different Deadwood Dick figures. Dick comments, "I see that counterfeits are being shoved on the market—that is, *sham* Deadwood Dicks. We have one here in Eureka . . . I wish to meet this chap and learn where he obtained the right to use my copyrighted handle?"[65] While ostensibly speaking in metaphor, this Wheeler character has the power to go beyond the bounds of his fictional existence and recognize his status in the marketplace.

In the Beadle and Adams dime novels, overtures to the readers are always conducted by the authors themselves, in the course of their narratives. No clear image of the assumed audience emerges, because there are no specific appeals or offers. However, throughout the writings of four of the major Beadle authors, there is a recognition of the contract between author and audience, and the principles on which it rests. In Buntline's work that relationship is almost personal and certainly separate from the reliable history which he narrates, while Ellis and Ingraham bring notions of contract and competition into the fiction itself. Finally, in Wheeler's stories the (overtly commercial) contract has become part of the tale, the characters themselves discussing and guaranteeing the quality of the publication which they compose. It is a good introduction to the twentieth-century dime novel, which inverts these developments, making the tale (and its author) part of the contract between publisher and audience, producer and consumer.

In the Street and Smith stories, the sense of commerce is strong. The nickel series Rough Rider Weekly is typical of their publications. The tales are still of frontier adventure, and costumes, codes, and cryptograms remain prominent. But now the formulas are not connected to any discussions about writing, and the individual authorial voices have disappeared. Reactions to the marketplace saturate the language of the fiction and are no longer confined to rhetorical flourishes.

The vocabulary reflects the firm's concern with finance and competition. Two ruffianly mountain guides explain their arrangement: "That's what you call it—a monoperly. That's what these yere big trusts have. That is what is good in any big business. That's what Jack an' me has. . . . We wanter continue ter be ther official guides, an' we don't want other people buttin' in."[66] In *Ted Strong, King of the Wild West*, Ted, the hero, has "executive ability," his gang is his "organization," and his horse is described as a machine, "quivering like a thing made of steel springs."[67] Praise is expressed in terms of money—Ted makes "the rest of the gang look like thirty cents" (*Ted Strong's Rough Riders*, p. 4); and it seems impossible to describe any rough rider except in competitive terms— Ben, the strongest man in the troop, has broken all the records for wrestling and weight lifting, while Bud, the fastest cowboy in the West, holds the steer-roping championship for Texas.

There is no authorial self-reference. Rough Rider was authored by four men, but they all wrote under the same byline, "Ned Taylor." Since they were Street and Smith authors, it is very likely that their formula was dictated to them to the same degree as Gilbert Patten's, and doubtless they were briefed to create continuity. The stories show only small differences in style and attitude: those by William Wallace Cook express the most enthusiasm for business; Harry St. George Rathborne's include the most practical jokes; the writing of W. Bert Foster, who was used least frequently, comes closest to the Beadle authors' kind of wordplay; and John H. Whitson's tales all revolve around sports scenes.[68] When these authors, very occasionally, address their readers directly, they do not talk about themselves or their methods of composition. In anonymous, indistinguishable voices, they either instruct their readers about the West or they invite them to participate in the games which the fictional characters enact. For example, when Ted is held up by a high-wayman, he begins to inch his way imperceptibly toward his assailant. The author interrupts the action to explain how this is done:

> It was a trick that he had learned from an Indian, and that he had perfected with a good deal of practice, thinking that it might be useful to him in some case like the present.
>
> You can try it yourself, if you wish, in your own room or anywhere, for the matter of that. . . .
>
> It is done as follows.
>
> Bring the toes closely together, and then, with a slight start, bring the heels together.
>
> Bring the toes close together again and repeat.[69]

If Buntline's rhetoric has disappeared, so has the textual self-reflexion of Ellis, since (in a Foster narrative) double entendres are expressly disavowed: Stella says to Ted, " 'But there's another chance.' 'What is it?' 'Fort Chance—no pun intended.' "[70]

In these publications, there is still a direct commentary on the construction of the fiction and, in time, an invitation to the audience to participate in the composition of the tales. But all this is communicated outside the stories, at the end of the weekly issues, by an editorial voice:

> Beginning with the next week the readers of this weekly will find that the stories are increased over one-third in length. This is in response to a general demand to have the stories issued oftener than once a week. It is impossible to do that, but we have made the stories longer to show our appreciation of the favor with which our readers have received them. With the increased length there will be no change in the price of the weekly and no lowering of the quality of the stories.[71]

This announcement begins a running dialogue in which it becomes increasingly clear that the publishers are addressing themselves to an audience of juvenile males. Their appeals come to a head when a full-page advertisement offers a set of six postcards of the rough riders "entirely free" to "every boy who says a good word for Rough Rider."[72] The response to that incentive is published in a new feature, "A Chat with You." The letters praise Ned Taylor and the rough riders and ask questions about Western life. The editorial responses capitalize on general attitudes and illusions. From the first, readers believe that "Ned Taylor" must be a Westerner. The editor encourages that notion, presenting him as a "cowboy author . . . procured at considerable expense."[73] (At the time that remark was made, he was actually William Wallace Cook, who was being paid less than $60 an issue.) He also flatters the readers: "Ted Strong is typical of the brave, manly and chivalrous young American. It is like looking in the glass when our boys read about Ted in the ROUGH RIDER WEEKLY, as they see in the character all their own noble and admirable characteristics."[74] Many editorial replies resound with competitive assertions about the popularity of the paper and accusations about second-class imitations by other firms. At this time, the series was foundering badly, and the whole enterprise is obviously an attempt to save it.[75] It is this dialogue which replaces that (more subtle and less separate from the fiction) which is discernible between author and reader (or the author's idea of the reader) in the nineteenth-century dime novels.

The twentieth-century narratives were increasingly shaped by the dialogue on the letters page.[76] At first, the relationship between the fiction and the letters shows up in inconsequential details only. In one issue, a reader asks about lions in America. There is an editorial reply, but this is supplemented three issues later, when a lion is introduced into the action as a means of threatening Stella, as an opportunity to refer to Roosevelt's sportsmanship, and as an excuse for another disquisition on the mountain lion. From the first appearance of the letters page, the editor stresses Ted's existence, inviting boys to visit his ranch. In time, the narrative echoes this theme. A group of townsmen discuss the rough riders. The postmaster, Hogg, says,

> "This here Ted Strong has a gang of boys, all dressed out in uniform like reg'lar soldiers. They act as deppity marshals. He's a-waitin' for 'em, now."
> "Ho! ho! ho!" laughed Jim Rose. "There ain't no sech fellers at all. Yer must have been readin' thet in a book."
> "It's a Kid's story," said Bill Stone. . . . "Ther ain't no such thing as ther young rough riders."
> . . . there sounded the clatter of hoofs on the road. . . . There was no doubt but that these *were* the young rough riders. Hogg was right and the two wiseacres were wrong.[77]

When readers respond badly to Ted's companion, Stella, the editor at first tries to cajole some interest in her in his replies to letters. Paralleling that encouragement, Ted says, "I rather think it's a case of where the public opinion will have to be educated!"[78] That is the last time the text tries to dictate to its readership. From then on, the magazine acts the servant to its audience, adapting characters and inventing incidents according to suggestions printed on the letters page. (One letter, for example, asks to see more of a comic figure, Carl Schwartz; in succeeding numbers, he becomes much more prominent both in the plot and on the cover.)

The most telling debate occurs in the last months of 1906. It concerns the relationship between the hero and heroine, which had always been platonic. In Rough Rider issue 130, a letter says, "I hope Ted is not in love with Stella," and the answer is, "Ted and Stella are by no means in love with each other. They are simply friends, but oh! such steadfast friends!"[79] That answer has to be revised in reply to a letter in number

132—"I hope Ted marries Stella"; "Ted and Stella are very good friends, and think as much of each other as if they were sister and brother."[80] The 140th issue ends the equivocation. When another reader writes, "I think Stella and Ted should marry," the editor throws open the door of the author's study and invites all the readers in:

> So you think that Ted and Stella should marry? What do the rest of our readers think about it? We should like to have their opinion on this question. Perhaps some think that the interest would cease in Stella in that case. Perhaps she would have to stay home and look after the household duties and could not find time to accompany Ted on his chase after outlaws. But then, again, she might be with Ted in camp all the more. In that case we might hear more of Stella. There are two sides to this question, and we should like to have it decided by our readers.[81]

In order to keep its audience, Street and Smith told them that they could fashion the narrative themselves; the stories became overt bargaining tools between publisher and public.

Whereas Buntline and Ellis fictionalized their dialogue with the readers, Street and Smith denied their authors that possibility by taking over the dialogue and making it a literal barter in which the author had no place. He functioned as a minor laborer, working to plans supplied by the negotiators. The characters, acting in a world shot through with commercialism, are ciphers adaptable to the audience's demands. Dime fiction changed from a game to a mere counter in the game played between editor and reader in another part of the magazine.

Pulp magazines finally institutionalized the dialogue between editor and audience as part of the formula. For example, when Street and Smith turned Wild West into a pulp, they established a department called "The Wranglers' Corner," which invites readers' comments to "Help us to pick the stories that you like."[82] Prefacing the letters is a piece by the editor, who pretends to be joined in his Corner by the various series characters from the fiction. He reports what they say to each other and, in time, the characters respond directly to readers' letters. When readers are invited to contribute stories to "The Wranglers' Corner" (for payment) in the 1940s, the characters comment on these pieces too. Occasionally, authors are mentioned in this department, but the main emphasis is on direct contact between readers and fictional figures, orchestrated by the editor. Such features, which proliferated in the pulps, were plainly promotional gambits designed to create the atmosphere of a club and thus foster loyalty in readers. In this scheme, the authors were pushed even further out of the picture than in dime publications.[83]

In the pulps, the commercial nature of the relationship between editor and audience also rises to the surface. Thus, the editor of a Street and

Smith publication, *The Popular Magazine* (1903–28), could say directly that which the firm articulated more circuitously in Rough Rider Weekly:

> A number of months ago we made a statement in these pages to the effect that it was our intention to pattern THE POPULAR MAGAZINE after the suggestions received from our readers as conveyed in the Criticism Contest. It was a distinct effort to fashion a publication on the cooperative plan. We had no desire to instruct the reading public as to the class and scope of literature it should read, but rather to publish that which had been selected by the majority. This occupation of magazine publishing is, in our opinion, entirely a business proposition. . . . We publish THE POPULAR MAGA-ZINE as a money-making enterprise, and we follow the line of least resistance in catering to our public.[84]

Another evidence of the commercial impulse was the chorus of advertising voices which joined the editorial overtures in the pulps. The rhetoric of the advertisements echoes closely the escapism at work elsewhere in the magazines. Generally, advertisements do not concern Western products, but they do promise consumers a kind of heroic omnipotence with products which will improve their health, income, and social status. A parallel results between lead stories (which show rugged Westerners winning unattainable women and unbelievable riches by vanquishing hosts of enemies single-handedly), editorial departments (in which editors offer readers instant authorial recognition and financial rewards for contributing to their pages), and advertisements (in which, for example, Charles Atlas promises consumers stunning new physiques in three weeks for a modest fee).

In time, it becomes clear that the different kinds of power offered to readers are actually the bait by which the publishers fitted their audience into their commercial scheme. Publishers' priorities were revealed when they began to make efforts to attract advertisers and put their readers to work to impress these potential sponsors. In 1924, Street and Smith incorporated an "Advertising Prize Contest" into *Western Story Magazine*. The rubric ran in part:

> Perhaps you too wonder why our magazines carry so little advertising.
> Let us take you into our confidence.
> The real truth is that advertisers, almost as a whole, have hesitated about using fiction magazines because of a conviction that the purchasers of such magazines buy them for the stories they contain, and do not read the advertisements. You, as readers, and we, as publishers, know this to be wrong. We know you read the advertisements in our magazines, and that you can help us prove it to the advertisers. Therefore, if you will tell us why you think one advertisement in this magazine is better than another and if your letter proves to be the best one received on the subject during the month, we will send you $5.00.[85]

Gradually, publishers codified the role of the audience more and more. In *Zane Grey's Western Magazine* of the 1950s, the readers' creative contribution is limited to answering quizzes, mostly on Western history and geography. When *Far West* began in 1978, it carried a form which the editor called a "questionnaire." Actually, in contrast to Rough Rider's, this "reader survey" involves no questions and leaves no room for the readers' individual voices. It is a list of answers, with a box beside each for the reader to tick statements about presentation (such as, "I prefer one long story and one or two short stories") which assume that the fictional matter is fixed.[86] Having long since integrated the pulp novelist into the machinery of production, pulp publishers succeeded in formalizing the reader's role also, posing questions which allow only a limited, predetermined range of responses. They created a smoothly running machine in which the input and the output were under their control but others paid for it to run.

The rationale behind dime and pulp publishing—selling the fictional product to as many people as possible as profitably as possible—remained the same for 150 years. However, the dynamics of the marketplace varied throughout that time. Changes in audience type, in the autonomy of authors, and in the use of advertising directly affected the conventions of dime and pulp Westerns.

When the dime novel was invented, the Beadles did not define their audience or their fiction's content precisely but instead focused their dictatorial powers on the presentation of their novels. Their writers realized that the fiction was part of a commercial policy of repetition and conformed to the same general pattern in plot, characterization, and scene; but they had scope enough to construct their own images of their audience and create their own overtures to that imagined group. The four major Beadle and Adams authors chose to talk to their readers about the commercial paraphernalia of the dime novel, identifying the fiction more and more closely with its market function. Buntline's candid admission of the competitive commercialism of his task—which has to do only with his presentation of the story, not the events or characters—evolved into Ingraham's dramatization of the novel as code or game, which brought the fiction closer to an acknowledgment of its status in the publishing field. Ellis developed the integration of the dime novel's literary and marketplace properties when his text became a self-conscious participant in the exchange between writer and reader. Edward Wheeler's characters completed the last refinement in that interplay, by becoming independent of their author to the extent that they wrote their own plots, devised their own identities, and fought their own publishing battles. The voice which recognizes the systematic interchange between producer and consumer no longer belonged directly to the author, but to the characters. By the end of Beadle and Adams's reign, the author, inasmuch as he figured in the text, was rapidly becoming superfluous.

Street and Smith involved themselves much more fully than their predecessors in issues of audience and content. The publishers tried to clarify their picture of their audience and took steps to establish direct communication with the buying public: they published readers' letters to the editor and substituted their own, corporate voice for the authors' as the only form of direct address in their publications. This enlargement of the publishers' role considerably diminished the authors' function. Writers became absorbed into the publishing apparatus: when a Street and Smith editor praised William Wallace Cook in 1928 for "hammering out" stories,[87] he was clearly treating the writer as part of the equipment for producing the publishers' demands. Cook, for his part, developed an imagination entirely immersed in images of machinery and business. The effect on the fiction is exemplified by the stories in the Rough Rider Weekly series, many of which were written by Cook. These Westerns are products of, and paeans to, financial and technological efficiency. Cook and his fellow writers spend more time praising modern business methods and gamesmanship than talking about the wild West.

Pulp publishers generally entrenched the dime novel formulas. Their major innovation was seeking advertising revenue. The attempt to woo advertisers led publishers to downgrade their audience, alongside their authors, to the position of ciphers in their marketing strategy: when the pulp editor invited the audience to participate in production, he meant the offer literally. The audience's contribution became as codified as the authors'; thus it was shown for a second time that to comply with the publishing apparatus was inevitably to become a part of its mechanism.

TWO

The Western Formula and the Disappearing Frontier

At the turn of the twentieth century, Owen Wister and Frederic Remington set out to "sell" their fictions of the West to an American audience, in a very different way from the dime novelists. They inherited their fictional materials from the same source as the dime and pulp authors—Fenimore Cooper—but they worked under different conditions and published in different media. The timing of their production was important, too: Wister and Remington popularized the modern version of the Western formula just as the frontier seemed to be disappearing. Instead of being caught up in a struggle against the rules of formulaic production, they were mainly concerned to oppose the pattern of Western history with their own personal visions of the West. Thus they created fictions which, while certainly romantic and escapist, also reflect, if indirectly, some of the tensions of the times.

Around the end of the nineteenth century, the Western wilderness was seen to be disappearing in the face of America's rapid industrialization. With developments in immigration, urbanization, manufacturing, and transportation, the last large area of free land—the Great Plains—seemed to be filling up with railroads, barbed wire, farmers, and businessmen. This impression was somewhat confirmed in 1890, when the director of the census announced that "the unsettled area has been so broken into by isolated bodies of settlement that there can hardly be said to be a frontier line." In 1893, Frederick Jackson Turner articulated the meaning of this event. In his famous address, "The Significance of the Frontier in American History," he said that the frontier experience was responsible for the unique character of American life; now that the frontier was closed, the first phase of America's history was over.

The perception that the frontier was disappearing, coupled with the difficulties accompanying modernization, stimulated interest in the West among some members of the Eastern establishment. The two Easterners who contributed most to national enthusiasm for the Far West were Wister and Remington. Both went west for the first time in the 1880s and found, to their delight, the healthfulness, masculinity, and individualism which they felt had died out in the settled, Eastern sections of the country.[1] However, they also realized that the open, wild West which they were encountering was in the process of changing. Their reaction was to record, and thus preserve, the frontier in art. Remington tells how, on his first Western trip, he met an old frontiersman who told him that the West was dying:

> The old man had closed my very entrancing book almost at the first chapter. . . . I knew the wild riders and the vacant land were about to vanish forever, and the more I considered the subject the bigger the Forever loomed.
> Without knowing exactly how to do it, I began to try to record some facts around me.[2]

After a few visits west, Wister was also very aware of the need to preserve the wild West in art. He describes how, in 1891, "fresh from Wyoming," he began to mull over the need for a literature of the Far West:

> Why wasn't some Kipling saving the sage-brush for American literature, before the sage-brush and all that it signified went the way of the California forty-niner, went the way of the Mississippi steam-boat, went the way of everything? Roosevelt had seen the sage-brush true, had felt its poetry; and also Remington, who illustrated his articles so well. But what was fiction doing, fiction, the only thing that has always outlived fact?[3]

At this point in his meditations, Wister began his first short story about the West.

Wister and Remington published their artistic versions of the frontier predominantly in *Harper's Weekly* and *Harper's Monthly* and, to a lesser extent, in *Century* and *Collier's*. According to Frank Luther Mott, *Harper's Monthly* was "the great successful middle-class magazine" of its time—lying between the dime and pulp publications on the one hand and the high-toned literary quarterlies on the other—and the other periodicals frequented by Wister and Remington were of a similar character.[4] At 25¢ to 35¢ a copy, these magazines cost more than the pulps, they were more expensively produced, and their contents were certainly more serious and varied: they carried a mixture of topical commentary, biographical sketches, travel articles, and fiction. Above all, their illustrations far surpassed those in cheaper periodicals in both quality and numbers; indeed, their large woodcuts and halftones were their great innovation and their major selling point. At the same time, however, *Harper's* and *Century* were caught up in the demands of the commercial world, most obviously by being in the van of large-scale magazine advertising; they carried, from the 1880s, numerous advertisements for personal and domestic items, food and drink, patent medicines, and newly invented gadgets. Also, their pieces were decidedly middlebrow; they were not trying to appeal to an elite readership. In the late nineteenth century, Harper magazines led the way in publicizing the West of the Indian, the cavalryman, and the cowboy to a vast, mainly Eastern audience.

This was the context in which many of Wister's and Remington's pieces first appeared, although both men republished most of their work as hardcover books. The publishing conditions of the magazines did impinge on these authors' output to some extent, though not nearly as directly or completely as dime and pulp methods affected their writers. Both men were paid by the word or the page, and both were directed by their editors to concentrate on the Western scene; when Remington tried to alter his subject matter near the peak of his career, a *Harper's* editor rejected his illustrations.[5] However, both Wister and Remington were paid at much higher rates than dime and pulp authors: eventually *Harper's* paid Wister 10¢ a word and Remington came to command $500 to $1,000 per reproduction in *Collier's*.[6] Also, the editorial insistence on the West merely confirmed the direction of these artists' tendencies, and both had the freedom to be selective or even to alter the terms of their commissions. Beyond the editorial strictures, the magazines gave a certain cast to their publications. Wister and Remington were conscious of inserting new Western material into Eastern publications, aimed mainly at an Eastern, urban audience. Also, in the same way that the magazines were popular and commercial without being assembly line products, Wister and Remington contributed to the development of the Western formula without themselves being formulists simply imitating a fictional model.

Wister and Remington's position, as middlebrow authors writing mainly for an Eastern audience, is also echoed in the formal details of their work. In both the literary and the visual pieces, they went beyond the recording of Western images. First, they demonstrated the coming together of the two halves of the country, by foregrounding love stories which symbolize the meeting of East and West and which act out the consequences of that event. Second, they created formal devices to set these plots within temporal and spatial conditions which defy change. In such ways, these artists created popular, romantic works and also tried to counter the dying out of the heroic West which they believed they were witnessing.

Very soon, Wister's plot was adopted by imitators like Emerson Hough, who turned it into the new version of the Western formula, supplanting the dime novel model. Remington's writing did not undergo the same process. His fiction was very nearly a mirror image of Wister's and was the alternative model available to the formulists—one which they chose to ignore. This chapter looks, firstly, at the plots of Wister and Remington, to see, in detail, what was taken up by the formulists and what was rejected. Then it considers the structures which both men created to protect their West against the encroachment of time and space. Finally, it examines, briefly, the way in which one formulist—Hough—reworked the material carved out by these artists.

OWEN WISTER'S WESTERN ROMANCE

One theme runs throughout Wister's reactions to the West, in his diaries, his essays, and his fiction: the desire to reconcile Eastern and Western values. By writing about the West in the major magazines of the Eastern middlebrow establishment, he was, to some extent, achieving his goal. However, his major act of synthesis was his novel, *The Virginian* (1902), whose plot, characterization, and structure are all informed by the resolution of conflict. Whereas Fenimore Cooper demonstrated the rift between East and West, Wister dramatized their union. Yet, various critics have talked of a vague sense of threat remaining at the end of *The Virginian*.[7] A close reading of the novel reveals that the impression of unease has a precise cause, for, at one important level, the author failed to reconcile the opposing elements in his work.

In his own life, Wister enacted, to some extent, a synthesis of Eastern and Western qualities. He was a genteel, Harvard-educated Philadelphian who first went to Wyoming in 1885 for his health. He so enjoyed the vigorous outdoor life which he found in the West that he made fourteen more Western trips in the next fourteen years, eventually buying a ranch in Jackson Hole. His professional writing career began as a direct result of his experiences on these trips. Giving up his law practice in the East, he made the West the most prominent subject of his fiction.

Wister abhorred contemporary political conditions and the populist masses of Eastern cities, and he saw the West as a potential antidote to the general degeneracy of the more settled sections of the country. This was the reaction which he recorded in his journal on his first encounter with Wyoming:

> I feel more certainly than ever, that no matter how completely the East may be the head waters from which the West has flown and is flowing, it won't be a century before the West is simply the true America with thought, type, and life of its own kind—We Atlantic Coast people, all varnished with Europe . . . will vanish from the face of the earth. We're no type—no race—we're transient. . . . All the patriotism of the War doesn't make us an institution yet. But this West is going to do it.[8]

He saw in the West healthfulness, individualism, and what he called "pure Anglo-Saxonism." However, his optimism was recurrently undermined by an apprehension that the West might not, after all, transform America, but instead be overcome by Eastern values. Only two weeks after his first meditation on Wyoming, he confided to his diary:

The nouveau riche element in New York will damn this western expanse of virgin soil if it doesn't look out. The one idea of Western city people is to have a town as good as New York—in New York the English importations at present antagonize. But will they continue to? If not, good day to my theory of an American civilization here—It will slowly New Yorkify, and rot.[9]

As the Western journals continue into the late 1890s, they give witness to Wister's increasing pessimism concerning his country's future, his hatred of its "putrescent" politics, and his sense that a national disaster was imminent. This private record shows him becoming less and less sanguine about the frontier's own development and its ability to affect trends in the East.

When Wister began writing essays and fiction in 1891, he intended his work as a corrective to the moral decline he witnessed around him. First, the East had to understand what the West was really like: Wister said that one goal of his writing was to correct the "Alkali Ike" impression of the West perpetrated by the comic papers,[10] and, in his 1895 preface to *Red Men and White*, he claimed realism and authenticity for his tales. His next aim was to act out a meeting of East and West. He gave notice of his desire to unite the country most obviously in his *Harper's Monthly* essay, "The Evolution of the Cow-Puncher" (1895). He opened the article on the history and conditions of the cowboy with the meeting of an English Lord and a Western cowboy, and ended it by voicing a hope for the future of the country, based on his belief in the heroic cowboy spirit as a wellspring of national regeneration.

The plots of his fiction also demonstrate, repeatedly, the differences and the acts of reconciliation between East and West. Many of his earlier pieces of fiction set up conflicts between Eastern and Western ways, or between women and men. Wister's first short story, "Hank's Woman" (1892), is about conflict between an Old World, Christian, white woman and New World, heathen, "little black Hank,"[11] which ends in both their deaths. "How Lin McLean Went East" (1893), his next tale, tells how a Western cowboy of Eastern origins returns east, only to discover that he now belongs wholeheartedly to the West. He is superior to men in the East and cannot reconcile himself to urban ways, even though his adherence to the West means that he must break with his family. Wister's major work, *The Virginian*, restates these polarities, but it also crystallizes a reconciliation of East and West, taking that subject as one of its main themes. The unification of contrasting customs also provides one of the few structuring elements in this episodic novel.

The Virginian contains various relationships and many adventures, but its three most sustained strands are three cases of opposition which become resolved in the course of the novel. The first is the story of the Eastern tenderfoot narrator, who initially finds the West and its inhabitants incomprehensible. At his first arrival, he is divorced from his physical environment: "I stared out through the door at the sky and the plains; but I did not see the antelope shining among the sage-brush, nor the great sunset light of Wyoming. Annoyance blinded my eyes to all things save my grievance: I saw only a lost trunk."[12] He is excluded yet more rigorously from the rituals of the fraternity which he encounters and tries hard to pierce: "Steve looked at me, and looked away—and that was all. But it was enough. In no company had I ever felt so much an outsider. Yet I liked the company, and wished it would like me" (p. 13). Although the narrator always remains a visitor to the West, he does become more fully part of the land. Through the adventure with the hen, Em'ly, he achieves friendship with the cowboy hero and, at the same time, he begins to perceive the land around him more and more clearly. This movement is finally completed beyond *The Virginian*, in Wister's last Western tale, in which the narrator is among old cowboys and his wish to belong is fulfilled: "They had made room for me, they had included me in their company."[13]

The other two conflicts focus on the hero, who is himself a synthesis of opposites. The Virginian is in a clear line from Natty Bumppo, embodying many of the contrasting characteristics of his prototype, but harmonizing them where they remain in conflict in Natty. The Virginian is the late-nineteenth-century version of the untutored "son of the wilderness," who engages in savage acts and has some difficulty in trying to woo his social superior. At the same time, he is naturally wise and moral, a dandy with innate gentility who is above the law of the courts and indestructible. The reader watches the Virginian undergo, like Natty, a rite of passage from prankster boyhood to a manhood forged out of sorrow and battle. But the Virginian goes further than Natty, in creating harmony out of his opposing inclinations to savagery and civilization. He both proves his natural superiority as violent frontier man and enters the hierarchy of the cattle trade, winning promotion from cowboy to foreman to rancher. He even enters the business world at the end of the novel. Also, unlike Natty, he wins the hand of the Eastern woman and settles into family life.

Before this harmonious end is reached, the hero has to participate in conflict, first with the villain Trampas. Wister makes this battle between good and evil a prominent part of his novel, but he does not exploit the formal contrasts involved in it as vividly as Cooper does those in fights between Natty and his enemies. Both hero and villain are dark in coloring and clothing, they are not presented in balanced tableaux, and the final showdown is not couched in a dualistic syntax. Furthermore, when the Virginian finally kills Trampas in a duel, the author's description camouflages the hero's act:

A wind seemed to blow his sleeve off his arm, and he replied to it, and saw Trampas pitch forward. He saw Trampas raise his arm from the ground and fall again, and lie there this time, still. A little smoke was rising from the pistol on the ground, and he looked at his own, and saw the smoke flowing upward out of it. [P. 481]

Unlike Cooper, Wister seems concerned to avoid laying greatest stress on violence in his Western scene.

He emphasizes formal contrasts much more in the other conflict, between the Virginian and Molly, cowboy and schoolmarm. He sets up a version of the conventional pastoral debate between nature and culture or rural and urban values, in this case linked specifically to Western man and Eastern woman. The opposition between the two protagonists is clear, for they carry with them the marks of their separate geographies. Molly's dependence on time past and ancestry, her pacifism, and her adherence to false social and intellectual standards contrast clearly with the Virginian's independence, his often violent mastery of other men, and his natural gentility and wisdom. Wister uses two spatial comparisons repeatedly to point up the contrast. He puts side by side the actions of each at the same moment in widely separate places, and he constructs dualistic tableaux, trivial and significant. In one instance, a scene symbolizes the contrast between Molly's painstakingly correct speech, and all it stands for, and the Virginian's dialect: dark-haired man and fair-haired woman sit on either side of a table—"The inkstand stood between them" (p. 365)—to write letters to the East. Each of their meetings is couched in martial terminology, and the wedding, even, is spoken of as capitulation and conquest: "Thus did her New England conscience battle to the end, and, in the end, capitulate to love" (p. 482).

By underscoring the contrasts between Eastern woman and Western man, Wister made their marriage that much more dramatic a resolution of their differences. At one level, Wister was simply acting out the conventional wedding which ends the pastoral romance. But he was also doing something important and novel within the development of the Western formula. By resolving the differences between East and West presented in his love story, he healed one of the divisions exposed by Cooper—the Western hero's unfitness as a mate for the genteel heroine. This problem, presented by Cooper in *The Pathfinder* especially, was largely sidestepped by the dime novelists. They tended to supply Eastern heroes for their cultured heroines and never really foregrounded the love story. So, as many critics have pointed out, Wister was the first to create a Western hero who was handsome and chivalrous enough (partly because of his Southern origins) to marry an educated Easterner. The wedding enacts the first full reconciliation of Eastern civilization and Western wilderness in the popular Western genre. Countless later Westerns imitate the love story in *The Virginian* and repeat its romantic happy ending. The centering of the Western hero and his successful romance with a cultured heroine was Wister's main deviation from the dime novel plot and the major element of what became the new version of the Western formula.

The fact that the formulists adopted *The Virginian* as their new model makes it all the more important that the apparent harmony of the wedding masks real discord. The novel is somewhat structurally disrupted after the marriage scene: while the narrative describes a harmonious union, the symbolism and structure of the text continue to communicate unease and division. Wister created a Western hero diverse enough to effect a fusion of East and West, but not a text which can sustain the pattern at all its levels.

By the time of the marriage scene, the novel has firmly established certain associations in the reader's mind. The Indian attack, the rustlers' hanging, and the Virginian's traumatic reaction to that event are linked intimately with the settings in which they occur. Thus "the ominous wood" (p. 315), mountains, and cottonwoods come to symbolize somberness and evil. When the Virginian travels through the mountains, after the lynching, he succumbs to a trancelike state, in which he "looked at the pictures in his mind" (p. 395), and he behaves like a "little kid," a regression which the narrator sees as dangerous; however, "once out of these mountains, I knew he could right himself" (p. 413). This symbolism is repeated in the moments before the final duel, when the shadows cast by the mountains and cottonwoods reinforce the sense of a trap closing on the two participants; more casually, when the Virginian is recovering from his near fatal wound, he is said to be "out of the woods" (p. 358).

In the last chapter, after the wedding, these symbols unexpectedly cluster around the hero and heroine's retreat into their isolated Eden. They camp among trees in the mountains, a double imprisonment, and, in a phrase echoing the description of the Virginian's nightmare, the scene "in his mind . . . became a picture" (p. 483). In established Western typology, the setting sun represents eternal life. Here, the change which marriage brings to the Virginian is "like a sunrise" (p. 494). He seems to be regressing to a childhood state again. Molly wonders, "Was this dreamy boy the man of two days ago? . . . his face changed by her to a boy's" (pp. 494–95). Furthermore, the dualistic scenes set up by Wister to establish the polarity of the contrasts involved are not modified. When the husband and wife swim in opposite pools with the island between them, they are still repeating the configuration of the letter-writing scene. All this means that the display of this closest union, the marriage of East and West, is not convincing at any but the plot level, for the validity of the cowboy's adaptation to the East, the modern West, and marriage is undercut by the network of inappropriate imagery and ambiguous statement on which it rests.

The Virginian figures as the pinnacle of Wister's literary achievement and the climax of his effort to fuse fictively the polarities which he observed in his country. All his other Western fictions prepare for, or decline from, this novel. There are feints at the same concerns in earlier works, like *Lin McLean* (1897), when Lin marries an Eastern girl. After *The Virginian*, these kinds of unions die out. The story "The Right Honorable the Strawberries" (1928) suggests a different attitude to the meeting of East and West. In it, the English visitor survives to settle in the West, while the Western cowboy who has tried to protect him is killed. The plot reads like an oblique acknowledgment by Wister of either the West's failure to survive as a regenerative force or his own failure to marry East and West in fiction convincingly. In any case, only the structured novel puts so much emphasis on conflict and its resolution, clearly associating the marriage of man and woman with the reconciliation of West and East. The harmony achieved in the novel's final stages and in its ending, in particular, is an apotheosis within that piece of fiction, within Wister's work, and within the Western genre as a whole. When the novel turns out to be coherent in symbolism and structure in only thirty-five of its thirty-six chapters, the repercussions reverberate widely.

FREDERIC REMINGTON'S ALTERNATIVE ENDING

Frederic Remington was a better painter than novelist, and his fictions are not finely wrought. But they are significant both in relation to the work of Wister and to the Western genre. The two important points about Remington's storytelling are that he worked in a diametrically opposite direction from Wister and that he developed Fenimore Cooper's themes in a unique way.

Remington thought about the West in the same way as Wister—as a last enclave of sincerity, independence, and virility—but he did not rate its potential for rejuvenation as highly. Both men could see that the wild West was disappearing, but, while Wister stressed that its spirit lived on, Remington emphasized its death. As early as 1889, in "Horses of the Plains," he predicted the diminution of Western types, human and animal. By 1898, he was comparing, in *Crooked Trails*, modern and historical West, only to disparage the former and glorify, with some melancholy, the latter. In 1900, he wrote to Wister that there "ain't going to be any more West."[14] Like Wister, he informed the East about the West, but he developed the integration no further.

The difference is reflected, first of all, in Remington's use of the first-person narrator. He, too, went west as a tenderfoot Easterner (to Montana in 1881). He used a naive narrator in his early writing, a tenderfoot

civilian who travels to ranches and army posts to report on these unknown places and serve as mediator between East and West. In the
articles and stories which appeared in *Harper's* and were collected into
Pony Tracks (1895) and *Crooked Trails* (1898), the "I" plays a central, comic
role, acting as focus and contrast. But the figure never becomes more
fully assimilated to Western ways. Instead, as Remington's writing becomes more fictional, the mild contrast which the narrator provides mu-
tates into a savage, destructive conflict which is contained in the new
focus, the heroic protagonist.

His most tortured hero appears in the work which contrasts most
directly with Wister's—*John Ermine of the Yellowstone* (1902). The novel
was written partly in response to *The Virginian*. Since 1893, Remington
and Wister had been personal and professional friends, working together
on various enterprises. But, as Ben Vorpahl shows, they had slowly developed in separate directions and had lost confidence in each other's
artistic abilities.[15] By 1902, Wister had begun to criticize Remington in
private letters. Remington can be seen to have carried his disapprobation
into *John Ermine*, which he was spurred on to write by *The Virginian*'s
great success.

John Ermine tells the story of a white boy, White Weasel, who has been
reared by the Crow Indians. In his adolescence, he is handed over to a
white hermit whom the Indians venerate. The old man rechristens the
boy "John Ermine" and reeducates him in the ways of white men. In
time, Ermine reenters white society by way of an army outpost, which
he joins as a scout, soon winning the soldiers' admiration for his bravery
in battle. He encounters Major Searle's daughter, Katherine, an Eastern
beauty who has come west to visit her father. He falls in love with her,
proposes marriage, and is rejected with horror. When he tries to murder
her (Eastern) fiancé, he is killed by a Crow scout who bears an old grudge.

The novel completely reverses the method of *The Virginian*. While
Wister deals in resolution or reconciliation and uses authorial devices to
emphasize that end, the thrust of *John Ermine* is toward rupture and
destruction. Ermine is like the Virginian in many ways, particularly in
his embodiment of contrasting forces. But he cannot harmonize the
oppositions in his own makeup or in the community around him. His
mixture of Indian and white sensibilities causes him agonizing conflict.
He has two names, at times he is referred to as two separate characters,
and he prays to two gods. In his final despair, he appeals to them both:
"O Sak-a-war-te, why did you not take the snake's gaze out of her eyes,
and not let poor Ermine sit like a gopher to be swallowed? God, God,
have you deserted me?"[16] Ermine understands that two-sidedness is at
the root of his tragedy, but he ascribes that characteristic to the white
soldiers. Whereas he apprehends vaguely a possible unity behind his
beliefs—"Sak-a-war-te and the God of the white men—he did not know

whether they were one or two" (p. 133)—he unreservedly identifies duality in the white attitude and blames that as the cause of his humiliation. He accuses the officers, "You have two hearts: one is red and the other is blue; and you feel with the one that best suits you at the time" (p. 236). And he tells his hermit friend savagely, "The white men in the camp are two-sided; they pat you with a hand that is always ready to strike" (p. 264).

As well as being half red and half white, Ermine sometimes mediates between Westerners and Easterners in the West. On one occasion, he introduces the Indians to the soldiers' relatives from the East. But he brings these two sides together only; he does not intend to reconcile them: "He had thought out the proposition that the Indians were just as strange to the white people as the white people were to them, consequently he saw a social opening. He would mix these people up so that they could stare at each other in mutual perplexity" (p. 153). The resultant clash causes his death. When he brings Katherine and a Crow scout face to face, he intervenes to protect the girl from the Indian's touch. Having thus insulted the Crow, he is eventually killed by him.

Starting out with the same model as Wister, Remington developed from it a very different conclusion. He did not leave the contrast entirely unstated, for he made several oblique gestures to Wister's novel in his text. At first, Ermine looks as if he is going to be as successful as the Virginian, winning admiration from his male companions and attracting Katherine's interest. At this stage, one soldier, talking of love, says, "I don't see how men write novels or plays about that old story; all they can do is to invent new fortifications for Mr. Hero to carry before she names the day" (p. 182). Of course, Remington's story does not turn out like this at all, but the synopsis neatly summarizes Wister's love plot. The names "Molly" and "Mrs. Taylor" are introduced peripherally, but during crucial courtship scenes, in connection with Katherine and her mother. Most tellingly of all, when Ermine proposes to Katherine, he invites her to "come to the mountains with me. I will make you a good camp" (p. 223). This is precisely where the Virginian takes Molly after their wedding and the two are shown as spending an idyllic month in pastoral isolation. Katherine, on the other hand, derides Ermine, accuses him of trying to turn her into a squaw, and runs screaming into the house. Remington was clearly pointing out the other possible result of an East-West meeting.

John Ermine has a dimension beyond its contrast with *The Virginian*: it is the centerpiece of the fiction in which Remington took further Cooper's vision of the frontier, and so suggested an alternative development for the whole genre of popular Western fiction. Remington's three long works—*Sundown Leflare* (1899), *John Ermine*, and *The Way of an Indian* (1905)—start with the Leatherstocking myth of the hero caught between two races and two times, then play out the implications of that situation to its violent conclusion.

It is worth recapitulating, briefly, Cooper's vision and the imitations it inspired, to show Remington's place in the history of the popular Western. Cooper worked to a dualistic design when he brought together the historical romance and the frontier saga to create his innovative Western fiction; and he repeated the principles of counterpoint and opposition at every level of his work, in theme, characterization, plot, scene, and even syntax. He never exploited either of the possible consequences of this dualism. That is, he neither involved his hero in a sentimental reconciliation with wilderness or civilization, nor did he let his hero be destroyed by either of these forces. He froze his frontier hero into unresolvable stasis, locked between savagery and civilization, while also providing a romantic, Eastern hero to end each novel with the conventional wedding. Some subsequent writers, like Robert Montgomery Bird, echoed Cooper's ending unchanged. Others, most predominantly the dime novelists, exploited the possibilities for sentimental reconciliation by creating genteel heroes who merely disguise themselves as savage frontiersmen. Wister's hero was the first genuinely to encompass capacities for civilization and wilderness within his own personality, and Wister, as we have seen, tried hard to reconcile East and West with this figure. Only Remington developed the implications of destruction inherent in the polarization which Cooper presented.

The first work in which Remington clearly echoes some central characteristics of the Leatherstocking tales is *Sundown Leflare*. The half-breed hero, Sundown, is similar to Natty in various ways, but he always remains a comic version. Thus, when he is introduced as a translator who mediates between Indian and white men, the cross in his blood is revealed casually: "Sundown was cross-bred, red and white, so he never got mentally in sympathy with either strain of his progenitors. He knew about half as much concerning Indians as they did themselves, while his knowledge of white men was in the same proportions."[17] Similarly, although Sundown, like Natty, wins his name as a young man because of extraordinary abilities (he can see unnaturally far at sunset), it turns out that the christening is based on trickery (he has secretly acquired a pair of binoculars and uses them under cover of twilight).

The most important coincidence between the two is that Sundown is locked into a similar time scheme to Natty's. The book consists of five stories in which Sundown gradually becomes more intimate with the Eastern narrator and at the same time tells him about adventures from farther and farther into his past. The five stories correspond structurally to the five novels in the Leatherstocking cycle. In them, Sundown gradually becomes older and more civilized, but simultaneously he tells tales which show him in younger and younger, and more and more purely

Indian, guise. Thus, in the last story, he attains communion with the white narrator. Sundown says,

> "Now I tole you dees ting—what was de great medicine—but I don' wan you for go out here een de village un talk no more dan I talk—are you me?"
>
> "I am you," and we forgathered. [P. 105]

But the direct cause of this identification with a white man is Sundown's description of his elevation, as a young man, to medicine man in an Indian tribe—that is, to full Indian status.

Sundown undergoes an experience akin to that of Natty and Chingachgook, who slough off the layers of age until they achieve the primal innocence of *The Deerslayer*, but out of the process he achieves a more circular immortality than them. The mythic time scheme in the Leatherstocking tales results from the order in which the books were written. Although Natty ostensibly dies at the end of *The Prairie*, his death has little force, since it is implied that, setting with the sun, he will surely rise again with it. Furthermore, Cooper brought him back to manhood thirteen years later in *The Pathfinder*. The interdependence of mythological and chronological time is more intricate than this in Sundown's case. In each episode, he is involved in straightforward chronology in his developing relationship with the white narrator and, simultaneously, he articulates a mythic, inverted time scheme, when he presents himself in moments from the past. These strands are dependent on each other: as Sundown grows older, he brings himself into being as a younger and younger, and more fully red, man; but these stories of his youth depend on his increasing age and familiarity with the white narrator for their articulation. Each version of time feeds into the other, to create a perpetual cycle.

As if in response to the dominance of this double time scheme, which is the only element ordering the disparate tales, Sundown articulates circular repetition in his language. He always uses a mongrel verb construction, made up of present, imperfect, and infinitive forms. He describes a simple action, "I was geet two pony, un was go to log house" (p. 29); or, with a slightly more complicated construction, he says that the priests "all time wan' tak care of me when I die. Well, all right, dees Enjun medicine-man she tak care of me when I was leeve sometime" (pp. 98–99). Since he seems not to know the perfect tense, all his verbs are in the present, whose main use is the description of habitual acts, and the imperfect, which describes continuous actions without definite time limits. He has a vocabulary only for the ongoing present and unfinished past; he does not verbalize finitude and ending any more than he experiences them. Remington's conclusion, in this respect, is a more extreme version of Cooper's. Both heroes are eternally displaced and disjunct from the rules of human time. Both are assigned to cycles which perpetually repeat but never proceed.

John Ermine is even more clearly a descendant of Natty Bumppo. He is an orphan and a celibate who, having proved his natural gentility by superior behavior in military service, approaches a woman of higher social rank than his own. But in Ermine's case, the consequences of that mistake are more severe. When Natty is turned down, he returns to his Indian companion and his wilderness life; Ermine's rejection results in his death.

As I have already indicated, Remington's novel stresses the divided circumstances of the Western hero's existence just as much as Cooper's work did. But Remington shows that the meeting of savagery and civilization not only traps the frontiersman, but destroys him. In various ways, Remington suggests that this ending is both true and inevitable. He uses repetitions and prophesies to lend the ending force. More explicitly, the hermit recognizes the reality of the action—"like the raising of a curtain, which reveals the play, the hermit saw suddenly that it was heavy and solemn—that he was to see a tragedy, and this was not a play; it was real, it was his boy, and he did not want to see a tragedy" (p. 263). The same character admits the necessity of the conclusion: "I do not understand why men should be so afflicted in this world as Ermine and I have been, but doubtless it is the working of a great law, and possibly of a good one" (p. 267). Once, even, the author intervenes to show that Ermine and his Indian companion cannot help but bring about their own demise: "Neither of the two mentioned people realized that the purpose of the present errand was to aid in bringing about the change which meant their passing." Long before the end of the novel, the author points out that these frontier types are already dead—"America will never produce their like again" (p. 88). Remington was signaling that, both in the world of his novel and in the real West, the frontiersman was doomed from the beginning to extinction by the agents of Eastern civilization.

In this scheme, Remington's last book, *The Way of an Indian*, acts as an endpiece, showing what is left after the contending forces of East and West have been played out.[18] Its emphasis is all on death and endings. It tells of the boyhood, maturation, and death of Fire Eater. There are no contrasting strains in this figure; he is a full-blooded Indian who belongs to the Cheyenne tribe, whose downfall has already been mentioned in *Sundown* and *John Ermine*. At the beginning and the end, the hero is alone, thinking about the afterlife. Between these two points, although he does undergo the various stages of initiation into manhood and leadership, all his experiences are clustered around with images of death, all his victories are petty, and all his attacks on the white man, futile. He has no mythic time scheme and the one gesture at regeneration is the hero's pretended rebirth, acted out to avoid the tribe's censure for his failure in battle. At the end, the tribe is massacred by the army, and Fire Eater is left, the last of his line, with his dead grandchild in his arms. It is no accident that the most memorable image of the work concerns the introduction of new life to violent death. The chief takes his grandson to show him a dead soldier, just before the final defeat. The baby, soon to freeze to death himself, stabs the dead corpse.

> Pulling his great knife from its buckskin sheath [Fire Eater] curled the little fat hand around its haft and led him to the white body. . . . Comprehending the idea, the infant drew up and drove down, doing his best to obey the instructions, but his arm was far too weak to make the knife penetrate. The fun of the thing made him scream with pleasure, and the old Fire Eater chuckled at the idea of his little warrior's first *coup*.[19]

In these three works, Remington developed the darker and more resonant side of Cooper's vision, which had been ignored for over fifty years. Henry Nash Smith said of Cooper, "if he had been able—as he was not—to explore to the end the contradictions in his ideas and emotions, the Leatherstocking series might have become a major work of art."[20] Remington's interest in contradiction was limited to his heroic type; even so, his achievement is very rare in popular Western fiction. I have found no other author working with formulaic materials (until the anti-Western writers in the 1960s) who explores to their violent conclusion these contradictions in the image of the wilderness man at the disappearing frontier.

Remington's vision never became popular: while *The Virginian* immediately became a bestseller and the model for the Western formulist, *John Ermine* sold only moderately well and has been almost forgotten since early in the century. Indeed, *John Ermine* did not even retain its plot in its own dramatization. When Louis Evans Shipman turned the novel into a play in 1903, the public disliked the ending, and he persuaded Remington to help him revise it. The new ending ran: Ermine shoots Katherine's fiancé dead. He is accused of murder, but successfully defends his action as self-defense and eventually wins Katherine as his bride.[21]

Yet *The Virginian* is a divided novel about ultimate harmony, whereas *John Ermine* is a uniform expression of rupture. The dissonances in *The Virginian*'s design indicate the importance of *John Ermine*'s overt recognition that the wilderness Westerner inevitably failed to integrate with society. That such a central work as Wister's should betray the same concerns, in stifled form, suggests that, although Remington was alone among popular Western writers in dramatizing this irreversible conflict, he had realized a crucial aspect of the genre, which had been present, but muted, since Cooper. Popular Western fiction may have lost some better alternatives when Remington's design ended with him.

DEFENDING THEIR WEST: THE ARTISTIC
STRATEGIES OF WISTER AND REMINGTON

Would I might prison in my words
And so hold by me all the year
Some portion of the Wilderness
Of freedom that I walk in here.

Owen Wister, 1889[22]

Although these artists wanted to inform the East about the West, they did not rest with documentary accounts. Their work is highly stylized, despite its inclusion of realistic details. Their observations of the West were only the raw material which they reshaped to fit into certain literary traditions and, more significantly, into their own artistic structures. They designed their fictions in such a way that they resist the shapelessness and transitoriness of the actual West which they claim to represent.

The formal patterns in Wister's and Remington's art are different, and they correspond to the artists' contrasting attitudes to the West. Wister's plot in *The Virginian* and his continual utterances about the survival of the cowboy spirit show that he was unwilling to accept the death of the wild West. He put together *The Virginian* when he was with his wife in Charleston, South Carolina, the place of their honeymoon four years before; he composed within society, always trying to harmonize the South he wrote from, the West he had visited, and the East to which he belonged. Remington, on the other hand, retreated to his island refuge in the St. Lawrence River to write *John Ermine*. He accepted that the wild West was irretrievably gone, and he turned his attention to a West which was firmly fixed in the past, with no connection to the contemporary Western region. In 1907, he proclaimed, "my West passed utterly out of existence so long ago as to make it merely a dream."[23]

Remington was an illustrator before a writer or a fine art painter, and the composition of his Western scene—both visual and literary—was influenced by his early artistic habits. For example, as an Easterner who spent much more time in the East than the West and produced many more illustrations in his studio than preparatory sketches on location, he seems to have relied heavily on photography at the start of his career.[24] Using a camera may well have affected his perspective; a foreshortening of foreground figures and a lack of focus on background details were always characteristic of his work. Also, the technology of illustrative reproduction in late-nineteenth-century magazines limited Remington to black-and-white prints for much of his career. He himself complained that this situation led him to concentrate on form at the expense of color, even when working with watercolors and oils.[25] More generally, the frame which surrounds painted figures was important in all his work, for he made a boundary line the major structuring principle

"A Cavalryman's Breakfast on the Plains," c. 1890. Courtesy Amon Carter Museum, Fort Worth, Texas.

"The Fight for the Waterhole," 1901. Courtesy The Hogg Brothers Collection, The Museum of Fine Arts, Houston.

"The Sentinel," 1909. Courtesy Frederic Remington Art Museum, Ogdensburg, New York.

"Sundown Leflare's Warm Spot," first illustration, 1898.

"Sundown Leflare's Warm Spot," second illustration, 1898.

"Sundown Leflare's Money," illustration, 1898.

"Sundown's Higher Self," illustration, 1898.

"The Bronco Buster" (large), 1909. Courtesy Frederic Remington Art Museum, Ogdensburg, New York.

in his fiction as well as his art. To whatever extent technical conditions shaped his work, however, they were not wholly responsible for the distinctive patterns which he developed: these patterns became only more pronounced after he ceased illustrating, and his writings suggest that his design was due at least as much to his vision of the West as to the constraints of his media. The chronological development of Remington's composition can be seen most clearly in his canvases. These then need to be put alongside his more complex, double-faceted works—that is, the texts and illustrations which he conceived, together, as imaginative recreations of the West.

Whatever else it may be, the West of America is a geographical region. Yet this best-known artist of the area was no landscapist. In most of his paintings his background—whether Montana, New Mexico, or Colorado—is represented by a few horizontal strokes or an unformed wash of colors. Many of his studies of single horses, cavalrymen, or cowboys are given no background at all. Only in his later years, as the effects of Impressionism finally began to interest him, did he shape his background creatively. Even then, he was concerned not with detail or shape but with contrasts of shade, color, and texture. When Remington did fill in his background at all, he did it with figures of animals, men, or buildings, smaller echoes of the shapes which occupy the foreground of the picture, not with elements of a natural landscape. There is one exception: when portraying an Eastern setting, he sketched in the forms of densely growing trees or foliage. But his Western setting is an empty scene.

Because of this relatively empty backdrop, the viewer's attention is focused on the figures. Remington's Western type is well known: he is a rugged, often mustached rider, who is authentically dressed in the fringed buckskin of the frontiersman, the chaps and gunbelt of the cowboy, or the stripes and braid of the cavalryman. These figures change hardly at all throughout the thirty years of Remington's art.

What does change with regard to these figures and what comes to seem most important about them is the way in which they are arranged into increasingly stylized configurations. From the first, Remington presents his repetitive types in coherent units, not allowing them to disperse across his landscape or face in too many directions. Sometimes a simple line of figures results, as in his canoeing pictures and his depictions of cavalry on the march. Often figures are grouped into a clump well forward in the picture, all moving in the same direction and focusing on the same point. This is the arrangement of the figures in one of Remington's earliest paintings, the watercolor "Arrest of a Blackfoot Murderer" (1887).[26] Sometimes the containment suggested by this grouping is emphasized by a building or fence which keeps the figures well to the fore of the canvas. This use of pictorial space results in an impression of harnessed energy, perhaps even circumscribed movement, however vigorous the action of the figures. Throughout Remington's work, these layouts reappear, particularly in scenes of stagecoaches or of the cavalry.[27]

As time passed, Remington also began to structure his scenes into more distinctive and more rigid patterns than these, strengthening the suggestion of circumscription hinted at in the earliest canvases. In later pictures, he repeatedly arranges his figures into one of a limited number of diagrammatic patterns, whose components are a circle and a straight line.[28] The circle can be composed of men sitting around a campfire, men on foot surrounding a hunted animal, or men and horses forming a protective barrier against attackers. The circle is nearly always backed by a line which is parallel or diagonal to the baseline of the picture and usually represents the horizon. A second, vertical line tends to intersect the circle at its perimeter or its center. These three components become more starkly diagrammatic through time.

The canvas titled "A Cavalryman's Breakfast on the Plains" (c. 1890) has in its foreground a group of cavalrymen, standing, sitting, and squatting around a campfire. They all face in toward the fire, their faces reflecting one another in their impassivity. Echoing this arrangement are two more circles of men round fires, set one behind the other, giving some depth to the setting. The postures and appearances of these figures imitate those of the foreground. These three circles are placed diagonally, right to left, across the canvas, in receding perspective. Cutting off the scene and limiting its depth, is a row of horses standing in a parallel diagonal line. Beyond their heads is only the uninterrupted blue of the sky. The animals create a horizon which shuts off the wide plains of the title from the circled enclosures of men.

In a later oil painting, "The Fight for the Waterhole" (1901), Remington makes his scene more extensive, by opening it up to the plain and the mountains. As usual, these areas are not detailed; the plain is a flat wash of bleached-out yellow, the mountains a more shadowed line of purple peaks. In the foreground is the waterhole, whose color echoes the mountains' tones. It has a circular rim, around which five cowboys lie, pointing their rifles outward. In the center is a small pool of water, circular like the upper rim and flanked by horses. In this design, the circle is much larger than in the previous example, and it is backed by the horizontal lines of the plain and the mountain ridge. The line of the waterhole rim connects each cowboy to the next, and their positions echo each other around the circle. The lines of their long-barreled rifles, pointing away from the circle's center, indicate that the force is centrifugal.

In one of Remington's last pictures, this diagrammatic layout is clearest. "The Sentinel" (1909) is, pictorially, one of his shallowest scenes. A single hunter stands flat against the canvas of a wagon, flanked on either side by a large spoked wagon wheel. The emphasis is all on the circular and the vertical, for the pattern is unelaborated now by narrative or depth of perspective.

The overall impression made by these pictures is that Remington developed artistically not in his representation of individual figures but in his arrangement of them into certain configurations. This is also true in his illustrations to his own writings. In his written texts, he finds verbal equivalents for these visual patterns and thus he reveals something which is only implied in his canvases: that these increasingly rigid structures resulted from his growing unease with Western space.

In *Pony Tracks*, Remington's first collection of journalistic writings, the structures which I have described are evident in both the illustrations and the text. In the same way that figures are grouped together against an empty background in the illustrations, the stories are mainly set in man-made oases, whether cavalry post or ranch, and the adventure often results from the inhabitants of these outposts venturing into the wilderness in a group. As always, the emphasis is on the animate figures, not the scene in which they are set. Remington shows that he appreciates the vastness of the Western panorama, be it in Mexico, New Mexico, or Wyoming, and he does not attempt with words, any more than with images, to sketch in its details. He gestures toward the landscape without describing it: "It is one of those marvellous vistas of mountain scenery utterly beyond the pen or brush of any man. Paint cannot touch it, and words are wasted."[29] He makes it clear that the landscape is simply too big for the artist: "All this made a picture, but, like all Western canvases, too big for a frame" (p. 169).

In his second collection of short pieces, *Crooked Trails*, Remington regiments his literary and his visual material more strictly than in *Pony Tracks*. He also articulates his reasons for doing so: they have to do with his attitudes toward both history and geography. First, he tells several stories set in the historical West, creating in them various fictive frames which intercede between the narrator and the action. Thus, two tales of the seventeenth- and eighteenth-century wilderness are presented as documents—one a memoir and the other a letter—which retain the original spelling, vocabulary, and typeface. In this way, Remington establishes a clear demarcation between the material of the Western story and the introduction by the Eastern narrator. When the West is less ancient, he indicates its separateness from the present by multiplying the number of narrators through whom the story passes. Accompanying these historical tales are illustrations which order their figures into lines and avenues more rigorously than in the previous collection. The depiction of British soldiers for "Joshua Goodenough's Old Letter," for example, marshals the group into identical rows, stressing the lineal regimentation by showing them crossing parallel tree trunks which bridge a chasm. All this emphasis on boundaries is apparently motivated by the author's belief that the heroic Old West needs to be marked off from the trivia of the contemporary era. His concern to preserve the past is articulated in his introduction to the seventeenth-century memoir, when he declares, "to those [who disbelieve this tale] I say, Go to your microbes, your statistics, your volts, and your bicycles, and leave me the truth of other days."[30] He sees truth, too, in "Joshua Goodenough's Old Letter," "which I publish because it is history" (p. 92).

In the same collection, Remington suggests that there is also a geographical reason for his marking the human off from the landscape: he has to emphasize regimentation because he is beginning to feel that the landscape is threatening to overwhelm the human figure. This is a new development. In *Pony Tracks*, the narrator could say of the black cook William, "He was the first impression my companion and myself had of Mexico, and as broad as are its plains and as high as its mountains, yet looms up William on a higher pinnacle of remembrance" (p. 62). Now the humans do not dominate the scene nearly as surely. The sense of an overwhelming land is clear in "Pestiferous little man disturbed nature" (p. 75) and "I felt rather insignificant, not to say contemptible, as I sat there in the loneliness of this big nature which worked around me . . . I somehow did not seem to grace the solitude" (pp. 26–27). The author is beginning to reveal a nervousness, an unease about this vast Western space. Before, he showed respect; now he hints at fear.

Having established strategies for containing his figures in his short stories and his illustrations, and having gestured toward his motives for doing so, Remington proceeded to undermine his patterns. In the course of his three long fictions, he begins to express his discomfort with his own stylization. The relationship between text and illustration becomes more complex, and gradually the diagrammatic configurations change their character.

Remington's discomfort with his stylization is suggested, briefly, in an early article. In the midst of all the frames and lines I have described, the narrator suddenly criticizes rigid patterns in art: "soldiers in rows and in lines do not compose well in pictures. I always feel, after seeing infantry drill in an armory, like Kipling's light-house keeper, who went insane looking at the cracks between the boards—they were all so horribly alike" (p. 64). The ramifications of Remington's contradictory reactions toward and against rigid composition are worked out systematically in *Sundown Leflare*, his first extended piece of fiction. Here, Remington presents his hero within a variety of confining patterns, but he also displays a resistance to these patterns.

As I have already shown, Sundown is caught within several, fairly complex structures. The time scheme he inhabits is a unique combination of forward-moving present and backward-moving past, each dependent on the other for its continued existence. His mixed racial characteristics and his highly codified speech also set him off from the narrator and the reader. All his stories pass through at least two narrators (in the opening tale, four). As the book proceeds, the figure Sundown is removed behind more and more guises, since he appears in a different costume in each tale, and recedes into a more and more remote past.

The illustrations tell a different story from the written text. The most obvious discrepancy between the two is that, while the text always shows Sundown to be comic, in the illustrations—from the frontispiece of him in shabby, ill-fitting work clothes to his final appearance in Indian headdress—he looks increasingly romantic and heroic. With reference to stylization and the use of painted lines to fence in human figures, the illustrations again tell their own story. At first, the illustrations become increasingly stylized, thus corresponding to the fiction, which accumulates more and more frames. For example, in "Sundown Leflare's Warm Spot," the third story in the book, there are two illustrations. The first is of Sundown arguing with the Indian, Snow Owl. They stand opposite each other, at either end of a very approximate circle of seated Indians. The second illustration shows the two men dueling, and in it one half of the scene reflects the other, each set in perfect parallel lines. Sundown and Snow Owl sit astride horses which are angled toward each other, and, following the same lines, their lances cross. Repeating that pattern are the lines of trees which intersect with the horizon. By the next story, "Sundown Leflare's Money," Sundown seems to be trying to break out of this stylized arrangement. In the second illustration, he is on his horse in the foreground, shooting back at a train which crosses the picture in a diagonal line behind him. By the story, we can tell that his shots are directed at a face which just perceptibly peeps through the wheels of the train. The main impression of the illustration, however, is of the foreground unit (Sundown on his horse) shooting at the confining back line (the diagonal train). By the final illustration, he seems to have escaped this kind of circumscription. He sits on a hillside with an Indian, pointing out the panorama to him. The figures are in quite small perspective and positioned to one side. With lines, planes, and shadows, Remington gives an unusual amount of detail to the landscape, which could imminently swallow up the small figures.

There are two Sundowns, then: one appears in the written text as a comic anachronism circumscribed by an accumulation of narrative structures; the other is illustrated as a hero transcending the bounds of Remington's usual protective strategies. What happens in the illustrations seems a last attempt by the artist to break out of the rigid formations with which, more and more, he was depicting his Western scene.

In *John Ermine*, the tension between text and illustration has gone, because they both now insist on scenes of confinement. However, Remington's fictional "framing" still seems to bother him, because he points out, here, the danger of enclosure. The action takes place in a vacuum, in that general historical and geographical coordinates are supplied, but immediate visual details of the land are omitted. Enclosure is part of the fiction's theme. Ermine is taken from the Indian camp to the hermit's cave, then to the army post, all of which are portrayed as confining in some way, in both text and illustrations. For example, the introduction of Ermine and Crooked Bear to Indian life is judged by the hermit: "They had entered from opposite doors only, and he did not wish to go out again, but the boy did" (p. 53). This sentence is close to the illustration of the hermit and Ermine meeting. It is a dark, shadowy scene inside a cave. All the figures are close together: the hermit sits with his arm round Ermine and these two form the centerpiece of a half circle, closely flanked on either side by an Indian and a huge dog.

The theme of enclosure is injected with a specific sense of threat when the framing process becomes associated with Eastern woman. (There is a similar, less strong association of Molly and confinement in *The Virginian*.) Ermine first sees Katherine's image in a photograph, which becomes more real to him than the woman herself. Remington uses a particularly self-conscious simile when he makes Katherine look at Ermine "for all the world as though he had stepped from an old frame" (p. 184). She also thinks that Indians should be kept in cages like animals at the zoo, and she moves around the post within her protective retinue of admirers. Because of Katherine, Ermine renounces his trip out to the hills, to remain within the camp, where he will ultimately die. He stays inside his tent, dreaming about her; he is dangerously like the disappearing Indians who "draw their robes more closely over their heads as they dreamed" (p. 268). The illustrations support these effects, either showing dark indoor scenes or tracing closed patterns of figures. The word and the picture have come together again, to emphasize the self-enclosement of a past which is dead.

In Remington's final book, *The Way of an Indian*, the structures become so rigid that they trap the participants. Arrangements that were once defensive now clearly become self-destructive. In the written text, the diagrammatic forms are translated more directly than ever into language. Everything except the patterns created by characters' movements is quite vague. Not only is there little landscape detail, but there is no precise dating either. This is an amorphous, long-gone past which does not connect with the present. (The death of the chief's baby before the end makes impossible any prolongation of the race.) Further, the hero, known at different stages as White Otter, the Bat, and Fire Eater, is not described in any detail. The author says simply, "He was a boy—a fine-looking, skilfully modeled youth—as beautiful a thing, doubtless, as God ever created in His sense of form" (pp. 12–13). It is as if, by now, the author has chosen his heroic type and wants to develop his treatment of proportion, contrast, and shade. This development in his writing imitates that, much earlier, of his art.

As in the illustrations, Remington emphasizes shadow a great deal in this piece of writing. He talks about size and distortion, and makes the hero's shadow an extension of his character, indicating his mood. Repeatedly, he describes scenes, often highly ritualized, of circles and straight lines. In these descriptions, the familiar visual configurations reappear in verbal form:

> "I will go down the hill, and make my pony go around in a circle so that the camp may send the warriors out to us," saying which, the Bat rode the danger-signal, and the Chis-chis-chash riders came scurrying over the dry grass, leaving lines of white dust in long marks behind them. [Pp. 68–69]

> while the robe aspirants sat in a circle . . . the pipe made its way about the ring without stopping.
>
> Iron Horn then walked behind the circle sticking up medicine-arrows in the earth. . . .
>
> Resuming his seat, he spoke in a harsh, guttural clicking: "What is said in this circle must never be known to any man who does not sit here now." [Pp. 127–29]

The depiction of stylized configurations is now the primary aim of both text and illustration, and it has its consequences. In Remington's earlier work, the emphasis on layout seems defensive: figures are protected from disintegration in an overwhelmingly featureless landscape, and the fictive past, increasingly stylized in composition, is curtailed by narrative structures which protect it from the present. However, here the configurations which the Indians adopt prove to be destructive, not defensive. In one of the climaxes of the book, fighting Indians, led by Fire Eater, pack themselves into a waterhole and line themselves round its rim to battle with the white men. (The strategy is very like that adopted, apparently successfully, in the painting "The Fight for the Waterhole," several years before.) Now, the arrangement simply enables the besiegers to attack on all sides, drawing in the net of their circle to massacre the Indian group.

As the strategy boomerangs fatally on his protagonists so, perhaps, it did on Remington's creative abilities. He never changed the patterns through which he presented his artistic and fictive vision; he only made more rigid the lines which he had adopted from the first, repeatedly blocking off groups of figures from the empty space around them. The rigorousness of his defensive structures possibly became claustrophobic to him; they certainly became artistically sterile. Perhaps, in the end, the ambiguous consequences of Remington's method were one reason why he was most enthusiastic about, and most artistically successful with, his bronze sculptures. These represented little development in Remington's artistic vision, because they simply repeated the figures and poses already familiar from his canvases. However, they were different from his paintings in at least one important way: they provided the artist with an escape route from his problems with Western space. These forms did not need a frame, and, with them, Remington could concentrate on lines of movement unlocated in any scene. They were solid and unbreakable. Their cohesion and configuration could not be threatened by the time or place in which they were set.

If Remington seems in awe, almost in fear, of the Western landscape, Owen Wister does not. Whereas Remington denied space, Wister concentrated on it in all its aspects, using it as the main component in his strategy to preserve the wild West. Although he admitted on one level that the West which he admired was dead, he wanted to prolong its life in fiction. The plot of *The Virginian* demonstrates one method by which Wister tried to keep the spirit of the wild West alive. This plot line is supported by Wister's general portrayal of the Western scene in his fiction. He creates a West immune to the passage of time, largely by concentrating on the land's spatial qualities.

Wister strains to convey the Western landscape in all its size and detail. None of Remington's inhibitions are visible in his method. He situates his scenes exactly, with a wealth of detail, using various metaphors to describe more vividly the natural setting: "Fort Robinson, on the White River, is backed by yellow bluffs that break out of the foot-hills in turret and toadstool shapes, with stunt pine starving between their torrid bastions."[31] Remington conveys a sense of extensive landscape only by omitting its description; in contrast, Wister uses the vast emptiness as one of his major effects. From his earliest writing, he concentrates on this aspect of the land: "I . . . saw the desert everywhere flat, treeless, and staring like an eye without a lid."[32] In *The Virginian*, especially, his attention shifts from the details of the landscape to its spaciousness. The narrator characterizes it as "this voiceless land, this desert, this vacuum" (p. 58), and he is entranced by its size and atmospheric effects of light and color, rather than by specific sights. The empty landscape is shown to be healthy and clean, in contrast to the grubby, littered towns which man has built on its surface, staining its purity. In this novel, space becomes a moral touchstone.

Later, in *Members of the Family* (1911), the author shows interest, briefly, in space divorced from landscape—space as an abstract quality, the medium of energy. He uses the principle of the movement of energy through space to structure one story in that collection. Its sections are given headings like "The Storing of the Energy," "The Energy Is Transmitted," and "The Vibrations Spread." Wister introduces the action with a pseudoscientific commentary on this business of movement through space. (He was imitated, almost fifty years later, by Jack Schaefer.)

Force, as you may know, is like the King, and never dies. It endlessly trans-
mits itself through the same or some other shape. Drop a stone in a pond,
and the wave-rings may seem to expire as they widen, but they do not;
through friction or impact or something, they merely become invisible. You
can stop a cannon-ball, but you cannot kill its speed. . . . Scientific men have
told you all this as they have told me, and judging from the delightful events
which I shall proceed to narrate, I should not wonder if the scientific men
were right.[33]

The important point about this description is its emphasis on immortality. Wister's thoughts seem to run: if movement through space cannot
die ("You can stop a cannon-ball, but you cannot kill its speed"), then
space contains an element of immortality which might preserve the Western scene. This is the kind of logic Wister applied when he treated the
West in essays and fiction.

Within this Western scene, with its emphasis on the spatial dimension,
Wister tried to create a nonchronological time scheme. He began this
process in his 1895 essay, "The Evolution of the Cowpuncher." In the
scale of chronology, Wister presents the cowboy as an isolated orphan:
"These wild men sprang from the loins of no similar father, and begot
no sons to continue their hardihood."[34] Wister had no desire to relate
the cowboy to his recent or contemporary relations in the East, because
they were the businessmen, the money worshippers he so detested. Instead, he asserted that the cowboy was related to the great heroes of all
ages. In tracing this descent, Wister reckoned by a kind of typological
time, or a time scheme which connects mythic types. Although the essay
is titled "The Evolution," the cowboy's ancestry is shown to be composed
of one static type, the vaguely defined Anglo-Saxon, who cannot be
changed by the course of history. The model of the adventurous, powerful man simply reappears at irregular intervals, unaltered except in
superficial costume. So, the cowboy in the West "showed once again the
mediaeval man. It was no new type, no product of the frontier, but just
the original kernel of the nut with the shell broken" (p. 610). On the
continuum of typological time, the cowboy is the immediate successor
to the knight of Camelot, "his direct lineal offspring among our Western
mountains" (p. 606). In this early essay, Wister replaced chronological
time with mythic or typological time as his main measure.

In the same year as the essay, 1895, he rewrote the specific relationship
between space and time in America, when he claimed that, at that period
in the late nineteenth century, space was reordering time. In the preface
to *Red Men and White*, he explains:

Never, indeed, it would seem have such various centuries been jostled together as they are today upon this continent, and within the boundaries of
our nation. We have taken the ages out of their processional arrangement
and set them marching disorderly abreast in our wide territory, a harlequin
platoon. We citizens of the United States date our letters 18—, and speak

of ourselves as living in the present era; but the accuracy of that custom
depends upon where we happen to be writing. [P. vi]

He goes on to say that the further west one travels, the more ancient
are the inhabitants' characteristics. In this description, he comes close to
saying that American space has reordered time from a diachronic to a
synchronic arrangement. He also echoes Frederick Jackson Turner's
thesis, that "the United States lies like a huge page in the history of
society. Line by line as we read this continental page from west to east
we find the record of social evolution."[35] This theory was very much in
the air when Wister wrote *Red Men and White*, having been presented by
Turner just two years earlier. Wister, however, was the first Western
author to attempt to embody in his fiction this idea of a relationship
between space and time in the American West.

His ideas achieve their most complete fictional expression in *The Virginian*. In this novel, the space of the landscape brings into being a mythic
time scheme. In its opening pages, the novel uses the immensity of Western space not only as a moral absolute, but as a medium through which
the mythic temporal link can be brought into being. Wyoming is "a world
of crystal light, a land without end, a space across which Noah and Adam
might come straight from Genesis" (p. 13). In this space, Genesis, the
mythic past, becomes a distant spot on the Western map. Thus, when
the narrator says of the Virginian, "He had plainly come many miles
from somewhere across the vast horizon, as the dust upon him showed"
(p. 4), he is placing the Western hero in the pantheon of mythic figures.
The personal and mythological facets of the Virginian are linked spatially, for the "somewhere" can be equally Judge Henry's ranch and the
locus of Genesis. In this Western environment, even the Easterners, the
narrator and Molly, partake of this direct historical connection. Celebrating his rite of passage from tenderfoot, the narrator feels he is "living
back in ages gone" (p. 375), and Molly, in her Western cabin, can commune with the portrait of her Stark ancestor, "across the hundred years
which lay between them" (p. 324). Again, time is expressed as space, in
this case as the distance between the girl in her chair and the portrait
on the wall.

These large-scale rearrangements of geography and history are supported by Wister's treatment of time as a more localized measurement.
In *Lin McLean*, the eponymous hero has already voiced his contempt of
time in response to the Eastern narrator's conventional attitude: "Hours
and hours! You're talking foolishness. What have they got to do with
it?"[36] In *The Virginian*, there is an attempt to erase that measure. In aside
after aside, time is a poison, a threat wielded by Eastern woman—"if you
do this, there can be no to-morrow for you and me" (p. 475)—or an
irrelevance—"Days look alike, and often lose their very names in the

quiet depths of Cattle Land" (p. 283). (Only on the honeymoon island—
a contradiction again—does time become a regular beat as action is plotted by days and nights.) The novel takes place within these temporal-
spatial brackets, in which space is the more important dimension. The
formulation is not fully worked out, nor does it appear systematically
throughout the story; nevertheless, Wister here establishes a reordering
of time and history which later Western authors, like Jack Schaefer,
explore more thoroughly.

Clearly Wister was creating a bulwark against passing time: the process
of history cannot touch his heroic cowboy, because he belongs to nonchronological time, he does not measure action with time, and in his
Western milieu space is the main dimension. Like Remington, Wister
was becoming increasingly dissatisfied with the modern age and was
desperately retrenching, trying to shore up a way of life which was disappearing before his eyes. However, in his preface to *The Virginian*, he
acknowledged that he was fighting a losing battle. By the time he wrote
this introduction, which was after he had finished the novel and several
years after he had written some of the chapters, the West he admired
was a thing of the recent past. He described one way in which this development directly affected his text: for book publication in 1902, he
had to revise the chapters written late in the nineteenth century by changing all the verbs in the present tense into the past. He commented that
"time has flowed faster than my ink" (p. ix).

As time moved on for Wister, he came to admit the death of the wild
West more openly in his nonfiction, but simultaneously stepped up his
efforts to deny time in his fiction. In his 1911 preface to *Members of the
Family*, he gives notice that the wild West is definitely past: "Time steps
in between the now that is and the then that was with a vengeance; it
blocks the way for us all; we cannot go back. . . . The nomadic, bachelor
West is over, the housed, married West is established" (pp. 7, 10). But,
as if in response to this admission, he switches from the casual symbolism
of *The Virginian* to a last, direct denial of time in a short story in this
volume: "Wind River horsemen mostly looked and acted as if there was
no such thing as being behind time, there being no such thing as time"
(p. 164). Omitting the finite verb in that crucial subordinate clause, Wister avoids limiting his claim for nontime to the past of the story.

When he admitted the temporal element back into his fiction, it was
a clear sign that he had reached the end of his Western storytelling. In
1928, in his last collection of Western tales (*When West Was West*), Wister
reaffirmed that the Western landscape was indestructible: "the breath
of the wilderness, the eternal, impassive witness of our deeds and lives,
came through the open door" (pp. 205–6). However, he also admitted
that the heroic era was dead: "but it was gone, the true, real thing was
gone. The scenery was there, but the play was over" (p. 210). Until this

publication, the author had bent his energies to using that scenery—landscape and space—in such a way as to preserve the vitality of the play.

When West Was West was Wister's requiem to the wild West, his ultimate acknowledgment that the place was made up of time as well as space, and that time destroyed it. The tales are full of death and decay, and the final story encapsulates the author's renegation of all his attempts at preservation. His fictional defenses against time have fallen. Titled "At the Sign of the Last Chance," the tale concerns a group of old cowboys who, after a bout of reminiscences, admit the death of their era symbolically, by making a ritual out of burning the saloon sign. The symbolism is clear: words are being burned, words which represent the heyday of the wild West. There is little movement in the story, either by the old shuffling men of the present or in their stories of the past. The scene is mostly indoors and there is minimal interest in land or space. Everyone's attention is absorbed by time, and the men punctuate their conversation with wrangles about precise dates and periods of time. One character, in particular, addictively glances at a clock which is no longer there, to plot his way through the day: "Henry from habit turned to see the clock. The bullet holes were there, and the empty shelves. Henry looked at his watch" (p. 444). Time has asserted its properties completely. The author has renounced the effort to redefine time and thus protect his heroic West against its ravages. "Yes, now we could go home. The requiem of the golden beards, their romance, their departed West, too good to live for ever, was finished" (p. 447).

Both Wister and Remington saw a West which they wanted to make known to the East and to preserve in the face of industrialism. By writing about frontier life at all in the major Eastern magazines, they achieved some part of their goal. Moreover, they both constructed plots which enacted the meeting between East and West and the consequences of that event. Beyond these obvious levels, however, they did something more creative and more complex. They both tried to mold the frontier which they observed into a shape which would prolong its life artificially. To do this, they employed defensive strategies. The one tried to immure his figures against space, having early admitted the victory of time. The other, striving to create the wild West as a present reality, tried to bulwark his characters against time. Remington preserved an embalmed West, an era he accepted as dead, and he blotted out space by his concentration on figures, marshaled into protective configurations. Wister sometimes used the modern West as a fictive milieu, and he wanted to link the old to the new era, as well as the West to the East. He wished to keep his West alive. He used space to deny time and preempt the temporal measurement.

To some extent both writers succeeded in preserving their version of the West, since Wister's vision has been immortalized in the Western formula and Remington's style, in the visual arts, has been copied by a small but prolific "school of Remington" and has been imitated endlessly in the designing of cinematic scenes.[37] Moreover, both men succeeded, to some degree, in convincing their audience to accept these accounts as alternative versions of history. Theodore Roosevelt certainly regarded them as historical documents, speaking of Remington's work as "truthful presentation" and "the real thing," and saying of Wister's stories that "they have a really very high value as historical documents which also possess an immense human interest."[38] Wister, especially, received a large number of letters from his readers, with comments like "Your 'Virginian' is *not* a creation—however much you may cherish him. He is *real* . . . and I have known him."[39]

Yet, despite these successes, both men's texts are marked internally by failure and tension. There are, of course, the failures of imagination and artistry in the content of their work. More interesting, however, are the tensions and failures evident in their formal aspects, because these arise from the unsuccessful attempt to flout cultural fact with patterned fiction. When Remington fictionalized the destruction of West by East which he felt he had observed, he could play out the movement artistically without paradox. However, when he tried to preserve his Western types by manipulating his Western scene, he could not sustain the illusion: the fictional Western space which he carved out for his characters finally closes in on them. Wister, who tried to overturn history more completely, failed on two fronts. His fictional reconciliation of East and West is badly undercut by the language in which he couched it, and his fictional denial of time is eventually rendered unworkable by the very element he sought to erase.

HISTORY AND THE FORMULIST: EMERSON HOUGH

Three years after Macmillan published *The Virginian* and *John Ermine*, they brought out a comic version of the Western formula: *Heart's Desire* by Emerson Hough. Hough was one of Wister's many contemporaries to produce an imitation of *The Virginian*, showing that it was the new model for the Western genre. His work is important because it demonstrates what happened to Wister's prototype when it was imitated by a formulist who had also experienced the frontier in its closing years. The evidence shows that, however harmonious and even trite Hough's work appears, there remains some tension embedded in the details of his writing. The implication is that, as long as the romantic Western was in the hands of those who had actually experienced the closing of the frontier, it remained a fractured form.

Although Hough's Midwestern upbringing was different from Wister's and Remington's lives in the East, his experience of the West was very like theirs.[40] The influx of southern European immigrants into America in the late nineteenth century disturbed him deeply, and he venerated the Anglo-Saxon "race," particularly American Southerners with their chivalric code of honor. In the 1880s he went west, to New Mexico, and was impressed by conditions there. Believing that the West could bring about national regeneration, he admired, and was admired by, Theodore Roosevelt. In time, he worked to preserve the Western wilderness in direct ways: not only did he record the frontier in factual works about cowboys, outlaws, and frontiersmen (one of which Remington illustrated), but he instigated various conservation measures, particularly in connection with the wildlife in Yellowstone Park.

His writing habits betray one major difference with his Eastern contemporaries: where they tried to create distinctive works, he adopted given fictional models. Throughout his career he published in the popular general magazines, and, because his rate of payment was only average for a long time (*Collier's*, for example, paid him 3¢ per word) he was always churning out material as fast as possible. He accepted directions from editors readily: when he put together the novel *Heart's Desire* from a number of short stories, he worked closely with his editor at Macmillan. In fact, it was his practice to submit a scenario to a publisher, then wait for his approval before writing it up into a novel. In all sorts of ways, Hough looked for saleable patterns to imitate, and he valued successful marketing of his material above its artistic worth.[41]

Hough also accepted a given version of events in the West, and he saw Western man as part of, not apart from, America's historical course. Like Wister, he set down his ideas about the West in nonfiction, and in *The Story of the Cowboy* (1897)—his first book-length publication—he established his vision of the heroic cowboy. This work differs from "The Evolution of the Cow-Puncher" in one crucial way: whereas Wister presented the cowboy as a manifestation of an unchanging type, Hough tied him firmly to both chronology and environment. While lamenting the diminution of the Western spaces and the cowboy population, he maintained that the heroic West had not wholly disappeared. He said that the old had mutated into the new West, the latter symbolized by the Johnson County War of 1892, which brought the syndicate power of businessmen into play in a Western conflict. The contemporary West was a degenerated landscape, but its relationship to the older scene was discoverable:

> To-day the Long Trail is replaced by other trails, product of the swift development of the West, and it remains as the connection, now for the most part historical only, between two phases of an industry which, in spite of

differences of climate and condition, retain a similarity in all essential features.[42]

If Western man was fully involved in the process of time, he was also very much part of the space around him:

> The cowboy was simply a part of the West. He who did not understand the one could never understand the other. . . . If we care truly to see the cowboy as he was, and seek to give our wish the dignity of a real purpose, the first intention should be to study the cowboy in connection with his surroundings. [P. 339]

Hough's fiction conforms to his prescription by incorporating historical details in direct ways. Three of his most famous Western novels are slotted into sets of specific historical circumstances: *The Girl at the Halfway House* (1900) presents the birth of a railroad town (modeled on Ellsworth, Kansas); *The Covered Wagon* (1922) describes a journey along the Oregon Trail in 1848; and *North of 36* (1923) fictionalizes the first cattle drive from Texas to Abilene in 1867. His other major Western novel—*Heart's Desire* (1905)—romanticizes a more private piece of history: the changeover of White Oaks, New Mexico (the place of Hough's first stay in the Southwest) from a frontier to a railroad town. The author constantly reminds the reader of the historical context by interrupting the action with historical facts and observations, thus bringing directly into his text the kind of information which Cooper and others put in their footnotes. Although his characters act out fictional adventures, they witness or participate in verifiable events, and they interact with figures like Billy the Kid, Wild Bill Hickok, and Jim Bridger. Hough integrates his Western cast fully into America's history.

The historical change acted out in these fictions seems, at first sight, to be both sanguine and predictable. For example, *Heart's Desire* deals with the same general situation as *The Virginian* and *John Ermine*—the coming to the West of civilization, here represented by Eastern woman and her railroad—but Hough treats this development in a much lighter tone than his predecessors. The inhabitants of Heart's Desire accept right from the opening of the novel that change is inevitable. There is no argument about the coming of the railroad; one of the most philosophical Westerners says:

> I ain't goin' to say that the old days'll last forever. We all know better'n that when it comes right down to straight reasonin'. A country'll sleep about so long, same as a man; and then it'll wake up. I've seen the States come West for forty year. They're comin' swifter'n ever now.[43]

The only struggle is to ensure that the men of Heart's Desire will profit—in jobs and compensation—by the railroad's arrival. In all Hough's work, the omniscient and omnipresent narrator makes leaps forward within and beyond the time spanned by the novels, explicitly reminding the readers that they are viewing this action retrospectively. This means that the larger outcomes of the novels are avowedly predictable, since historical developments, like the successful arrival of emigrants in the Willamette Valley in 1848, are known. Each act does not have unlimited possible consequences.

The predictability of the specific ending (the marriage of hero and heroine) is suggested, too. Hough adheres strictly to stock moves which, by the conventions of the sentimental novel, imply certain results. In the later novels, he underlines the conventional sequence of events with a device which, presumably, he borrows from Zane Grey: he ends chapters and important scenes with an incantatory phrase which looks toward the ending. Also, during the action, both author and characters talk a great deal about the inevitable result of all this activity. The author recurrently talks of fate, destiny, and the immortal gods, and characters voice the same belief in predetermination. In *Halfway House*, the hero assures the heroine repeatedly that fate means them to marry; when she finally agrees, he cries, "I knew it must be so . . . I knew it was to be."[44]

With all this emphasis on inevitable harmony, the ritualistic conflicts in the action, especially those between hero and heroine, seem perfunctory. Ostensibly, Hough follows the same pattern as Wister, by first establishing contrasts between the two lovers, then demonstrating their reconciliation. But the differences suggested at the beginning are never genuine (as those between the Virginian and Molly are); they are merely misunderstandings or superficial paradoxes. For example, in neither *Heart's Desire* nor *North of 36* are the hero and heroine separated by geographical associations as firmly as Molly and the Virginian. In the earlier novel, both are Easterners, and in the later, both are Texans, though the heroine, Taisie, has just returned from being educated in the East at the beginning of the novel. The difficulties in the romance are invariably due to mistakes. For much of the action in *North of 36*, the heroine distrusts the hero because, although he is a sheriff and a Texas Ranger, he seems to collude with the villain who is trying to steal her land inheritance. Taisie herself represents a paradox when she changes from a cultivated pastoral figure to one who casts off her sex—"I'll be only a man now"[45]—to join in the trail drive. Of course, both these contradictions are untrue. It turns out that McMasters' villainy is only a pretense, and Taisie adopts only the clothes, not the behavior or characteristics of a man. Once these misapprehensions are resolved, the two can wed.

But underneath all this easy harmony and superficial conflict, one level of real conflict does eventually emerge. The farther the frontier West receded into the past for Hough, and the more closely he copied the symbolic love story of *The Virginian*, the more signs there are that he became prey to the same doubts as Wister. Hough's early novels, *Halfway House* and *Heart's Desire*, largely follow the older formula, from the dime

novels and Cooper, in their characterization of the love story. In both
novels, the heroes are Easterners in the West, and they fit easily into the
wedding compact at the end, despite their adventures. Thus, the hero
of *Halfway House* is content to return to domesticity:

> Although all the primitive savage in him answered to the summons of these
> white-hot days to every virile, daring nature, Franklin none the less felt
> growing in his heart the stubbornness of the man of property, the land-
> holding man, the man who even unconsciously plans a home, resolved to
> cling to that which he has taken of the earth's surface for his own. Heredity,
> civilization, that which we call common sense, won the victory. [P. 179]

In the novels which Hough wrote after the First World War, however,
the endings become a little less convincingly harmonious. Hough wrote
The Covered Wagon in response to the *Saturday Evening Post* editor's re-
quest that he follow the Wister prototype more closely than formerly,
and this work brings its hero into closer contact with violence than the
two earlier novels. Perhaps for this reason, its final scene of reconciliation
involves two minor discordances. Unusually for Hough who, while lamenting the death of the old West, accepted the rule of chronology,
there is a defiance of time: when the hero and heroine finally come
together, "then both were young again. . . . He kissed her in contempt
of time."[46] It is more a sentimental than a structural gesture, but it jars
in any case. The more literal false note is sounded when the heroine
tells a lie in the final lines. She has spurned the hero throughout the
book because his rival wrongfully labeled him a thief, but now she maintains that she never believed that lie. Such an obvious untruth seems a
strange declaration to preface immediately the lovers' final embrace.

These hints of discordance develop most vividly in *North of 36*, Hough's
only novel with a violent cowboy hero and the book in which the love
story most resembles *The Virginian*'s. During the action, the heroine has
been named repeatedly as an evil force. McMasters has made clear his
desire for her, but she believes him guilty of theft and treason and rejects
him. In the course of the trail drive, misunderstandings are revealed,
and they prepare to wed. Naturally, this event brings about a change in
their relationship; but, as in *The Virginian*, it also stimulates a host of
discordant images and descriptions, which suggest an underlying unease.

All these images cluster around the final scene, in which hero and
heroine agree to marry, and they all contrast with earlier characterizations in the novel. For example, throughout the action the heroic symbols
are McMasters' guns and red shirt cuffs. Near the beginning, he declares,
"I'll give Miss Lockhart anything on earth but my guns" (p. 97). He is
equally adamant about retaining his dyed cuffs, because they are a legacy
of his family's pride during the Civil War. However, when he comes to
propose to Taisie at the end, she notices:

His collar and his cuffs were white—pure white, in good linen. Once—she vaguely remembered it now—he had not worn white; had explained to her some reason for the dull red of his linen.

And there was another change, she was sure of this—he was unarmed! The heavy weapons no longer swung at his belt, nor even showed in his saddle holsters. For the first time since she had known him she saw him weaponless. [Pp. 420–21]

Whiteness and pacifism are the pastoral woman's characteristics; the hero has capitulated to the standards of a woman who has been labeled, at the least, as bad luck. Furthermore, throughout the novel the hero has been characterized as unchanging and in control. Now, the author comments, "Sometimes we feel some such indefinable change in a man who has suffered a great sickness or met with some great reverse" (p. 421) and "For the first time she saw his fingers tremble as he half reached out a hand, withdrew it" (p. 425). Like Will in *The Covered Wagon*, McMasters contravenes Hough's usual scheme by denying time in this last scene: he says to Taisie, "There is no past" (p. 429). There is one last hint of unease. Declaiming on the mistakes of their past, McMasters says, "Taisie . . . what fools we've been! Ah, what a blind fool I was!" (p. 29). The final sentence, four lines later, reads: "Her head fell forward upon his shoulder, drowsily, although it was morning, and though the sun shone all around them, brilliantly, blindingly." The undercurrent of suggestion is that this move is as foolishly mistaken as any of the past.

The ending matters particularly in Hough, because of his emphasis on destiny and inevitability. Thus, when he failed to produce the thoroughly harmonious ending to which all his narrative points, he created a text which is just as fractured as Wister's. This happened despite the fact that Hough set himself a much easier task than Wister—copying another's fiction, rather than creating a new romantic pattern. Most of the conflicts in *North of 36* are eminently superficial. At the same time, there is a genuine contrast between the narrative and the imagery, and it occurs at exactly the same point in the novel as in *The Virginian*: the coming together of hero and heroine, which represents the marriage of wilderness and civilization. Hough solved the easy conflicts, as if realizing that resolution was the essence of the new formula, but he was left with the genuine one. Yet again, the details of the text reveal the author's doubts about his romantic portrayal of resolution between the wild West and the East.

Robert Warshow and John Cawelti have identified the main characteristic of the formulaic product as its dissociation from reality. It is "an ideal world without the disorder, the ambiguity, the uncertainty, and the limitations of the world of our experience"; a type which "appeals to previous experience of the type itself," not experience of reality.[47] A detailed reading of *North of 36* suggests that it took some time for the

Western formula to achieve that state. For all that Hough's novels are derivative and predictable, in the end they proved susceptible to the author's real-life experiences. Having witnessed the frontier in the 1880s, he found it difficult to sustain his sanguine attitude to changes in the West in the twentieth century. After the First World War, especially, he began to fear that America had lost touch with the frontier ideal forever. From then on, he could not sustain both an acceptance of historical change and a thoroughly optimistic interpretation of the joining of East and West in his fiction. Although his novels do not admit this change overtly, in the shape of their plots, a note of unease creeps into his introduction of the Western hero to domesticity. The Western romance had to wait for the next generation of formulists—Zane Grey and the like, who were one stage further removed from the nineteenth-century frontier—for its happy ending to become convincing at every level of the text, and the new version of the formula to become entrenched.

THREE

Escaping from the Pulps

From before the First World War until after the Second, the most famous, successful, and prolific authors of popular Western fiction were Zane Grey, Frederick Faust (as "Max Brand"), and Ernest Haycox. These were the men who carried Wister's formula into the world of mass production. In doing so, they smoothed out the last traces of ambiguity or unease in Wister's model, but found themselves caught up in a new set of tensions, to do with their own positions as writers. The conflict arose because these authors desired both to publish popular, profitable fiction and to transcend the artistic limitations of commercial production. The resultant tension had a direct effect on their work: while the battle between nature and culture in their plots is purely ritualistic, the struggle between individual author and commercial formula, played out in the narrative technique, is very much alive.

These authors' involvement in the marketplace is clear. Each of them repeated Wister's formula many times, with some variations, in the commercial magazines before reprinting their novels in book form. In this way, Grey and Faust became mass sellers: the former is famous as one of the first Americans to earn $1 million by writing, while Faust's massive income supported his lavish lifestyle in both Europe and America. Haycox, too, came to command high rates for the magazine serialization of his novels: by the 1940s, he received over $50,000 for two serials. Faust used 20 pseudonyms to publish 196 novels, 226 novelettes, 162 stories, and 44 poems. Not all of this output is Western fiction but, apart from his Dr. Kildare stories, he is best remembered for his many Westerns, most of which were published under the name "Max Brand." Grey was less prolific. He wrote 33 books of Eastern fiction, outdoor adventure, and juvenile stories, as well as 59 Western novels, with which he set a record by appearing in the top ten bestseller list nine times from 1915 to 1924. Haycox's production was the most modest of all. He published 24 novels and almost 300 short stories.[1]

These works usually appeared initially in pulp or slick magazines, then as cheap hardcover books, then, sooner or later, as paperbound reprints. Every step of this process was accompanied by commercial decisions about production and promotion by members of the publishing firms. However, the commercial circumstances which bore most directly upon the authors were those surrounding the production of pulp and slick magazines. A description of the policies and constraints of the magazines in which Grey, Faust, and Haycox published should convey something of the commercial context in which these authors worked.

In the pulps, which I discussed in chapter one, the most important content was the fiction. Because these magazines were developed on the premise of low production costs combined with large circulations, they carried little in the way of illustration. Nor did they ever have many advertisements: they could not provide lavish displays, and advertisers believed that the pulp audience was limited to low-income consumers of inexpensive goods. Thus, the fiction was the main product for sale and out of it, publishers concocted various selling strategies. Most obviously, they used characters and, sometimes, authors to conduct dialogues with the readers and thus instill in them a sense of loyalty to that publication (and, simultaneously, fill a few pages at no extra cost). More generally, editors thought of the fiction as a sales device in itself; one thirties' pulp editor said, "Serials are nothing more than sales promotion efforts."[2]

These conditions and attitudes directly affected pulp authors. The need for low production costs kept authorial rates down (usually to 1¢ or 2¢ per word in the twentieth century), so that authors had to turn out great quantities of material at speed to earn a living wage. Inevitably, this pressure encouraged the use of formulas. Furthermore, editors, in search of vast circulations, were determined to give audiences what they wanted, the editorial consensus being that "if there is one trait that the pulpwood reader has it is his predilection for sameness."[3] Thus, editors wanted writers to adhere to tried and true fictional patterns. The general understanding was that authors earned a loose rein by showing that they would conform to the usual genres.

The slick magazines were quite different from the pulps in makeup, but they tended to create a similar commercial environment for their authors. Slicks were cheap monthly and weekly miscellanies made of rag content ("slick") paper, a more costly kind of paper than pulpwood, with a very good surface for illustration. They took off toward the end of the nineteenth century when Frank Munsey, S. S. McClure, and Cyrus Curtis realized that there existed a vast untapped audience of lower-middle-class readers who were not attracted to the contents of magazines like *Harper's Monthly* and could not afford the 25¢–35¢ price.[4] These publishers won this audience with attractive slick magazines whose contents were a lighter mixture of popular fiction, journalism, and service departments than *Harper's* and, most importantly, whose price was 10¢ for a monthly or 5¢ for a weekly. This formula produced massive new rates of circulation: whereas *Harper's Monthly* was considered highly successful in the 1890s with sales of 200,000, by 1897 the slick *Munsey's Magazine* claimed a circulation of 700,000. In the twentieth century, the figures become even more fantastic: in the 1920s, *McCall's*, *Collier's*, *Pictorial Review*, and *The Ladies' Home Journal* each had between 2 and 2½ million buyers; by the late 1940s, *The Saturday Evening Post* had pushed its circulation up to 4 million.[5] The low price, which remained throughout this time at 10¢ to 15¢, was made possible by the massive amounts of advertising attracted to these magazines by their mass circulations, and by their attractive makeup.

The inclusion of huge amounts of advertising accounted for the greatest difference between the slicks and the pulps. The advertisements in slick magazines were much more numerous than those in the pulps, much more lavish in illustration, and much more subtle in their appeals. They seem to be directed at an audience who considered themselves more sophisticated than the readers of pulps, though they probably were not much more affluent: the goods advertised are generally domestic and personal items of middle-range cost. The volume of advertising brought new pressures on publishers, too. The slick publisher had to please his advertisers even more than his readers, since his profits came from advertising revenue, not circulation. He became a dealer in consumer groups as well as editorial wares; he was selling to advertisers access to a particular section of the buying public. From about the 1920s, advertisers' demands for guarantees about both the size and the nature of a magazine's readership caused publishers to invest in more and more market research into their audience's social circumstances.[6]

These changes in turn affected the role of the fiction within the magazine. Slicks tended to publish genre fiction similar to that in the pulps, but it was just one element in the miscellaneous contents: fiction shared space not only with numerous non-fictional articles and service departments, but also with the advertisements, which were spread throughout the publications. Also, with publishers' attention concentrated more on advertisers than on readers, there was much less editorial rhetoric surrounding the fiction than in the pulps. While there were often pages given over to readers' letters, they did not necessarily discuss the fiction at all; and characters never appeared as spokesmen outside the fiction.

The same priorities were reflected in the treatment of authors. Although some slicks made huge profits, this prosperity was generally not passed on to the writers, who were paid about ½¢ to over 1¢ per word. However, as competition became increasingly intense, magazines did start to vie for certain "showcase" authors, and these few came to command as much as 15¢ per word. Nevertheless, payment to writers remained a minute part of a magazine's budget, and even the most famous authors had to fit into the overall concept of the magazine. Those periodicals which carried authors' biographies kept them short, and slicks in general expected reliable, formulaic material from authors. With large production costs and the obligation to please both readers and advertisers, publishers had more to lose than ever and thus were more cautious than ever. Also, while methods were being developed to gauge consumers' social backgrounds, editors had no finely tuned research tools for discovering the reasons for readers' preferences in editorial material: McClure was typical in considering his own taste sufficient yardstick, and Frank Munsey always relied on trial and error, saying "I keep on experimenting, creating and killing, till I happen to hit the public's taste."[7] Once editors hit on a successful formula, they repeated it endlessly. Thus, while writers could feel that they were addressing a rather more sophisticated readership in the slicks than in the pulps, they were still locked into a system which demanded formula and repetition.

All these conditions are relevant to an understanding of Grey, Faust, and Haycox, since at least one of these authors appeared regularly in every magazine mentioned above. Although there is no evidence that any of the three was subject to sustained close supervision by magazine or book editors, they were all prey to the general pressures of commercial production. Their main avenue of escape from these strictures lay in their writing; the details of their fiction contain these authors' limited and fruitless rebellions against the publishing machine from which they profited.

ZANE GREY

When Heywood Broun observed that the substance of any two Zane Grey books could be written on the back of a postage stamp, he was not exaggerating by all that much.[8] Grey's plots are certainly repetitious and formulaic, with their simplistic characterization, regenerative violence, and predictable happy endings. Yet Grey's attitude to repetition was not at all simple. On the one hand, he emphasized the repetitions in his work to create a mythological context for the Western formula, thus distancing his fiction both from the historical actuality which proved so troublesome to Wister and Remington, and from the marketplace in which magazine serialization placed his novels. On the other hand, he also tried to subvert the pattern of repetition and insularity: for a time he added some discussion of social issues to his stylized adventure stories and, simultaneously, he moved from a simple to a complex narrative technique. This combination of characteristics allowed him both the conformity expected by editors and audience and the signs of artistic progress for which he yearned. Ultimately, the limited rebellion implied by his changes was stopped short by his publishers. Before that happened, however, Grey's most interesting novels demonstrate the author's contradictory impulses—toward and away from repetition—colliding and struggling for supremacy.

Grey worked seriously and doggedly at his fiction, convinced of his novelistic abilities despite a long apprenticeship of rejections. He gave up his Manhattan dentist job and staked all on his writing in 1903, but he had four failed books—an Ohio River trilogy about his pioneer ancestors in the eighteenth century and the story of his experiences in 1907 with Buffalo Jones, the hunter—before he found success with *The Heritage of the Desert*, which was accepted simultaneously by the pulp *Popular Magazine* and by Harper and Brothers for book publication in 1910. He soon moved into the slick magazines, and his contract with Harper for at least one book a year became permanent. He continued to work very hard at his craft, devising daily exercises to improve his novelistic technique and doing research for each novel: not only did he make several trips west every year, finding sights and characters to use in his fiction, but he also undertook melodramatic experiences, like the walk across Death Valley which he later wrote into *Wanderer of the Wasteland* (1923).[9]

He also distanced himself from the give-and-take of the marketplace by insisting on his artistic autonomy. When Bob Davis, editor of the Frank Munsey pulp magazines, suggested an idea for a novel, Grey took him up on it, and it eventually resulted in a tale which appeared in Davis's *Munsey's Magazine* and became a Harper book entitled *The Light of Western Stars* (1914). But Grey was very careful to separate Davis's idea from his own execution. He wrote to Davis:

> I have taken your idea of a splendid girl, an American Beauty, developing and finding herself in the west. I have taken your idea of a wild, raw, simple, strong cowboy rising through love of her to some plane near her level.
>
> With these characters standing warm and living in my mind, I shall commence the marking out of their destinies. This, of course, will be my labor, my evolution of the single idea . . . you have given me a fine idea, for which I am grateful, and shall show it in more than words. But please leave the evolution of that idea to me.[10]

There are more letters in this vein and Grey even sent Davis a receipt for his idea, promising him the dramatic rights on the novel in return. Obviously, Grey did not consider himself a tool of the publishing machine in the way of the dime novelists.

The magazines which serialized his novels also bolstered his image as an autonomous artist separated from the exigencies of the marketplace. He published for a brief period in pulps like *Popular*, *All-Story Weekly*, and *Argosy*, which always heralded his appearances reverentially on the cover and inside. In *All-Story* and *Argosy*, the editor compared him to Dickens, Scott, Harte, Twain, and Stevenson. Every one of his novels was dubbed a "masterpiece," and when *The Desert Crucible* (published in book form as *The Rainbow Trail*) appeared in *Argosy* in 1915, the editor dressed up a commercial decision to serialize as an artistic necessity: "if taken at one gulp it would not be appreciated. The novel must be read carefully—thoughtfully"; "like any monumental work of art, it's bigger than it seems to be at first glance—you have to study it slowly to get its real meaning." Zane Grey was puffed almost as a god among men: his book "will leave you with a picture of the desert . . . that will be far more vivid than you could get by going to the country yourself—more vivid because Zane Grey is a genius who sees with an eye more penetrating than those of us ordinary men and women." This publicity is very different from the presentation of hired hacks like William Wallace Cook, whose name was not even known to his readers. The editor still pretended to discount his own contribution—"when it comes to editing this magazine you folks who read it are the doctor and the whole box of pills. I'm just the blank you write the prescription on"—but no one suggested that Zane Grey would bow to the public's advice.[11]

When Grey graduated into the slicks, he was puffed in a much more subdued way than in the pulps. With their subtle advertising pitches and their glossy, expensive format in which fiction was only a small part of the contents among the articles and topical commentary, the slicks did not go in for the brash exaggerations of the pulps. However, they obviously considered Grey a big name: *The Country Gentleman* always announced his fiction on its cover; *McCall's* called him "One Of The Great Novelists Of Our Times"; and *The Ladies' Home Journal* declared that "No other writer of our time has succeeded in crystallizing the big, free spirit of America as has this master writer of adventure in the unspoiled West."[12]

In any literal sense, of course, Grey's artistic status as characterized by himself and the magazines' rhetoric was a mirage. Although Grey never wrote to order, more than one magazine editor did censor his fiction, in deference to the assumed moral standards of the pulp- and slick-buying public. Even at the peak of his career, his attempts at artistry were thwarted by both his magazine and book publishers.

Yet there was one level at which the claims about Grey's separateness from his environment ring true: the method by which he created his fictional world. Grey's novels very much follow Wister's formula, by revolving around love stories set in the West, between representatives of virile wilderness and degenerate civilization. But Grey worked up the repetitions of character, setting, and plot into a quasi-mythical pattern. By stressing echoes from classical mythology, he emphasized that his world of adventure was cut off from its historical background and he underlined this impression by gesturing toward the limitations of his settings and characters. Within this self-enclosed world, East and West can come together harmoniously.

Grey was certainly not the first to discover parallels between the characters, settings, and events in the popular Western and in mythological and romance tales. Right at the beginning of Western fiction, Fenimore

Cooper presented Leatherstocking as an American Adam. Joel Porte has elucidated the classical allusions in Cooper, even comparing *The Last of the Mohicans* to the *Iliad*, and *The Prairie* to the *Odyssey*.[13] In the twentieth century, Wister and Hough, among others, related the cowboy to chivalrous types and commonly used pastoral figures like the cultured heroine in white who also dresses up as a boy. Stephen Fender has discussed the presence of pastoral conventions in the Western formula in some detail.[14] But these authors did not exploit their debt to romance beyond some scattered references. Even Eugene Manlove Rhodes used his town, Arcadia, in the novel at one time titled *Bransford in Arcadia* (1914), more as an excuse for various jokes than as an opportunity to match his love story closely to the pattern of the pastoral form. Zane Grey, in 1910, was the first author of popular Westerns to exploit systematically the connection between the Western formula and traditional narrative patterns.

Grey repeatedly organized his fictional action into the sequence identified by Joseph Campbell as the "monomyth," the principle of action in all mythological tales. It consists of the progression, separation-initiation-return.[15] A particularly neat example of this organization can be seen in *The Rainbow Trail* (1915), the sequel to *Riders of the Purple Sage*. In this novel, the hero, Shefford, has experienced the Call to Adventure[16] in the East, prior to the opening of the tale, from Venters and Bess, who tell him about the unresolved issue of the preceding book. He travels west and is adopted by the Indian Nas Ta Bega (his Supernatural Aid) who leads him into the desert, thus helping him to Cross the First Threshold and enter "The Belly of the Whale." After this Departure, Shefford undergoes his Initiation through the Road of Trials, the Meeting with the Goddess, and, perhaps, Atonement with the Father: he slowly learns Western skills, he finds Fay Larkin, and he resolves his belief in God. Finally, the Return consists of the Magic Flight (through the desert, from Mormons); the Rescue from Without (when cowboy Joe comes for them in a boat); the Crossing of the Return Threshold (the hazardous river journey); and the Return with the Boon (the carrying of the captives east to their friends).

Grey's pattern is not always as perfectly cyclical as that: whereas the departure is always physical, the return may be symbolic only, signified by a marriage which returns the Easterner to a more domestic existence. That design is evident in the earliest works in the pulps, like *Heritage of the Desert*, *Desert Gold* (1913), and *Light of Western Stars*, whether it be man or woman who has come west. In that variation, there usually takes place, within the incomplete cycle, another movement which is exactly circular. At the center of *Heritage of the Desert*, for example, the Eastern hero, Hare, goes into the desert to save Mescal, the Indian heroine. A mysterious, disembodied voice calls to him and he crosses the river, to find a dog which guides him across the desert. He suffers sandstorms, heat, thirst, and pain from cacti and burning lava before he reaches the canyon and the "Goddess," Mescal. The desert imagery here is particularly close to Campbell's description of a dream landscape. They leave, cross a river, flee from rustlers, cross the sandbar, and arrive back at the oasis from which Hare departed. "I've travelled in a circle!" Hare realizes.[17]

Grey's fiction also contains a profusion of romance imagery, since it stresses chivalry, love, education, religiosity, and adventure. Conventional romance types appear repeatedly: the beautiful, virtuous heroine who is associated with white dress, music, or flowers in the midst of the desert; the solitary, dark, armed protector who is obviously equivalent to the knight; sometimes the dark woman who represents sensual temptation to the knight, who quickly spurns her; and the vicious, duplicitous villain who assumes fair shapes to tempt the heroine and carry her off. Finally, the stories contain the main activities of the romance genre: the hero's education, in which the heroine plays an instructive role, and the hero's rescue of the heroine from the villain.

Generally, Grey seems to cull his models indiscriminately from a variety of traditional fictional types from different eras. However, there is one constant note in his use of prototypes: he always reconstructs them so that any lasting conflict disappears and his final resolution remains unmarred. For example, *Wanderer of the Wasteland* (1923) tells of Adam who, thinking that he has killed his brother, flees into the desert for fourteen years to expiate his sin. When he eventually returns to civilization, he discovers that, after all, his brother has survived. The biblical analogy is indicated ("Cain and Abel—the old bitter story"), but here "Cain" turns out to be no fratricide.[18] Similarly, in *Riders of the Purple Sage*, the pastoral retreat is recognizably Edenic, but it is Eden with the Fall written out: the snake which Venters and Bess encounter is still friendly to man. In the same book, as Jane and Lassiter flee, he tells her not to look back at the conflagration. Unlike Lot's wife, she does not, and so this couple achieve their paradise safely. Whenever there is some acknowledgment of the traditional narratives which stand behind these stories, this fiction puts forward a more sentimental version, and nothing disturbs the harmony of Grey's happy endings.

If Grey's constant adherence to traditional forms can be read partly as a strategy for distancing his fictional world from any contemporary or realist context, there are other pointed indications of this perspective in his early and late novels. For example, the description of landscape sets a note of insularity. Although Grey's landscapes are very detailed, their boundaries are often emphasized. An extreme example is the impenetrable valley in *Riders of the Purple Sage*, but less dramatic settings also stress their limits. The boundaries of the wilderness scene which opens *Horse Heaven Hill* (1959) are located at all four compass points:

the open country spread like a fan to the north and west . . . soon to heave
into mounds and hills, timber-topped and shaggy. . . . South of the little city
the sage had given way to wheat. Here Wadestown was the most northerly
outpost, located on the railroad that ran almost east and west, and which
served as the border line of the wilderness.[19]

Characters articulate the restricted scope of the fiction more explicitly.
There is an example near the end of *Horse Heaven Hill*, in which the
heroine, Lark, has managed to stop the slaughter of some wild horses
for chicken feed. She speaks to her cousin Marigold:

> "If only they'd stop that cruel wild-horse driving!"
> "I like horses, but not as you do. You, Lark, you suffer agony. I could
> tell that. Forget about the wild-horse drives. Blanding will quit after he
> catches that bunch."
> "Oh, he will! That's fine. Then he'll not go down to my range to drive
> my wild horses?"
> "No, he won't!" declared Marigold. "But someone else will, Lark. You
> must reconcile yourself, or forget it. . . . Now I must run and dress. We will
> not speak of these things again. Kiss me, Lark."[P.212]

That is the last we hear of the doomed horses, for the rest of the book
is taken up with the happy wedding of the hero and the heroine. One
hint after another reminds the reader that events in Grey's works have
little to do with the larger world of reality.

Grey established his methods for stressing the self-enclosure of his
fictional world in his early work, and he returned to them strongly in
his late novels. In the middle years of his career, between 1918 and 1925,
however, he set about trying to develop his writing in some way. When
he did this, he did not break with the familiar types and patterns which
had proved so popular and profitable for him. Instead, he tried to introduce a measure of consequence and complexity by tacking on a limited
amount of social commentary to his mythic pattern and changing his
narrative technique from a simple to a fairly elaborate organization. The
latter development is quite subtle, but a comparison of his earlier narratives with those of his middle years shows that the change is real.

Grey's early method of presentation is demonstrated clearly in *Heritage
of the Desert*, the first novel with which Grey broke into the pulps, and
one which contains a precise cyclical pattern. In the novel, events have
little connection with a past or a future beyond the story. The background to the tale—the Mormon history and the hero's past—is disposed
of in summary in the first few pages. Thereafter, the emphasis is all on
the present. When asked for the story of his past, Hare answers, typically,
"There isn't much to tell" (p. 6). The one hint of a mystery deriving
from the past comes to nothing. Naab tells Hare that Mescal's father was
Spanish, her mother, Indian, and her only surviving relative is Eschtah,
the Navaho chief. He adds, "Some day I'll tell you the story" (p. 38). Yet,

when Hare asks for the story, on the day he is to marry Mescal, Naab responds, " 'You ask about Mescal,' he mused. 'There's little more to tell.' 'But her father—can you tell me more of him?' 'Little more than I've already told' " (p. 295). Then he repeats information already known to Hare and the reader.

Events are presented chronologically, with no repetition of incidents or any major recapitulation in the time scheme. There is little sense that happenings bear any causal relationship to one another; they simply occur in a familiar sequence. Even at the most detailed syntactic level, Grey depends on sequential arrangements. The habit can be seen in his blanket use of the semicolon. Repeatedly, he uses this punctuation to arrange his material into lists, whether he is describing scenes and characters by their various attributes, conveying the passage of time, creating parentheses, or organizing parallel constructions for climactic effect. Also, by frequently omitting prepositions, he avoids stating causation: for example, in the sentence, "Precedence was given to the first and elder wife—Mother Mary; Mother Ruth's life was not without pain" (p. 60). Whether or not the effect was intentional, there is evidence that the practice was conscious. In his diary of 1905, Grey told himself:

> The skill with which a writer deals with the small connecting words, particles, and pronouns is the best evidence of the extent to which he has attained a mastery of the art of composition. . . . Work for clearness, sequence, climax. Do away with conjunctions, if possible. . . . Brevity helps action and makes strength and force.[20]

The result is a narrative which reads very like E. M. Forster's definition of a "story": "it is a narrative of events arranged in their time-sequence. . . . Qua story, it can only have one merit: that of making the audience want to know what happens next. . . . It is the lowest and simplest of literary organisms."[21] It is the form which elicits the response, "And then?"

That description identifies the main effect of all the novels up to *Wildfire* (1917), with the exception of *Riders of the Purple Sage*. With their repetitive cyclical patterns and distant settings, these works are stylized romances, lacking both social relevance and narrative complexity. Moreover, although they all make some gesture toward the past, the emphasis is on the present and sequential; indeed, the hero of *Wildfire* "had no past to think about . . . he felt absolutely free, alone, with nothing behind him to remember, with wild, thrilling nameless life before him."[22]

In the years between 1918 and 1925, when Grey was publishing regularly in the slicks, he tried to establish some links between his fictional adventures and the world of cause and effect. First he introduced topical debates into his work: characters still conduct the traditional pastoral debate about the relative merits of wilderness and civilization, but in *Man of the Forest* (1920) the argument specifically concerns social Darwinism, and in *Call of the Canyon* (1924), Flappers. Historical crises appear, too: the hero in the *U. P. Trail* (1918) rescues the heroine from captivity several times, but he also helps to build the transcontinental railroad and exposes some of the political intrigue behind it. Also, in terms of narrative technique, Grey began to order his events in a more intricate way than before. Initially, he tried for a relatively complex narrative by making his characters tell stories from the past. Then he began to arrange his novels into something other than a straightforward chronology, and eventually the force of the past becomes thematic in his work. One way of defining the difference between his earlier practices and his middle period is to accept Forster's distinction between the simple story and the more complex plot. He explains the second category: "A plot is also a narrative of events, the emphasis falling on causality. . . . The time-sequence is preserved, but the sense of causality overshadows it. . . . a plot with a mystery in it . . . suspends the time-sequence, it moves as far away from the story as its limitations will allow."[23] This is the kind of narrative for which Grey aimed during these middle years.

Of course, there is a basic incompatibility between Grey's repetition of the mythic round, which seems designed to confine his fiction to an unchanging formula, and his introduction of social criticism and complex plot, which involve a sense of causality and development. An early demonstration of the struggle between conventional pattern and a degree of formal complexity occurs in *Riders of the Purple Sage*. This novel was an early slick publication for Grey and his first attempt at an elaborate time scheme. It contains two parallel plots: that concerning Venters the cowboy and Bess the "outlaw" whom he rescues and, after a retreat in Surprise Valley, takes to the outside world she has never known; and that of Lassiter the gunman and Jane the Mormon landowner, whom Lassiter saves from Mormon despotism by taking her into the paradisal valley and closing its exit permanently.

These characters are much more interested in time past than are the cast of *Heritage of the Desert*. Both Lassiter and Venters are driven by the desire to find out about events from the past. For eighteen years, Lassiter has been trying to discover who kidnapped his sister: "Once I read about a feller who sailed the seven seas an' traveled the world, an' he had a story to tell, an' whenever he seen the man to whom he must tell that story he knowed him on sight. I was like that, only I had a question to ask" (p. 278). Venters tries to find out about the motives of the outlaws who steal Jane's cattle and about Bess's former life. He, too, is a searcher, or Forster's plot reader, with his constant question, "Why?"

Yet, despite this concern with past events, in the end the force of the past is subordinated to that of the present. Venters, in spite of his questioning intelligence, is caught between his curiosity about Bess's past and his desire to discount it. He makes an effort to forget her past (which he mistakenly believes dishonorable), convincing himself that it has no causal force: what she was before does not determine what she is now. The major relationship, that of Lassiter and Jane, confirms the priority of the present over the past. Both these characters have secrets concerning the abduction and death of Lassiter's sister, Milly Erne: Lassiter keeps from Jane, and the reader, the full story of Milly's fate; Jane keeps secret the identity of Milly's abductor. Only toward the end of the book are these secrets disclosed. Yet there is something strange about these stories, secrets, and revelations: by the time they are told, they are inconsequential not only to the reader, who has probably guessed the explanations, but to the other characters. When Jane finally admits the identity of the kidnapper, Lassiter says that he has already guessed it, from one of her reactions, but the knowledge is no longer important because under her influence, "I've outgrowed revenge" (p. 280). Jane tells him that there is one more secret concerning Milly's abduction: " 'There's one thing I shall tell you—if you are at my death-bed, but I can't speak now.' 'I reckon I don't want to hear no more,' said Lassiter" (p. 281). Even when she finally reveals that the man who ordered the abduction was her father, Lassiter maintains his response: "Jane, the past is dead. In my love for you I forgot the past. This thing I'm about to do ain't . . . because of anythin' that ever happened in the past, but for what is happenin' right *now*" (pp. 287–88).

When Lassiter frees himself from the power of the past, and helps Jane to do likewise, he fractures three patterns: his repeated questing, the Mormons' habitual domination of Jane, and the formal construction of the plot. Jane has recurrently refused Lassiter's Call to Adventure and is very nearly caught by the past and the trap the enemy is weaving around her. It is only when she sets the mythic pattern in motion, by leaving her home, that she frees herself. This action and the dialogue around it also stop short the creation of a complex plot. To a certain point, with the new emphasis on mystery and the importance of the past, it seems as if a plot (in Forster's terms) is in the making. When, however, the past is discounted, the novel settles for something less intricate, and we are back at mere successiveness or "story." In the end, the characters choose the present over the past, action takes over from deliberation, the mythic round gets going, and the author chooses story rather than plot.[24]

The novels in which the social criticism is most highly developed—*The Desert of Wheat* (1919) and *The Vanishing American* (1925)—are also those in which the time scheme is most sophisticated. Not only are the structures of these books fairly elaborate (with many flashbacks, recapitulations, and repetitions) but consideration of the past's power in the present is central to their themes. In both of them, the mythic paradigm is there, in the background, and events with mythological connotations (pastoral retreat, marriage to the heroine) finally save the heroes from the tragic consequences of their past experiences. However, the analogies with mythological patterns do not eradicate the effects of society and time past completely: Grey finally achieved a balancing of the three elements.

In *The Desert of Wheat* he returned to the portrayal of the hero as some sort of storyteller. This is an important book, despite its sentimentalism and romantic set pieces, because it is an unusually early attempt to depict the horrors of World War I. The first part of the book deals with the fight of Washington wheat farmers, led by Kurt Dorn, against I.W.W. saboteurs; and the second, with Dorn's war service, for which he has volunteered in an effort to exorcise his soul of its German taint. (He is a second-generation immigrant, with an anti-American father.) When Kurt goes to war, he is experiencing the separation-initiation-return cycle, which, in this least mythic of novels, is separated from the ritual romantic action of the first part. He learns the wasteful horrors of the American training camps and he undergoes the trauma of the front. Grey portrays the face of battle in the appearance and accounts of the French Blue Devils, in Dorn's own nightmarish, surreal killing of German soldiers, in an observer's account of the same act, and in the transformed, stricken Dorn who returns to Washington. Even once Dorn is in the American West, the effects of his war experiences are ineradicable: although he recovers from near death, with the heroine's nursing, he is left with only one arm. And he retains his battle experience in a nightmare convulsion which he undergoes repeatedly, reenacting in a trance his bayoneting of Germans. He even goes through the action immediately after his wedding, to the horror of the heroine.

Here are implications about causality, effect, and the nature of time not to be found in previous works. The past is fully operative in the present and its obsessive repetition has an ugly potency. The past has increasingly great consequences and the hero is a more grotesque "ancient mariner," wrenching his frame in the agony of having to act out his story again and again. In the end, the discord is resolved into a debate about social Darwinist principles. Kurt personifies the inescapability of a brutal past, and he adheres to the philosophy which generalizes that principle. Lenore, his wife, combats his determinism with her religious belief, which has motherhood at its center and wheat as its symbol. As a Western version of Ceres, she can heal the ravages of time and battle. Harmony is achieved by the mythic element overcoming the effects of war and time.

Grey's next few novels involve an obsessed character whose present, the repetitive expiation of his past, is reflected in the narrative technique. For example, there is an old frontiersman in *The Mysterious Rider* (1921) who is another "ancient mariner." He is harried by his violent past, the story of which he is compelled to tell again and again to those in whom he recognizes the mark of imminent death. Repeatedly the reader learns the beginning of Hell-Bent Wade's tale, but not its ending, and Grey's audience, along with Wade's, feels the power of "what happens next."

The Vanishing American contains Grey's most mature social criticism and develops the notion of the past as an agent in both the events and the syntax of the plot. This novel also comes closer than any other by Grey to breaking his formula. It focuses on an Indian who has been taken east as a child, has distinguished himself at university, and has now returned to his desert homeland, hoping to help his tribespeople but unable to mend even the rift in his own soul caused by his hybrid education. His dilemma is epitomized in his alienation from religious belief: he cannot accept either the white man's God or the Indian's pantheistic deities. In the East, he has fallen in love with a white woman who now comes west, wanting to help the Indians and marry Nophaie. At the reservation, she discovers all the corruption of the white officials which saps the Indians of their heritage.

Grey emphasizes the consequences of the hero's racial inheritance by making the first change to his formula. Nophaie ("the warrior") performs some of the conventional feats of a knightly hero: he becomes almost superhuman in his people's eyes by spiriting an Indian girl away from the lecherous missionary; he wins medals for his bravery in the Great War; and he thrashes the all-powerful reservation agents. But he is ultimately powerless to prevent tragedies: the girl is eventually seduced and dies; many Indians are dissuaded from war by the German superintendent and thus lose the chance to redeem the Indian's reputation; and the race as a whole, decimated by the plague, is vanishing. Society's treatment of Indians in the past has too great a weight now to be overturned; it has weakened Nophaie and his tribespeople irretrievably. Nophaie is Grey's least able romantic hero, being the only one who does not save his heroine from captivity or kill the enemy in a duel. He finds his true strength in his two pastoral retreats to desert oases, which eventually result in his acceptance of Christianity and his marriage to the white heroine. But the union also involves a recognition of death:

> The broken Indians and the weary mustangs passed slowly out upon the desert. Shoie, the tongueless, was the last to depart. . . .
> "It is—symbolic—Marian," said Nophaie, brokenly. "They are vanishing—vanishing. My Nopahs! . . . Only a question of swiftly-flying time! And I too—Nophaie, the warrior! In the end I shall be absorbed by you—by your love—by our children. . . . It is well!"[25]

This, again, is a formulaic marriage which heals, but this time it cannot overthrow the consequences of the past. Grey is, here, at his most mature, within his own coordinates, for *The Vanishing American* contains both the formulaic or mythic shape, the dramatization of a social issue and the formal requirements of a complex plot, without making one carry more weight than the others. The ending is a careful poise between creation and destruction, the power of formula or myth and the power of causality.

There is an ironic coda to this development. The conclusion of *The Vanishing American*, which seems to provide so neat a summation to Grey's attempts to mature within the framework of formula, saw publication only in 1975, when Grey's son published the final sections of the novel on their own. *The Ladies' Home Journal*, which serialized *The Vanishing American* in 1922, refused to accept the resolution created by a miscegenational marriage and made Grey rewrite the last pages. The same magazine which elevated Grey as a "master writer" also inhibited him from developing in the only way he could. In the end, however much of an artist he considered himself, he was caught in the same bind as the anonymous pulp hacks. Subscribing to the conditions of formularization, he was eventually trapped by them.

In the magazine version, Grey erased the racial problem by not only killing off Nophaie, but depriving him of his race and color:

> His eyes were those of an Indian, but his face seemed that of a white man. . . . "John, give me a room to die in. . . . It's got me," whispered Nophaie. . . . He clasped Marian's shoulders, held her away from him.
> "Benow di Cleash, I should have been dead hours ago, but I had to see you. I had to die as a white man. . . . white woman, savior of Nophaie, go back to your people. All—is—well."[26]

When Nophaie dies, he turns white, unlike all the other Nopahs, who turn black when the plague kills them. But Grey does not try to present this transformation as a reconciliation of white and red: both Marian and the trader dwell on the futility and pity of Nophaie's life and the white woman's love for him. The bleakness of the ending does not fit well into the pattern of Grey's work.

When *The Vanishing American* appeared as a book, in 1925, it contained yet a third version. In it, Grey managed to avoid miscegenation but still reinstate some of the scenes from the manuscript and so replace some of the balance between the harmony of his mythic pattern and the complexity of his causal time scheme. Nophaie still dies, but without turning white. The book ends with the original elegy, now delivered by Marian: "It—is—symbolic. . . . They are vanishing—vanishing. Oh! Nopahs! . . . Only a question of swiftly flying time! My Nophaie—the warrior—gone before them! . . . It is well."[27] By conjoining the sense of sorrow and a mood of acceptance in the final speech, Grey restored some of the design he originally created, while still bowing to public morals.

The incident well demonstrates the ways in which the constrictions of commercial magazines could reverberate on an author's work, even on that of a favorite, and highly paid, contributor. It was the job of the slick editor not to dictate to his audience but to please a majority of readers and advertisers. In this case, the inherent caution of formulaic production prohibited Grey from using racial types as he chose. But changes which were demanded for cultural reasons also boomeranged on to his relatively intricate formal construction. Only in the published *Vanishing American*, of all Grey's Westerns, did he not end with the hero and heroine's marriage, and the compromise ending articulates acceptance of the Indian's death, which does not fit into Grey's adherence to the comic half of the mythic cycle at all. The whole balance between formula and narrative technique which he achieved in the manuscript version is destroyed by the limits imposed, even on a successful and conventional author, by those who steered his work into the marketplace.

The book's publication in 1925 marked the end of Grey's more ambitious constructions. After that date, perhaps because his major attempt at a complex work had been thwarted, he reverted to ever more sensational romance and lapsed back into ordering his events sequentially. A novel like *The Shepherd of Guadaloupe* (1930) certainly exhibits much telling and retelling of the past, but now the device, like the story, seems stale—lacking a causal justification, it is simply a strategy to prolong the action. With the return of this strategy, Grey had arrived back at the "story," despite the appurtenances of mystery, secrecy, and revelation which the novel tries to sustain.

Grey's artistic progress was obviously limited, but he did achieve a measure of development. On the evidence of his fiction, it seems that his adherence to formula made it difficult for him to find an area which he could develop. He did not break with his repetitive materials or his mythic pattern. Instead, he tried to create consequentiality within the bounds of his formulaic action, by adding some social discussion and altering the relationship between events, from successiveness to causality. The details of his narrative changes illustrate one author's muted rebellion against the inhibiting powers of formula. His most successful novels—*Riders of the Purple Sage, The Desert of Wheat,* and *The Return of the Vanishing American*—are those in which an attempt at formal complexity and an adherence to formula or myth come together and struggle for supremacy. The tension resulting from the desire to be both artist and formulist was one of the most fruitful reactions Grey had to his task.

MAX BRAND

"Max Brand" was the main pseudonym of Frederick Faust, the most prolific and highly paid pulp writer of all time; the name was also the mechanism by which the author accommodated himself to an output for which he felt disgust and shame. Faust cared most about classical poetry and he considered his pulp writing a utilitarian, money-making occupation to be discharged as efficiently as possible. For him, his pulps held nothing of merit or personal significance, and he wanted to separate them from the rest of his life. He supplied a fictitious author along with his fiction, to take public responsibility for the work, fit in with all the marketplace requirements of a pulp author, and keep Frederick Faust completely out of the picture. (Faust's cover was not blown publicly until 1938, several years after he ended his pulp production.)[28] The split between Faust and Brand, between classicist and hack, which Faust assumed was completely absent from his stories, actually gives his novels a distinctive dimension. His enthusiasm for classical mythology shows up in the patterns by which he structured his fictional formulas. Also, he accompanied his predictable adventure tales with fragments of commentary which are not necessary to the action and which, when considered chronologically, tell the story of the author's reaction to his product.

Faust fell into writing Westerns when he was in New York in 1917, trying unsuccessfully to support himself on his poetry, which had won him Berkeley's most prestigious literary prize and praise from Benét, editor of *The Century*. Someone introduced him to Bob Davis, editor of the Munsey pulp magazines and when, at the editor's behest, Faust wrote a competent adventure story within a few hours of their first meeting, Davis realized that he had discovered a bountiful source.[29] From then on, Faust's output was prodigious, his many pseudonyms disguising the fact that one man was supplying so much of the market. Zane Grey may have been Faust's model for his Western fiction, but Faust's attitude to his writing was very different from Grey's.[30] It was a business for him, in which quantity and speed were the principles. Like Grey, he had a daily schedule, but it had all to do with quantity, not quality: setting himself a quota of four-and-a-half thousand words of popular prose in two hours every morning, he produced the equivalent of twenty-five books a year and, by the early 1930s, was appearing every week in *Western Story Magazine*, often in three different guises.

Faust did not fit the mold as easily as his fiction. He considered himself a poet who churned out pulp simply to support his family and finance his gargantuan lifestyle. (His daily schedule also included poetry: it called for six lines in four hours.) At the beginning, he was optimistic that he could sustain both poetry and commercial prose until he made his name as a poet. When he wrote his first Western, he could note, fairly flippantly, "It's silly stuff, I guess, but I like to run the narrative along regardless of whether it's literature or not."[31] But the longer he worked at his poetry, the less acceptable it became to publishers and readers, and it rarely appeared in print. More and more of his day was taken up with pulp. By 1936, he was saying, much more blackly, "I think long, dark thoughts for months. . . . I try to write better stuff. The habit of pulp has corrupted whatever little talents I have."[32]

Using his pseudonyms as a cover, he tried to distance himself from his pulp production as much as possible. He wrote to Bob Davis, "I am *not* Max, however, except to you. And if you ever introduce me or speak to me or even think of me aloud as Max Brand, I'll shoot you with express rifles and duck shot and bury you in a garbage can."[33] He realized that his fiction was false both to his own ideals and to the reality around him, and he was ashamed of it. He would not keep any of his books in his home, he kept his fiction a secret from his children (telling them he was "making shoes" when they asked what he did at the typewriter), and he condemned his audience: "a certain number of child-minded people, even millions of them, read this brainless drip and like it. Their minds don't have to budge."[34]

None of this fitted in well with the pulps which published his work, especially given their policy at this time. It has been seen in the case of Zane Grey, and it was true generally, that pulps adopted different public attitudes to their star writers than to their less well known hacks. As part of the general policy of flattering readers and fostering in them the sense of belonging to a club, some pulp editors introduced the most popular writers on the editor's page and had them say a few words (about their careers or the authenticity of their material) directly to the audience. This was another fillip to the democratic image: authors themselves attesting that they were "just common folks, same as you and me."[35] Since Faust was a major contributor to the pulps, under various pseudonyms, readers would inevitably expect some of these names to appear on the editorial pages.

But Faust did not want to claim any artistic responsibility for his work, publicly or privately. When he wrote to Davis about *The Untamed*, his first Western novel and a huge success, he insisted on the importance of the editorial contribution. In one letter, he reminded Davis, "The Untamed is not *my* book; it's *our* book"; in another, he admitted, "I quite realize that there is a field for my Western junk as long as I have you to put the jazz in it"; and in a third, he said, "I still fail to see why The Untamed has gone over, and it makes me feel that we can knock them dead with the sequel. . . . No question about it, I work a hell of a pile better with you than away from you."[36] Quite apart from his public, Faust did not want even his book publisher to know who he was. He wrote, again, to Davis: "Can't you tell them that Max Brand is a deaf mute with whom you alone can hold conversation through a system of intricate signs to which the F. A. Munsey Company holds the only code?"[37]

Faust published most of his Westerns, under various pseudonyms, in *Western Story Magazine*, the most popular Western pulp of the time and the one which gave its best-selling authors the highest level of visibility. His absence from "The Round-Up," the forum for authors' and readers' statements, is conspicuous. There are indirect uses of one or two of his pseudonyms: for example, "George Owen Baxter was in this morning, and he agrees with this C. O. Dodge fellow from Oroville, California, who says . . . [etc.]"[38] But neither Max Brand nor Baxter nor any of the other Faust authors ever speaks directly. Inevitably, some strain shows, especially when letters specifically addressed to these authors are published. When one letter demands a sequel from Baxter, the editor tries to conjure up the author for a reply:

> Well, Herman, tell you how it is: We have taken that up with Baxter several times. He is a perverse sort of cuss, that Baxter fellow is. In some ways we like it in him. He has strong opinions.
> "How about it, George?" we asked him. "In that 'Iron Dust' story, do they get married? Does the man go after the pony or the girl? Well, we asked him so hard that he wrote a sequel to it. . . .
> George is yet to write a sequel to "Wild Freedom." When're you going to get started on that, Baxter man?[39]

Baxter never answers and he never does produce a sequel.

Of course, Max Brand was *Western Story's* biggest star and the magazine made most efforts over him. Like Baxter, he was a silent presence.

> Stand up, Max Brand, and answer Wallace W. Harris, of Covington, Virginia.
> What? Max not present! Hark! It seems to us we hear the clicking of a typewriter. We'll bet he's out yonder in the mesquite with a lantern and his black piano, hammering away at another good yarn. Go down and put it up to him, Wallace.[40]

However much Faust wanted to distance himself from his fiction and its "child-minded" audience, the pulps could not sustain such an absence for long. Eighteen months later, *Western Story* created its own "Max Brand" to fill the gap. When the first installment of *Wooden Guns* appeared, the editor, in "The Round-Up," wished that the magazine carried pictures of its authors.

> Take Max Brand. My, but he's a fine upstandin' boy. If you want to see a typical product of the West, just cast your glance on Max. . . .
> One thing, though, Max isn't good at, and that's talkin'. No, sirs and ladies, when it comes to conversation, Max is sure weak. He's got all gifts the gods can hand out, save one, the gift of gab. If you're alone with him, and he likes you, you may get a little more than yes and no answers, by puttin' questions; but in a crowd, say, he might just as well be a hitchin' post, for all the noise he makes. . . .
> It's Max's eyes that sure get you most. Pale blue they are, and with a look in 'em that comes when the person as owns 'em has spent much time alone in the open places. Max looks at you—yes, he's a straight looker, but with a look that seems to go through, past you, and way, way out yonder.
> Gosh all hemlock, hope you haven't got tired with our talkin' so much about one of our children. . . . When Max brought "Wooden Guns" to our

desk, we up and asked him point-blank, before we even looked at the title, if he thought the story a good one.

"Don't know," he said. "Author can't judge his own work, but I'll say this much, had more pleasure doin' it than any story I ever wrote." Max would say nothing more; we made all the noise during the rest of the interview.[41]

In all the genuine reminiscences of Faust, he is famed as a charming personality, a great conversationalist, a man of erudition, energy, and wit who loved to entertain an audience of friends with Greek tales or details of astronomy. But if he would not talk in his own voice in *Western Story*, the magazine had to create a voice for him, and it fitted the purpose well to turn him into a Western hero.

The Max Brand who is sketched in by the pulp magazines is so far removed from the author who wrote the fiction that it would seem that Faust achieved his desire: to dissociate himself from his lucrative work. The question remains, of course, whether the fiction itself shows as little sign of its origins, whether the disdainful Faust is evident at all in the work of the pulp hack Max Brand. In fact, Faust's authorship makes itself felt in two ways. First, he used his knowledge of classical mythology to develop the same kinds of fictional patterns as Zane Grey. But Faust went further than Grey in creating a self-enclosed world of adventure: by and large, he sloughed off not only historical and social concerns but also, in time, references to mythic types beyond his own inventions. Second, within the adventure stories, there are subtle but discernible signs of their author's opinions. From Faust's earliest to his latest pulp Western, there is a progression from oblique to overt authorial distaste at the adventurous action.

The Max Brand pulp Westerns which Faust endowed with mythological dimensions are repetitive indeed: most of them tell of a man in the West who undergoes a transforming trial in the shape of a series of violent experiences. In the later Westerns, the hero changes from the Virginian type, who ends his adventures in matrimony, to the Leatherstocking kind, who remains outside societal relationships, wandering from one adventure to the next in a series of novels. The repeated use of characters emphasizes the impression that these adventures are ritual reenactments of the same story. The stories' lack of association is also clear. The Brand novels are written in a spare, brisk style which eschews philosophical or social commentary. Generally, they do not even indicate the date or place of the action. Like Grey, Faust chose the mountain desert as his landscape, but made of it an empty backdrop. His scenic descriptions are perfunctory, the action taking place in a blank area in which isolated constructions—a house, a farm, a town—come into focus. Sometimes a particular effect is made of the blankness: Kate Cumberland noted "with a blank eye" that the landscape "was a single mass of lifeless gray"; for Destry, "the world which he knew was now reduced to a great blank in which there lived a single face and a single name."[42]

What Faust did develop highly was his use of the mythic paradigm. Like Grey, he organized his action in his Westerns according to the sequence of separation-initiation-return. Also, he incorporated many more allusions than Grey to figures from classical mythology, the Bible, pre-Christian history, and Renaissance literature. This is a potpourri, but his fiction is most reminiscent of heroic romance: women and chivalry are less important than the hero's rites of passage on his road to manhood.

In the first chapter of his first novel, "Pan of the Desert" in *The Untamed* (1918), Faust introduces his hero on horseback, accompanied by a wolf dog and whistling: "It was fit music for such a scene, for it seemed neither of heaven nor earth, but the soul of the great god Pan come back to earth to charm those nameless rocks with his wild, sweet piping."[43] The hero, Dan Barry, is pastoral indeed: an innocent, indolent, good-natured boy who has been found wandering in the desert and adopted by a rancher. In young manhood, he is attacked and beaten by an outlaw, Silent. Inflamed by the taste of his own blood, Barry spends the rest of the novel on Silent's trail, finally killing him in a gunfight. This book contains a profusion of classical similes. Dan is variously likened to Pan, Fate, centaur, and Samson. His horse is called Satan, but also often referred to as a winged horse. After undergoing a false death in a burning shack, Dan, with his dog and horse, enacts his revenge quest, which involves many superhuman feats of shooting and tracking. Having killed the villain, he returns to the rancher and his daughter, to whom he is engaged. But the circle is broken at the last, for the hero wanders off again into the desert with his animals.

Two sequels complete the circular pattern. *The Night Horseman* (1920) records the rancher and his daughter waiting for Barry's return. He is involved in more duels, notably one against Mac Strann, most feared fighter of the area until he confronts Whistling Dan: "it was to Mac Strann as it was to Patroclus when Apollo struck the base of his neck and his armor of proof fell from him" (p. 238). The rancher eventually dies when Barry carries Kate off into the night on his horse. In the last book, *The Seventh Man* (1921), Barry, Kate, and their daughter live in paradisal isolation until Barry's horse is killed by a posse. In retribution, Barry kills six of the seven men responsible. Reverting increasingly to animalism, he retreats to a cave with his daughter. Kate retrieves the child and returns to the old ranch house. When Barry has completed his vengeance, he burns the wilderness home, then arrives at the ranch to claim his daughter. Knowing that he can never be changed, Kate kills him. And so the cycle ends, with its symmetrical pattern of ritual fires, chases, rescues, and killings. It does not follow one classical story, but weaves together recognizable events and relationships from different myths: the revenge quest, the journey into hell, the betrayal of Delilah, and the murder of man by wife in a struggle over the sacrifice of their daughter.

From about the mid-1920s, references to specific legendary figures tend to fade out, and heroes come to be labeled conjurers or players in a game more often than gods. At the same time, however, the action is arranged into increasingly neat mythical patterns.[44] Eventually, when Faust began his final two Western series in 1933, he dispensed with the classical references completely and made his heroes mythic figures in their own right, rather than copies of traditional types. The Montana Kid and Silvertip perform all sorts of superhuman feats, often in sequences which demonstrate the threefold structure common to many features of the romance.[45] Even when their tasks are very similar to those of classical heroes, however, the precedent is not acknowledged.

Silvertip first appears in *The Stolen Stallion* (1933). He is a mysterious loner who almost dies in the desert when chasing a legendary wild horse, which he eventually catches. Silver is a legend in his own right, but some of the deeds ascribed to him belong to heroes like Hercules (though this is not acknowledged): "He'd go in the dark into a hole in the ground and rip the heart out of a mountain lion with his bare hands," says one character of Silver.[46] At the end, the hero is asked where he will go next: " 'over the edge of the world, somewhere,' said Silvertip" (p. 202). The subsequent novels in the series do, indeed, take him into an increasingly mythical sphere. In *Silvertip* (1933), having killed a boy by mistake, he goes, in atonement, to a hellish valley, into the fortressed castle where the boy's family live and, as their prisoner, deep into the earth into a tiny dungeon. Silver himself sees this descent into the underworld as a necessary ritual: "He secured hope out of one strange thought—that he had appointed himself to redeem the lost life of Pedro Monterey, and that therefore he must suffer worse than death, and then be given the chance to use his hands and his brains."[47] He suffers for three days, then breaks free. He fulfills the three vows of revenge made by the patriarch of the family against his opponent in a range war: that he will burn his brand into the door, the forehead, and the heart of his enemy. Silver almost dies carrying out his tasks, but he recovers and, despite the Monterey daughter's offer of herself to him as a bride, he rides off for more adventures of the same type in subsequent novels.

The first two novels in the Montana series are *Montana Rides!* (1933) and *Montana Rides Again* (1934). In them, the hero makes repeated forays into Mexico, where he survives a number of superhuman battles and trials, rescues various captives, and declines several marriage proposals. By the last novel in the series, *The Song of the Whip* (1936), Montana is a legendary hero, about whom the Mexicans tell stories and sing songs.

Out of the Montana Kid, a gunman, and Mateo Rubriz, an outlaw, Faust creates a new pastoral: "The story of that long battle which had cemented their friendship was still epic through all the mountains; you could hear the shepherds singing the tale of it as they walked the high plateaus."[48] This is the new mythic hero, who enacts deeds on a par with those of classical figures, but admits no debt to them.

To identify his popular creations with a world of myth and legend even more pointedly than Grey, Faust used his literary interests beyond his commercial production. In his private life, he was a serious classics student, who poured his enthusiasm for classical heroes into poems like the epic *Dionysus in Hades* (1931). Apart from his simple, effectively naive lyrics, his poetry is classical in subject, tone, and vocabulary and is delivered in conventional metres and rhyme schemes. Faust believed that he kept his verse strictly apart from what he called his prose "junk."[49] Nevertheless, it seems clear that his popular Westerns—which move from acknowledging classical prototypes to introducing their own super-human figures—have the same combination of mythological content and patterned form as his poetry.

The authorial identity behind the formulaic fiction makes itself felt in another, more personal way than this. Through time, Faust's attitude to his popular work—as it progresses from aloofness to irony to disdain—becomes increasingly perceptible in the details of his texts. Because there is no overt authorial voice, the author's presence rarely makes itself felt in direct ways. Perhaps it can be seen most clearly in the snippets of information which are peppered throughout the stories: references to Egyptian diorite statues, explanations of scientific processes, and details of Aztec mythology, all of which bear a very tenuous relevance to the plot, appear in asides in the present tense which interrupt the past-tense narrative. More often, Faust's perspective is conveyed obliquely, through the actions and dialogue of his characters. For example, the author's desire to remain aloof from his work is reflected in a recurrent distancing device, which separates the action from both author and audience. Again and again, there are scenes in which the main action occurs at some distance from an observer who stands in the foreground, conveying the events to the readers. More highly developed than this device is a series of remarks by different characters, which can be read as self-reflexive comments on the novels. They point to the fictiveness of the action, its dependence on pattern and, finally, its lack of significance. Interpreted chronologically, these comments read like Faust's muffled protests against the formulas in his own pulp production.

All the novels are full of figures of speech to do with storybooks, fiction, the stage, actors, rehearsed scenes, and pictures, that call to mind the artifice of it all. Only when Faust was pressured into producing a particular story, however, did he extend these scattered references into a sustained analogy between the action in his books and the writing or reading of language. The case arose in one of the sequels to *The Untamed*. Faust himself planned the first sequel, and it is unclear who originated the second, *The Seventh Man*.[50] That novel ends so decisively (with Kate killing Dan) that it seems as if the author had no desire to prolong Barry's adventures. But readers protested so vigorously at Barry's death that Faust was forced to write one more addition, *Dan Barry's Daughter* (1923), which tells of Joan Barry's search for the truth about her father.

The play with books, words and writing in this novel amounts to an extended metaphor, which suggests a sustained parallel between the author's and the characters' preoccupations. The adventures of the heroine have much to do with the comprehension of language. On the first page of the book, Joan is distracted from the book she is reading by the sound of wild geese (which was always Dan's call to action). She begins to ask Buck Daniels, her adopted father, about her past. Perturbed, he tells her to go back to her book and "he studied her as if her face were a page on which strange things might have been written in the last few moments."[51] He refuses to answer her questions: "It won't do no good for me to tell you what's wrong. You got to find your own words and say it in your own way" (pp. 9–10). Joan is startled by the hint of mystery: "This was opening the book to an unexpected place. This was to find poetry instead of prose" (p. 12).

Joan sets off on a quest for the truth about her past and finds that the search has much to do with the interpretation of language. From the sky come down to her "the voices of a band of wild geese . . . like so many words, each a message in a foreign tongue and yet with a meaning to be half guessed" (p. 41). On her travels, she repeatedly encounters people who feel themselves to be reliving "an old story." She comes to understand the words of the song which she habitually sings and the language of horses and, once she uncovers some of the truth, she realizes that "I've lived in the center of a lie!" (p. 173).

Her adventures involve her and her friends in all sorts of danger, and eventually, with Buck's death, she decides that she must stop her wanderings to settle into marriage and domesticity. When she refuses to take the quest any further, she also gives up her concern with language: "A wedge of wild geese, flying low, sent down their wavering and dissonant chorus, but Dan Barry's daughter did not hear" (p. 353). If this process is abstracted to the level at which the author works with language, the ending hints at some sort of protest against the prolongation of the series and a refusal to revive these characters again.

In much of the fiction after *Dan Barry's Daughter*, potentially self-reflexive comments stress the insubstantiality of fiction, particularly in the first-person narrations. In *Fire-Brain* (1926), the narrator ends his story with a retrospective consideration of his adventures: "for a long decade, now, I have looked back to my other self as to something found in the pages of a book, interesting but unreal." In *The Blue Jay* (1927) the hero repeatedly talks of "fool story-books" and "idiotic romances," and in *Trouble Trail* (1937), the narrator complains, "it makes me sick the way people will swallow a fool story, just because it's an exciting one. It ain't the probable lies that go down, but the neat ones."[52] Because the author has set up a parallel between the contents of his own stories and language in general, these criticisms of fiction rebound on his own products.

Another major issue raised alongside this commentary on fiction is the question of whether a pattern can be broken once it is established. In his notebooks Faust attested in his own voice to his use of patterns:

> Of course if you go after the mechanics of Western stories as such you'll find that it's a simple group of rules by which one may cut the pattern of any number of yarns. And your bank account need never fail if you follow the rules, and clip carefully along the marked lines. And not so carefully at that.[53]

In the fiction, the dominance of pattern is raised as part of the problem about the hero's origins: is a man's character determined irreversibly by the pattern of his paternity and heredity? In the early novels, the signs are that the mold is unbreakable. In *Clung* (1920), which is about the racial inheritance of the Chinese hero, and in *Black Jack* (1921), in which the hero discovers that his father was an outlaw, the constant cry is "Blood will tell!" Both heroes unwittingly follow the patterns of behavior set by their fathers: Clung casts off his oriental habits only to find that he has inherited his true, white father's instincts; when Black Jack is rescued from his life of crime by a woman, he is still mirroring his father's career.

In later novels, however, this conclusion is reversed. In *Dan Barry's Daughter*, the message is clearly that patterns from the past can be broken. *Steve Train's Ordeal* (1924) underlines this conclusion, when the hero, born and bred an outlaw, becomes an honest man and delivers the money entrusted to him by a rich rancher. From this point, the stories are repetitive narratives about the possibility of change, with repetitively affirmative outcomes. The sheer volume of these repetitions suggests that this is an obsession of the author as well as his characters. *Happy Jack* provides as clear an indication that this is so as we ever get. In this novel, the question of change becomes a theory of ecstasy, propounded by an Eastern professor and embodied by Happy Jack, the gunman. The professor talks of "the lightning in humanity" which transforms a man's ability. Some of his examples are telling:

> There are men, for example, who seem to be asleep. Suddenly, they write a great book. Something that we don't know about has happened to change their brains. Something too small to be noticed, let's say!
> But from that moment on, it's a new man at work. Walter Scott was over

forty when he wrote his first novel, for instance. So was Fielding. They'd done nothing really first-rate, or anywhere near first-rate, before that.[54]

Faust wrote this when he was thirty-eight, about to publish, privately, his long poem *Dionysus*, the labor of six years. His final cry seems eloquent: "Ecstasy is the thing. . . . If only we can control it and teach it when and where to strike!" (p. 42)

At about this point, although the possibility of change continues as a theme, there also enters a new note, to do with the danger of patterns and the wastefulness of the action which they generate. These notions first appear strongly in *Destry Rides Again* (1930), the most famous and best-selling Max Brand Western. Childhood habits determine the course of the plot. Destry has always been a skilled fistfighter, and in his youth, humiliated all the other boys in town by beating them. Now, as a young man, he is accused of a stage holdup. He is tried by a jury made up of those whom he defeated in childhood. In retaliation for old injuries, they condemn him on flimsy evidence. He is sent to prison, and when he returns, six years later, he revenges himself on the twelve, by killing some, exposing others' corruption, and frightening the rest out of town. At the same time, he fails to realize that the man behind the whole scheme, who framed him for the holdup, is actually the only man in town whom he counted his friend—Chester Bent, another of Destry's childhood victims.

There are two patterns here, both of which are broken at the end. First, there is Bent's plan to destroy Destry, which very nearly succeeds. Throughout the action, Destry senses that there is one hand, which he cannot identify, behind all the attacks on him. The reader, who always knows the villain's identity, watches Bent plotting his intricate design and its web tightening around the ignorant hero. At the very end, Destry just manages to kill Bent in a shootout, but he acknowledges that his escape is accidental: Bent actually outdraws him, and it is clear that the villain who devises all the happenings is more powerful than the hero who enacts them. If Bent is performing some kind of authorial function, he shows that the role is an evil one. There is also the conflict between Destry and his victims which has been perpetuated since childhood antagonism. Only at the end, after all the destruction, does Destry realize the pointlessness of violence and the wastefulness of all the events which have made up the novel. He understands that he has been wrong to prolong a pattern of conflict established a long time before, and he resolves to give up the life of physical, superficial adventure.

In various novels after this, the villain who orchestrates the hero's life reappears and implications of waste and meaninglessness recur. These negative reflections ultimately climax in Faust's final two Western series. Both Silvertip and Montana harp on the constriction of writing and pattern, the need constantly to escape and the pointlessness of their careers. Both heroes appear in series and neither of them marries or settles in society, so they make no gesture toward a lasting resolution at any level. There is little in the formulaic action to counteract the impression of wastefulness that is conveyed in the dialogue.

Silvertip realizes the danger of patterns most clearly in *Silvertip's Search* (1935): "Somehow, he felt, there was a way of linking everything together.... It was not chance, either, that had distributed them in such a pattern, making Silver the exact center of the design. The meaning was simple: he was about to be filled with lead."[55] At the same time that Silver feels unable to give up his adventurous life, he recognizes that some of his actions are senseless: "There had been no reason, then, to kill that man who now lay with his face pressed against the trail high up in the hillside. There was no reason to have '*them*' on his trail" (pp. 39–40).

In the Montana series, there is clear recognition that these adventures are to be written about, with characters repeatedly promising to record events faithfully. The last of the series, *The Song of the Whip*, was also Faust's last pulp Western novel, so its conclusion incorporates three endings in one. It brings together all the characters from the previous Montana novels and it has all the traits of a Brand Western: a perfectly drawn monomyth, new myths enacted, and new myths written down. It is particularly full of songs composed about Montana, Mateo, and the beautiful Dorothea. Mateo finally roars to the Kid:

> My God! amigo, what a wonderful thing it is that in such a little world there should be two such men as you and I.... If there were a century between us, still it would be wonderful.... But to be alive in the same land, at the same time, that is enough to be put into a book, even into a Bible! [P. 259]

That would be an exuberant ending to Faust's Western fiction, but it is followed by a long scene which actually finishes the book, series, and pulp output. It is the clearest comment Faust made on all the preceding action, and its import is all to the effect that none of this should ever have happened. Brother Pascual takes Montana to the Rio Grande and asks him,

> "What land is that beyond the water?"
> "America, of course."
> "Is that your country?"
> "It is my country, Pascual."
> "Why are you so far south?" asked the friar.
> The Kid turned and looked at him with keen, wrinkling eyes.
> "You must travel straight on," said the friar. "You must not turn back."
> Montana was silent.

"When you come south," said the friar, "there is trouble. . . . Consider this. . . . A peon is flogged, and that was too bad . . . and to help the peon you crossed the river into danger. . . . How many men have died, since then because a peon was flogged?"

Montana could not speak a word.

"Young 'Tonio' has left his father's ranch; a dancing-girl has been riding under gunfire," said the friar; "a lady of great place has damaged her name—who can say how much? . . . A famous hacienda has been looted; a peon has been turned into a bandit; every Rural in Mexico has been turned into a savage beast; an outlaw has passed into fire and out again; and a poor friar has left his flock and gone wandering far into sin, I greatly fear. . . . Because El Keed rode south! Because he heard 'The Song of the Whip'!"

The Kid turned his head and looked darkly back through the cañon.

"As for the rest, they will take care of themselves if you are not with them. But if you are there—would you choose black eyes or blue, brother?"

The Kid rubbed his knuckles across his forehead. He sighed.

"I have to think," he said.

"Take time," said the friar. "But tell me what you have gained for all this riding and shooting?"

"Only the horse I ride on," said the Kid, "—and some spoiled clothes!"

"Well, think!" said the friar.

The Kid bowed his head. And El Capitan, finding his head free, reached for a tuft of bunch grass, sun-cured, sweet.

He cropped it, reached for another, began to wander step by step down the slope from grass to grass. The head of the Kid lifted. He did not turn it again as the horse wandered.

And the friar drew a great breath, for he saw that the Kid was looking steadily towards the north.

When he looked again, El Capitan was at a trot, moving north, north towards the brown river. [Pp. 260–61]

That silent, indecisive vignette is the last of Faust's Western hero in the pulps. While the words, of both the author and the other characters, have accumulated around him—discussing story, change, and futility— the hero's meaning and purpose have dwindled to this.

One of Faust's few slick Westerns appeared in 1936, just after the pulp publication of *Song of the Whip*.[56] Robert Easton records that Faust hated the slicks even more than the pulps. He worked on his contributions to the slicks "with what he described as nausea. . . . At least with the pulps he could write myths and enjoy himself, at times. Not so with the slicks. They were buying his mind, not just his story-telling skill."[57] His slick Western "Wine on the Desert" reflects this heightened distaste. It does not have the characters or the plot of a formulaic Western. It features only two men, one a cripple and one an escaped outlaw, and focuses on the slow death of the outlaw in the desert. In this story, instead of oblique commentary by the characters on formulaic fiction, the plot itself acts out the death of Western types. The new form, then, only underlines Faust's break with Western adventure stories.

All this suggests that even an author who distanced himself from his popular work and produced his repetitive material as automatically as Faust professed to do, still conducted some kind of rebellion against his commercial circumstances in his writing. Faust never developed the rhetoric of the dime novelists or the philosophizing of Grey, and he did not contribute to the editorial commentary designed to bolster sales of his kind of fiction. Even more rigorously than Grey, he divorced his fiction from its environment in the pulp magazines by presenting it in the form of a new mythology. Nevertheless, his attitude to his position as a formulist is present in the details of his fiction. The more novels Faust wrote, and the more rigidly conventional they became, the more overt were his hints about his unease at being locked into a repeating pattern and his desire to change from telling wasteful adventure stories. Of course, Faust never did forge a creative fiction out of his protest. Unlike the dime novelists, his reaction to the marketplace was completely negative. His increasingly overt distaste never resulted in changes, only in rather repetitive and fragmentary protests and, in the end, silence.

ERNEST HAYCOX

> You've got to spend three or four years digging yourself a rut so deep that finally you find it more convenient not to get out of it.
>
> Ernest Haycox, 1945[58]

It is entirely typical of Haycox's career that he gave this advice to writers just as he was about to break with the serial market and so climb out of his own twenty-year-deep rut, which, while extremely remunerative, had led him into dissatisfaction, compromise, and frustration. He was always vacillating and hesitating, and his novels vacillated accordingly. Haycox's Western heroes may take all the risks which their author evaded, but they became enmeshed in similar repetitions and doubts.

Haycox's long fiction is similar to Frederick Faust's in that it reflects the author's reactions to his formulaic output. But Haycox's development is more intricate than Faust's and it emerges, in the end, in a changed form, for Haycox always believed that he could make something of his marketplace writings. The stages of his development are laid out graphically. There is a clear parallel between his artistic attitudes, his mode of publication and the matter of his fiction. His move from the pulps to the slicks to books involved the falling away of strict conventions of presentation. At the same time, there began in his novels a questioning

"I'M SETH JONES OF NEW HAMPSHIRE."

Seth Jones, frontispiece, Beadle & Co. London edition, 1860(?). Reproduced by permission of the Huntington Library, San Marino, California.

No. 1   THE ARTHUR WESTBROOK CO.
Cleveland, Ohio   Vol. I

DEADWOOD DICK, THE PRINCE OF THE ROAD:
Or, The Black Rider of the Black Hills.

BY EDWARD L. WHEELER.

"Ha ha ha isn't that rich, now? Ha! ha! ha! arrest Deadwood Dick if you can!"

Deadwood Dick, cover illustration, Arthur Westbrook reprint, 1899. Reproduced by permission of the Archives—American Heritage Center, University of Wyoming.

Issued Weekly. By subscription $2.50 per year. Entered according to Act of Congress in the year 1905, in the Office of the Librarian of Congress, Washington, D. C., by STREET & SMITH, 79-89 Seventh Avenue, N. Y. Application made at the N. Y. Post Office for entry as Second-class Matter.

lo. 79   **NEW YORK, OCTOBER 21, 1905.**   **Price, Five Cents**

Ted Strong, cover illustration, Street & Smith, 1905. Reproduced by permission of The George Arents Research Library, Syracuse University.

Zane Grey's Western Magazine, cover illustration, Dell, 1951.

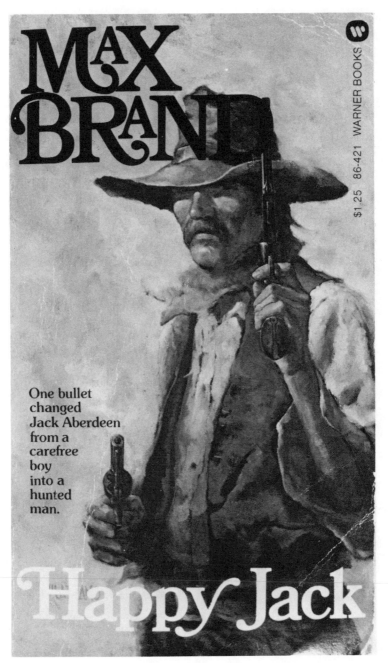

MAX BRAND

WARNER BOOKS

$1.25 86-421

One bullet
changed
Jack Aberdeen
from a
carefree
boy
into a
hunted
man.

Happy Jack

Happy Jack, cover illustration, Warner Books reprint, 1972. Copyright Dodd, Mead & Co., Inc.

Hondo, cover illustration, Hodder Fawcett reprint, 1966. Copyright
Bantam Books Inc.

Yellow Back Radio Broke-Down, cover illustration by Andrew Rhodes, Avon paperback edition. Copyright © 1977. Reproduced by permission of Avon Books, New York.

of formulaic rituals, which in time led to their disintegration and the rise of another, less definite set of laws to govern his characters' actions.

From the first, Haycox's experience of writing was tied up with the world of commercialism. He began writing short stories at the University of Oregon, and early in his career he came under the tutorship of W. F. G. Thacher, something of a pulp writer and winner of various commercial writing competitions.[59] When he had some little success, Haycox went to New York in 1924, to try to sell stories to various kinds of magazine. He received many rejections but finally succeeded in a small way with *Western Story Magazine* and *Detective Story Magazine*, and was advised by Frank Blackwell, editor of *Western Story*, to concentrate on mastering the technique of the Western.[60] Haycox returned west and followed this advice, publishing in pulp magazines exclusively for the next six years. At the beginning, he was fairly content to be pleasing the public; he was proud of his stories' entertainment value and believed that those who bought his work received their money's worth.[61]

When Haycox published in the pulp magazines, he entered a world of code and convention. There was a great deal of paraphernalia in the pulps, beyond the fiction itself, which was designed to answer the readers' appetite for vicarious adventure. Thus, the editors' columns and the letters pages fostered the fiction that readers were working Westerners: they were invited to write to departments entitled "The Round-Up," "The Camp-Fire," and "Come An' Get It!" Readers responded by underwriting the convention that the magazines' contents portrayed authentic Western life. The advertisements, too, exploited the audience's willingness to believe in a fantastical world, by promising overnight transformations—in physique, musical talent, or linguistic ability—which they authenticated with photographic evidence. Some advertising copy managed to use the sensational narrative typical of pulp fiction to tap the individual competitiveness of the business world: the University of Applied Science advertised a course in Secret Service training with the heading, "A Roar! A Flash! Two men dead—he escapes—Who is he?— $10,000.00 Reward. Follow Him! Thrills! Rewards! Await YOU! . . . Act Now. Don't let the other fellow enjoy what is rightfully yours."[62]

At the center of these similar fictions, and operating according to the same laws of fantasy as them, are the Western tales and their authors. The relationship between the author and the magazine is reinforced by various publicity devices, like advance notices, discussions in the editor's department, headlines on the contents page and synopses on the title page. For example, when Haycox's first pulp novel, *Free Grass*, appeared in *West* in 1928, the editorial announcement read: "Free Grass in the next issue of WEST is the novel that we have persuaded *Ernest Haycox* to write for us." Sometimes authors themselves participated in the magazine's strategy for publicizing its contents: when the first episode of *Free*

Grass appeared, Haycox contributed a letter to "Come An' Get It!" The
letter shows him both carrying the language of his pulp novels beyond
the pages of his fiction and employing the logic of the pulp magazines,
by authenticating one fiction with another.

> "The other day," Mr. Haycox says, "I happened to be leaning against a
> corral post swapping glances with a compact hunk of horse dynamite known
> as Cal Coolidge. . . .
> "Barring his cheerfulness, he seemed to be the dead image of Quagmire
> in my yarn, *Free Grass*. Shucks, I have shook dice with fellows like him, and
> with fellows like San Saba, too. . . .
> "*Free Grass* happened almost fifty years ago, which was a little before my
> time. But that doesn't make any difference. Types of men don't change in
> the West very fast. You'll see today, as I have seen, the very same kind riding
> the desert and the high bench as rode then in *Free Grass* from Texas to
> Dakota Territory. The fellow that says they don't, never got very far off his
> chair in the observation car."[63]

This letter suggests that Haycox participated in the codified world of
the pulps more directly than either Grey or Faust. On occasion, he was
able to fit his methods to those of pulp editors, readers, and advertisers.

The fiction which Haycox published in the pulp magazines clearly
subscribed to the standard conventions, too. Although Haycox's novels
do not stress their links with mythological patterns, they are highly stylized and repetitive. Again and again, they tell of a Western hero fighting
villains—often corrupt businessmen backed by Eastern politicians—in
defense of, or for the recovery of, his rangeland. In the course of his
battle, he encounters two women who represent a simple opposition—
the sensual contrasting with the virtuous, the Western with the Eastern,
the dark with the fair—and he chooses one of them as his bride. By the
end, he is secure in his home with his new wife.

The pulp novels also show characters, like their author, articulating
their allegiance to code and convention. The hero of *Free Grass* uses the
same language as pulp editors, readers, and advertisers to state his approval of ritualistic behavior. He is a Texan who has been east to college,
but now returns to the West, to help his father establish a new ranch in
Dakota. In the first installment, which is accompanied by Haycox's letter,
Tom Gillette lets his father know that he still subscribes to Western
values:

> "Shoulder to shoulder, fist to fist," mused Tom. "Play your own hand,
> ask no favours, ride straight, shoot fast. Keep all obligations."
> The Major nodded; a stray beam of light caught his eyes and kindled.
> "You have learned to express yourself well. Glad to know that what you
> have said is all I ever tried to teach you. That you still abide by the code is
> my greatest pleasure."[64]

After this, Haycox's pulp characters seldom discuss the code quite as openly, but they continue to talk and act in equally codified ways. Characters realize that they are playing some kind of game, and they are certain of its rules. The hero of *Dead Man Range* (1930) confronts one of his enemies with, "Now the next move seems to be up to me. Which I will make, according to rule."[65] He knows, too, the importance of his code: "No matter how little license he had for intruding on the quarrel, he had, nevertheless, lived too long with his own code to throw it over now" (p. 50). This code is so pronounced that it is recognizable to an outsider. When the Eastern heroine of *Smoky Pass* (1934, published in book form as *Riders West*) begins to understand Western men, it is the codified nature of their behavior which she picks up first: "They were, Nan knew, speaking in code" and " 'He knows,' she thought, 'but the code is not to tell.' "[66] All the familiar rituals are present in these novels: the captivity and rescue of the heroine and the tests of manhood represented by the bucking horse, the poker game, the fistfight, and the climactic gun duel.

After a few years in the pulps, Haycox began to realize the limits of his chosen genre and became increasingly unhappy with the defects of his fiction. His last appearance in the pulps echoes this change of heart, both in the author's public comments and in the details of his fiction. When the first installment of *Smoky Pass* appeared in the pulp *Short Stories* in 1934, Haycox still accompanied his fiction with a direct address to readers placed elsewhere in the magazine, but the mode of his expression no longer apes the artifices of the magazine. Haycox says, "I don't write about folks I haven't met—at least by proxy. I don't write about anything that I have not seen or somehow touched."[67] The qualifications are the outward signs of his private determination to remove himself from the pulps. The characters of *Smoky Pass* echo this change by acknowledging not only the rules of a formula, but the existence of narrative devices, too. There are various allusions to stories, beginnings, and endings. After the hero has killed a man near the opening of the novel, his friends talk: " 'Well,' mused Jubilee, 'here's the end of something.' 'No,' put in Townsite gravely, 'the beginning of something' " (p. 29). Halfway through the book, the heroine's ex-lover says, "There's nothing to do. The story's written. The ending will be a better one than I could furnish" (p. 221). And near the end, the hero hears gunshots lessening and "he knew the story out there was nearly told" (p. 291). In another part of the magazine, Haycox judged this work his first substantial achievement: "It has taken me a long while to reach the point where I can write a story that gets below surface action."[68] When he moved into the slicks, it was this self-reflexive note which he developed.

When Haycox broke into the slick magazines in 1931, he became enmeshed in many vacillations between his financial and artistic goals. Because he desired financial security, he tried to ensure the steadiness of his reception by staying well within his formula. He told Thacher that his only feasible plan was to mold his work for the slick market and so achieve a guaranteed income from thé white-paper magazines. But he was swayed by artistic considerations too. He wanted to improve his craftsmanship and, during the years 1931 to 1945, he became more and more dissatisfied with his repetitions. Reluctant to abandon the Western entirely, he vacillated endlessly, adding new, but never very important variations to his formula. He could not decide in which direction to develop, and he was scared of the chaos which might result if he left the tight form of the magazine serial. He never forgot his ambition to write a work of lasting value, though, and his private writings of this time show him to be guilty and defensive about his failure to experiment.[69]

The principles of slick publishing must have contributed to Haycox's sense of being adrift somewhere beyond the bounds of strict formula. In the world of the slicks, convention still operates, but at a much more subtle level than in the pulps. The values which can be discerned at the heart of slick magazines—in their fiction, articles, and advertisements—are just as traditional as those in pulp magazines. Moreover, by publishing in the slicks, authors seem to enter into the same kind of symbiotic relationship as in the pulps: at the same time that the editorial commentary puffs the fiction, the fiction itself dramatizes the values which the magazines and their advertising sponsors are trying to sell to the public. But all this works in a much less blatant manner in the slicks than in the pulps, because the slicks are appealing to a more sophisticated audience. The slicks do not, for example, call on the writer to comment on his fiction or enter into a dialogue with readers, and the editor's puffing of authors and stories is quite brief and relatively subdued.

Examples of the slick's rhetoric and the way in which it impinged on Haycox's work can be seen in both the editorial comments and in the advertisements. Editors flattered their readers, not by treating them as members in a club of virile Westerners, but by implying that they were sophisticated enough to share a quiet joke about the artifice, ritual, and repetition of the genre fiction which was a staple part of these magazines. For example, when the editor of *Collier's* announced Haycox's *Trouble Shooter* in 1936, he pointed out the pun in the hero's name: "His name was Frank Peace, which was appropriate, from one point of view—he was 'Trouble Shooter' for the Union Pacific." Similarly, the headlines accompanying the titles on the contents page implicitly recognize the ritualism in Haycox's adventure stories: "*Trail Smoke, Conclusion.* The only possible conclusion, in fact"; "*Man in the Saddle, Conclusion.* Gunfight, clinch, fadeout"; "*The Border Trumpet, Conclusion.* Clinch and fadeout." At the same time, however, in another part of the magazine, the editor praised Haycox for his traditionalism.[70]

Advertisers flattered their audience in a similar way. Instead of playing on readers' anxieties and lack of self-confidence, to sell them overnight transformations and miracle cures, slick advertising copy appeals to the readers' image of themselves as people of distinction and offers them modern, relatively luxurious goods like radios and automobiles (though always the lower-priced makes). Thus, an announcement by a watch manufacturer characterizes *Collier's* readers: "They are men and women whose success in the world is the reward of their judicious use of time. Active, fast-thinking leaders of a strenuous age. . . . We believe in Collier's readers—in their open-mindedness—in their need for fine time-pieces—*and in their ability to buy them.*"[71] The similarity between the values in advertisements and those in Westerns is occasionally thrown into dramatic relief. There is a nice instance of *Collier's* exploiting the commercial possibilities of Western stereotypes when it inserted a General Motors advertisement into the midst of Haycox's novel *Trouble Shooter.* The novel is about the building of the Union Pacific railroad; a few pages into its third installment, there appears a double-page advertisement for General Motors, which picks up the theme of the fiction. Across the two pages is a large, colored illustration of a wagon train passing through the desert. Against this, the heading proclaims, "Who Serves Progress Serves America! Your Money Goes Farther In A General Motors Car." The text of the advertisement continues:

> Just as in earlier days settlers followed explorers, homes and cities sprang up along the trails they blazed—new factories, new industries and new employment spring from the discoveries of industrial research today. PIO-NEERING NEW FRONTIERS. The hope of America still lies in exploration. . . . Out of such pioneering, as carried on by General Motors, have grown such diverse benefits as Diesel-powered locomotives, air-conditioning systems, and steady improvement in every car of the General Motors family.[72]

Haycox's fiction was certainly being fitted into the slick magazine's general philosophy, but the devices which made the connection were much less blatant than in the pulps.

As the rituals in the publishing media become less obvious, so the patterns in Haycox's novels lose some of their rigidity. The slick novels retain the basic shape of the action in the pulps, but there is a constant shifting of details as Haycox introduced new elements in one novel, then returned to his pulp habits in the next. Generally, the language of these later works is less clichéd, and their action contains fewer formulaic rituals than the pulp novels; they begin to deal with some of the events in the less predictable, historical West beyond the codified world of the fictional Western scene. Also, since the hero in slick tales often does not own the property for which he fights, he enters the scene of the range war as an unaligned newcomer, chooses to defend the weaker side, and expects throughout the battle to move on once the dispute is resolved. This means that he is more detached from the feud than the pulp heroes and deliberates more on his choice of action, on the significance of his role, and on the shape of events in general.

As the framework of commentary around the fiction decreases, the complexity of Haycox's self-reflexive narrative increases. The more freedom the author has to tinker with his formula and the more he vacillates over how to develop his writing, the more his fictional action is disrupted by the characters' comments about the pattern governing their behavior and their search for its significance. Clearly, heroes in the slicks recognize that they are locked into a pattern of repeating actions. *Trail Smoke* (1936) opens with the hero, Buck Surratt, riding into a new scene and hearing a shot in the night: "He had a part to play here, as he had known since the crash of that bullet had wakened him."[73] He discovers that he has ridden into a feud between cattlemen and sheepmen:

> He had crossed the desert to find ease and rest—the deep desire of his life; yet the echoes of that night bullet had laid an ancient pattern of trouble over these hills, and he was trapped in the pattern. The ways of a man's life, he thought wistfully, always caught up with him. [P. 20]

This note, of the inescapable pattern of a man's life, becomes the most insistent refrain of the book. During the fight, in which the hero helps the sheepmen and some small ranchers, he recurrently observes that the ways of a man's life trap him, that it has always been so, that nothing changes, that everything echoes from the past. His advice is, "The morning half of a trail is always fresh and full of new things, kid. But the afternoon half is a tedious journey, for there's nothing on it you haven't seen before" (p. 152). Even the final duel is familiar: "He had been through this before and the story was the same now" (p. 274). Throughout the action, the hero thinks that he will have to move on, for the girl whom he desires is engaged to his friend. In the end, however, he wins her and will settle with her on a ranch. The book ends with the usual kiss and the sentence, "He knew then that this was, for him, the end of the trail" (p. 293). While the hero finally breaks the pattern of his lonely, violent life by finding a mate, his commentary, if read as self-reflexive, survives until the very end. Its message is that it is bad to be unable to break out of a pattern.

At this time, just as Haycox finished *Trail Smoke*, he explicitly stated his desire to break the mold of his stories: he recognized that, so far, he had concentrated on the action-packed Western; now he wanted to work up characterization and theme.[74] John R. Milton has observed that the historical Western is the most literary version of the conventional Western adventure story.[75] This was the form Haycox now tried for, with *Trouble Shooter*. He retained his formulaic plot, but he set it within a specific historical event, the building of the Union Pacific Railroad. The hero now works for the railroad as troubleshooter, defeating enemies who plot to thwart the progress of the enterprise. This novel contains hardly any references to codes, patterns, or repetitions. The only self-reflexive note comes near the close when comments about ending and the emptiness beyond the end pile up. When the author found a new form, his characters stopped fretting over their inability to change.

But, of course, the change was not permanent, and soon Haycox returned to familiar stories of range wars. The self-reflexiveness reappears, and the novels of the *Collier's* years, from 1933 to 1943, constitute an extended debate about the value of the past and the influence of patterned behavior. In *Sundown Jim* (1938), a marshal comes into the country to break up a long-running feud, emphasizing the repetitious nature of the action and the destructive power of the past. Throughout *Saddle and Ride* (1940), the hero vacillates between past and present allegiances, finally accepting that the past is dead by killing his old enemy and marrying his new love. Yet this resolution does not last beyond the novel's ending. The first chapter of Haycox's very next novel, *Rim of the Desert* (1941), is entitled "Old Signals Rise Again," and its hero begins the debate all over again: "he was thinking back and remembering how this always went. It never changed. A man rode a thousand miles but the pattern caught up with him, and now it was hard to know whether to be glad or sorry."[76] Finally, the last novel in *Collier's*, *The Wild Bunch* (1943), provides the clearest summary of the recurring pattern. The novel is a late, tired repetition of the feud story which portrays a confrontation between the hero, Goodnight, and the villain near the opening: " 'Put in your chips and find out,' said Goodnight. Suddenly the high-nosed Bill laughed. 'That's typical,' he commented, turning to the smaller man. 'An arrival, a word, a threat and a showdown. It never varies. There's damned little originality in this country.' "[77]

Thus far, the self-reflexive commentary on the constrictions and repetitions of formulaic action is similar to that perceptible in the Max Brand novels, though it is more insistent in Haycox's case. But Haycox did not stop at acknowledging the repetitions in his stories; he tried to find a further significance in his adventure tales. His characters in the slicks echo this search by asking what kind of meaning is behind the constantly repeating pattern. Under this questioning, it becomes clear to the characters—and, presumably, their author—that if there are rules governing the action, they are brutal.

The hero of the late slick novel, *Alder Gulch* (1943), sets the tone with his pessimism. He wonders whether there is any meaningful pattern behind events and speculates on the brutality of the ritual in which he participates:

> At times he was his own great puzzle, troubled by the lack of order in him and the lack of meaning in the world around him; . . . he felt as though he were the only living thing on the planet, with all the forces of the earth, impersonal and relentless, seeking to destroy him. It was a game of survival—one man against the gods. Survival was the one hard and fast law.[78]

The more the rituals of the Western formula are examined, the more obvious become characters' animallike qualities. In the *Collier's* novels, characters (heroic and villainous) are fairly regularly represented as savages, primitives, or the lowest forms of life. For example, in *Trail Smoke*, men in a mob are described as wild dogs, savagely grunting, and the fistfight between the hero and the villain is much more gory than the ritualistic encounters in the pulp magazines. One rule of the game in *Sundown Jim* is "Dog eat dog" (p. 120), and in *Saddle and Ride* the hero and villain have degenerated to "two organisms destined to fight."[79] In *Alder Gulch* and *The Wild Bunch*, the metaphor of survival in the lawless jungle is introduced.

In 1945, Haycox graduated to the most prestigious slick of all, *The Saturday Evening Post*. His second novel in this magazine was *Bugles in the Afternoon*, which deals with the Custer massacre and is widely considered Haycox's best novel. It also seems to sum up the author's progress to that point. On the one hand, he continues to portray the formulaic love story and the rituals and codes of Western life, but on the other, he shows men to be brutes living in a meaningless universe. Although the fight at the Little Big Horn is the major incident in the novel, the plot follows the familiar Haycox model: it centers on a heroic cavalryman, his hatred for an enemy from his past, and his gradual transfer of his love from an old, faithless lover to a new, virtuous woman. Since the action is mainly set in a fort, there is much opportunity for the rituals of male group behavior and the military hierarchy. Yet at the center of this ritualism is repeated combat, which demonstrates man's essentially brutish nature. Even Custer's character is explained in Darwinistic terms: "survival and triumph and public acclaim were to him the same sources of life they were to the other public men who fought tooth and claw for them. Fame was a jungle in which predatory beasts roamed; there were no rules in that jungle, only a bitterest kind of fighting."[80] The most intellectual and articulate figure, the hero, sees only oblivion ahead for mankind; his nihilism accords with the setting, a landscape which is often described as empty and always as hostile. This mixture of formula and fatalism well represents Haycox's thinking by the time he came to the end of his involvement with the slicks. He was still fluctuating between the highly codified world of the formulaic Western and a naturalist scene in which characters have few certainties about life and little gloss of ceremony or humanity.

At last, in 1946, Haycox managed to break away from the magazines and from that date he published three books without first serializing them. He felt free, now, to create something more literary, less ruled by marketplace considerations: "I shall turn to a novel I've been stewing over . . . Oregon. . . . It is to be a full novel. I shan't be looking over my shoulder at the serial market."[81] Of course, in writing books for a popular market, Haycox was still caught up in the world of commercial publishing. But his writing was no longer circumscribed by the blatant sales strategies of the pulps and, less insistently, the slicks. The relative individuality involved in book publication was symbolized by the reduction in paraphernalia to the blandishments on the dust jacket.

With his work removed from the codification of the commercial magazines, Haycox made some changes to his fiction and brought to fruition a development perceptible throughout his career. These last novels still tell of fights over property and women, but they change the scene from range wars in the Far West to the trials of settlers in Oregon. Also, their characters are not easily divided into bad and good; in fact, many characters seem almost subhuman and about the only law they understand is self-preservation. Haycox can be seen to use the same kind of plot throughout his work, but where the pulp novels stress the codes governing the highly ritualized action, the slick novels question the values embedded in these codes. Finally, the unserialized novels bring to the surface the answer that the laws at the heart of the Western formula are those of social Darwinism.

In Haycox's first unserialized novel, *Long Storm* (1946), the language of social Darwinism is prominent. Again and again, characters assert that the old story of the strong against the weak repeats itself forever. The head of the shipping monopoly justifies his practice with a Spencerian argument about the laws of social progress, and, while the hero exposes the false logic of this argument, he too seems to subscribe to an interpretation of life which owes something to social Darwinism: "A man or a rock. It's all the same. Men will claw and rocks will rip. Nothing saves us except the power to fight back. We've got to do it. There's no other way."[82]

This interpretation of events begins to have a definite effect on the novel's formulaic shape. The hero's fatalism prevents him from making some of the stock moves expected of the formulaic Western hero. Most obviously, he decides not to kill the villain, Ringrose, because the act would have no meaning.

> He was exhausted and he was empty of whatever had been in him. . . . Even the thought that [Ringrose] might live to do evil again could not bring back Musick's anger. Ringrose was one more fragment blown through the world by a great wind; and the wind blew everybody, and nobody had power to prevent it. How could he change anything by holding Ringrose under the water until he was dead? [P. 280]

But some of the standard moves are still brought into play to rescue the hero from complete despair. He still marries at the end, and thus finds a positive value: his wife says, "I'm the only thing on this earth you'll ever feel sure of having. I am the one thing you'll never lose" (p. 287).

That romantic ending is one of the few staples of the pulp Western Haycox's late novels do not lose either.

The Adventurers (1955)[83] continues to present men as animals, and it takes further the erosion of the formulaic Western pattern. Early on, the ship carrying the hero, Sheridan, and his companions, Clara and Revelwood, sinks and the passengers react as a crowd of grunting, whimpering animals who stampede, clawing at each other brutishly. To survive, the protagonists save themselves from drowning, then crawl through a marsh. The experience convinces Clara and Revelwood that survival is the only important objective in life, and Revelwood's nihilism becomes complete, just before he is hanged for murder:

> There's nothing after death, I'm sure of that. . . . We're nothing—we weren'tmeant for anything. There's no plan, no hope, no future. . . . Did you ever stop to think if there were a God—and if He had any plan—He'd certainly not send such stupid, stinking bits of animal life down here to carry out the plan.[84]

The hero disagrees, but has no philosophy to suggest as a counterargument. He can sense that there is a pattern or set of rules governing events, but he cannot see it clearly:

> There was an answer, a form, a meaning, a feeling which once gotten would make a pattern for his life and give his days a meaning. He was sure of it and he was near to it. . . . but his mind . . . made some false motion of its own and the answer which had been so close faded away. [P. 124]

Even the final marriage brings no certainty. The hero says to his new wife, "Maybe there's some rules for us, but I can't see them . . . . Revelwood may be right, maybe not. . . . If there's something more, I guess we'll learn some day" (p. 313).

In the light of the nihilism in *The Adventurers*, the last novel, *The Earthbreakers* (1952), represents a reaffirmation of life, but at its lowest, animalistic level. This final work also reintroduces a definite pattern, which owes much to the tenets of American naturalism. The novel recovers the conditions of the early pulp fiction in its talk of East and West, its use of the hero as a law enforcer, and its reinstatement of property values. However, from the pulp code of stoicism and individualism, physical rituals and violence, issue naturalist images of sex and bestiality.

All the characters are governed by animalistic instincts. The settlers, including the hero, are constantly described as crouching, squatting, and straddling. Near the beginning, the consequence of coming to the West is personified in Stricklin, an ill man whom the hero finds collapsed in his tent. Burnett straddles him, holding him up to help him move his bowels. He makes the ill man crawl and sit, moving him from the horizontal position through the necessary stages of recovery, which also echo the stages of man's evolution. Men are repeatedly likened to animals, from the affable, oxlike giant, Eby, to the evil Lockyear who is like a stallion, knowing only his own existence, "dumb to half the pain he suffered in his search to eject himself into the receiving mare."[85] The settlers are like Indians, and the Indians, in turn, are changed to beasts by the alcohol Lockyear gives them. Edna, with whom the hero has sex, thinks that all women are sluts and life is only marriage, work, and babies. Rinearson, whose son Edna eventually marries, remarks of her, "In a year's time she won't remember the look on Moss's face, no more than a plowed field remembers who did the plowin' last season" (p. 378). The heroine, Katherine, echoes Revelwood in believing that people are only ants, and the hero, trapped by a tree and unable to dig himself out, becomes reduced as well: "he was a man without legs, he was a torso bedded in the mud, a stumplike animal crouched under the deadfalls, swaying forward and grunting as he worked" (p. 282). Relationships between characters are symbolized in the most repeated image in the novel, which is the picture of one being straddling another.

In the midst of all this animal activity, the hero finally sees a clear pattern at work. He understands that events are determined by laws to do with man's struggle for survival—that is, the kind of laws commonly expressed in naturalist literature:

> suddenly the shadow of the pattern was there, as something seen deep in water—unreachable and shapeless, yet throwing off the emanation of its presence. Nature built men and tested them to the limits of their endurance, and was unsatisfied with even the strongest; and this careless creating hand, failing to find the form and the substance sought for, built and smashed and built again. The very persistence of creation seemed to say that from the dust of the destroyed imperfects would sometime come the one dreamed shape. [P. 210]

Obviously, this new pattern contrasts greatly with the pulp ritual, which is violent but honorable. In *The Earthbreakers*, Haycox makes clear his rejection of the pulp code when John Gay, the community patriarch, says that he's had enough of "this Southern honor business" (p. 101). This statement reads like a jibe at the code of both Wister's *The Virginian* and Haycox's own *Free Grass*, in which Tom Gillette's father, relieved that his son has reembraced Western values, says, "I had feared you would forget—that you would absorb ideas less worthy a Southern gentleman" (p. 9).

At the same time, however, when Haycox switched from one set of conventions to another, he did choose a mode which can be seen as an outgrowth of his Western formula. In his own case, some of the Darwinistic imagery central to his late books appears in his very early pulp work. More generally, most Westerns show some reliance on loose, popular notions of Darwinian and Spencerian ideas: in Grey's fiction, characters discuss the merits of social Darwinism, and in Faust's, some element of atavism comes into the hero's makeup.[86] Haycox's use of philosophical ideas was no more precise than his predecessors', but he exploited the Western's impulses toward social Darwinism, where they simply appended them to the mythic pattern. When Haycox moved away from the elaborate codes which support his work in the pulps, and began to look for a meaning behind his repetitive adventures, he came up with naturalist images to do with violent action and contests between men. The main difference is that whereas the pulp mode plays on the ritualism and the ceremony of this behavior, the naturalist form stresses its brutality and animalism.

Haycox's work constitutes a progression from the codes of the pulp Western formula to the conventions of American naturalism. It took him some time to move from one genre to the other, and his really interesting writing results from his period of hesitation, when he feared to abandon one literary form before he found an alternative. The different ways in which his work was published and Haycox's own contributions to magazine presentation demonstrate clearly the author's move away from the strict and certain rules of pulp writing. Within the novels, the author's cautious attempts to change his literary mode are mirrored in the characters' comments on their own actions, as they perceive and discuss the repetitive patterning of events. In their self-reflexiveness and their questioning, the novels of the middle period carry a modern voice which is missing in either of the formulas in which Haycox felt secure. That this voice did not issue from any decision by Haycox to become more up-to-date in his literary practice, is proved by his final embracing of the kind of naturalism perpetrated by Norris and Dreiser at the turn of the century, which was well out of style by 1950, when Haycox produced his imitations. The temporary modernity achieved by this writer, then, was entirely the result of the interplay between author and formula which occurred when the formulist lost his certain coordinates.

CONCLUSION

Zane Grey, Frederick Faust, and Ernest Haycox all lived by the market, writing popular, commercial stories, but none of them took on board marketplace values wholesale in the way of the dime novelists. Although they all produced stereotyped, repetitive work, they also retained a sense of their autonomy, and all had ambitions for artistic development. Within their own field, they were lauded as the best: they were stars in the pulps, not part of the mass of anonymous workers, and for them magazine serialization was only preliminary to book publication. Out of the feeling for their own individuality and artistic potential, each developed a different attitude to the market which he supplied. Zane Grey always adhered wholeheartedly to the coordinates set by formulaic writing, and he believed he could develop artistically within them. Frederick Faust as ardently rejected all commercial values and despised the fiction which he produced in such vast quantities. While turning out pulp tales at enormous speed and raking in huge sums of money, he sought to dissociate himself more and more from the whole process. Ernest Haycox was not satisfied with his repetitive formulas, but he did not want to leave the security of the commercial field either. He compromised by investing his formulaic elements with significance and literariness, instead of changing them completely.

The authors' attitudes to the marketplace are reflected most directly in the paraphernalia of the magazines in which their work appeared. Neither Grey, Faust, nor Haycox absorbed the vocabulary or habits of commercial intercourse into their novels as the dime novelists did. This was partly because these three authors were more tied to traditional ideas of art and individualism than their predecessors in the field. However, the commercial dimension of their work was played out in the features pages of the pulp magazines. As stars of the pulps, these authors were brought into the dialogue between publisher and public by name and, in the case of Faust and Haycox, invited to participate in it actively. The magazines provided a kind of halfway house, in which the authors' reactions to the give-and-take of the marketplace could be acted out quite explicitly, beyond the boundaries of their novels.

What happens in the fiction is less direct. Its details reflect the literary consequences of commercialism, rather than the actual marketplace practices. Each author adjusted his artistic inclinations to his commercial circumstances by developing one area of his writing within the outline of his predictable formula. Zane Grey effected quite a technical change, concerning his presentation of narrative. He sought to add consequence to his tales by changing not the subject matter but the narrative technique. Frederick Faust's development is confined to an increasingly strong tone of irony which undercuts the action of his adventure stories. Ernest Haycox progressed most hesitantly, especially in his middle years, when he repeatedly introduced timid variations of his formula. During this period, his characters become infected by their author's nervousness, and an almost modern voice appears in his fiction for the only time. Although neither Grey, Faust, nor Haycox ever transcended the limitations of the Western genre—and none of them wrote the great American masterpiece to which each aspired—they all produced some work which is superior to their general output. Their best fiction grew directly out of the tension between a desire for artistry and an addiction to formula.

FOUR

The Last Few Spaces

Surprisingly enough, after all these novels, several recent authors have used the materials of the conventional Western once more and still have attained distinction, either of quality or sales. Three of the most important writers of this type are Alan Le May, Jack Schaefer, and Louis L'Amour. Le May is the least well known of them, although his best novel, *The Searchers* (1954), was made into a highly acclaimed film by John Ford. He deserves attention because, while his fiction belongs to the category of the popular Western, his writing is far superior to any of his more famous predecessors'. Jack Schaefer has achieved the highest literary reputation in the field, particularly with his novella *Shane* (1949). Louis L'Amour has attained sales figures outstripping even those of Grey and Faust.[1]

Le May, Schaefer, and L'Amour are among the last major authors of traditional Westerns and they all face the same dilemma: latecomers to an already overwritten genre, they must establish a place for their texts to set them above their competitors in the field. Le May manages to forge a new subject out of long-established practices. His novels move from using all the conventions of adventure fiction to taking the conventions as their subject. Schaefer and L'Amour have a different tactic. They develop the image of the empty space which only their works can fill. There are three kinds of space associated with the popular Western: the geographical space of the Western land, the spaces in historical accounts of it, and the now scarce spaces in the marketplace in which the fictional product is sold. Schaefer finds new ground for his Westerns by developing the first two themes; L'Amour, a much more commercial writer, makes use of all three.

ALAN LE MAY

Alan Le May's career as a writer of Western novels falls in two parts, before and after he began writing screenplays in Hollywood.[2] Because his work with films both interrupted and transformed his fiction, his career appears, at first sight, broken-backed. In fact, however, his novel writing develops in a way which is wholly consistent, both in terms of his own fiction and in relation to the tradition of the popular Western. From 1924 until the late thirties, he used the common paraphernalia of the formulaic Western to produce fairly repetitive, but well-written, Westerns (as well as some non-Western adventure stories). After four years in Hollywood, he returned to the same set of conventional plots, but he took the stock devices of the popular Western story not as the tools of his fiction, but as its subject. He is in a direct line from a dime novelist like Prentiss Ingraham, who also made his narrative conventions part of the subject of his fiction, though never so openly.

Le May published in the pulp magazines for a few years in the twenties, then throughout the thirties his work appeared in the slicks, predominantly *Collier's*. His Westerns of these years are fairly typical of the genre fiction in these magazines: they use conventional scenes and character types and, like many genre stories, introduce a mystery as the mechanism which puts the plot in motion. They are set in any of the Western states from Texas to Montana, at any time from the 1870s to the 1920s. The focal point, however, is always a ranch, run by an old man and his daughter. The hero—usually a foundling who has been rescued from a wagon train massacre and brought up by a plainsman—joins the ranch as a cowboy. Soon after the opening of the story, he is drawn into a mystery to do with a range war which threatens to destroy the heroine's ranch. The hero solves the mystery, kills the villain, saves the ranch, and wins the girl.

In amongst this action, there are various relationships between old and young Westerners and discussions about the disappearance of the frontier which show that Le May is aware of his inheritance from Cooper and Wister. At one point, one of his patriarchal characters, Horse Dunn, acknowledges *The Virginian* directly: "Amos was cursing bitterly, savagely, a continuous stream. 'I read in a book you're supposed to smile when you call me them names,' Dunn said. 'From the amount of 'em you're spilling I take it you're practically giggling.' "[3]

However, traditional thematic concerns never constitute the main point of Le May's stories. They operate, rather, as the evidence which shows Le May to be fulfilling the requirements of Western fiction and conforming to the traditions of the genre. The clearest demonstration of the author's shifting his emphasis away from the familiar Western themes occurs in *Cattle Kingdom* (1933), his only book to introduce an East-West debate of any length. The clash between East and West is represented, conventionally enough, in the relationship between the cowboy hero and the heroine, who is presented, at first, as an Easterner come to visit her uncle's ranch. The hero's love for her is unrequited, and she finds the West incomprehensible. Indeed, her uncle argues that it is virtually invisible to her:

Why, she can't hardly even believe that this country is here. . . . They've taught her that the country is all settled up—and they're right. Only, they don't understand this dry country. . . . If you told 'em that there's 500,000 square miles that can't carry eight head of cattle to the square mile, they'd say you lied. Marian can't believe her own eyes—didn't smart people tell her different back east? [P. 51]

The hero and heroine argue about Eastern and Western values, but, when Marian begins to be convinced by the hero's case, it is revealed that she is not really an Easterner after all, for she was born in the West to a Western father. "It was as if some false outer cloaking of ideas and habits, put upon her by her mother's seaboard world, had suddenly fallen away, leaving her revealed as what she was—a daughter of the dry land" (p. 256). This revelation means that, although the point about the West's superiority remains, there is no enactment of a reconciliation of East and West, as occurs in *The Virginian*. In fact, the geographical debate comes to be set aside completely: the hero "learned that she was neither east nor west, but all woman" (p. 262). Marian's viewpoint becomes part of the dynamics of the mystery, rather than a contribution to a thematic debate; at the end, it is disclosed that her presence alone has caused the story to change from a Western to a mystery:

That was all the story. One thing, only one, had warped that whole brief history into something mysterious and strange . . . that was the old fighter's abject humility, his pathetic, unreasoning panic before the disapproval of Marian, his niece. Without that, that first simple shootout would have ended where it occurred. [Pp. 286–87]

Obviously, mystery, not the culture-nature debate, is paramount in Le May's fiction. It is always a mysterious event that brings the hero and heroine together, and then complicates their relationship. Thus, in *Winter Range* (1932), the unsolved murder of a banker brings all the ranchers into town for the inquest. There, the heroic cowboy meets a rancher's daughter when she asks him to hide some evidence for her. He joins her ranch, but is alternately rebuffed and courted by her in a way that confuses him, until he realizes that she is trying to protect her father, whom she mistakenly believes to be guilty of the killing. The hero and heroine come together at the end because they have cleared up the mystery of the murder, not because they have overcome any fundamental discord between Eastern and Western values. All the ritual stages of the narrative—the Call to Adventure, the Trial, the Return with the Boon—are directed to the solving of a formulaic puzzle; they have little to do with notions of the West, and they are given no mythic gloss.

Because Le May concentrates on the investigation and solution of mysteries, his narrative devices, used to move the plot along, are the codes, clues, signs, and games so beloved of the dime novelists. Much of the dialogue proceeds by metaphors from poker (heroes who become involved in the mysteries usually say that they have "dealt themselves into the game"), and coded notes, camouflaged clues, and incomprehensible key words abound. *Gunsight Trail* (1931) is a good example of a story in which the hero, finding himself in the midst of puzzling circumstances, uses cryptographic devices to advance the action and work out a solution. He is first drawn into an unfathomable range war when a man staggers into his camp, utters a few incomprehensible sounds, then dies. The hero constructs a bluff around the sounds, pretending that he has understood, and is keeping secret, the man's last words, because he suspects that they are "a key to a door."[4] In his efforts to discover the murderer, and thus the villain of the range war, the hero writes cryptic notes and telegrams; he enrolls the help of a tracker for whom "the signs of obscure wilderness trails were his only newspapers, and the reading of those signs his only diversion" (p. 147); and, finally, he forces a senator to help the victimized rancher by writing a message with certain words in code appended, to authenticate the signature. It is clear that the hero is involved in two kinds of code: the heroic rules about bravery and morality, and the secret signals communicated by ciphers and written words.

Le May's interest in language as an encoded system is perceptible from his very first novel, *Painted Ponies* (1927). In it, the hero, Slide Morgan, is hounded by a community, partly because he has killed the vicious brother of a powerful cattleman, but mainly because a mystery about his past leads people to believe that he is a half-breed. Morgan begins to find out about his origins only once he recognizes that language can be a code which needs to be deciphered before it is properly understood. The realization begins when an old scout talks to him in Cheyenne: "Geer repeated the jargon. . . . Vague memories stirred in the back of Morgan's mind, as if some signal had reached him from a past which he could not recall."[5] The necessity of a technique for decipherment becomes clear when Morgan tries to understand the speech of a Cheyenne Indian. The workings of a coded language are obviously important enough to the author for him to describe them in some detail:

> The Laughing Coyote spoke rapidly in Cheyenne, using short sentences that yet seemed long; for in the Cheyenne tongue are many words made up of groups of smaller words, chained together into long polysyllables. Morgan could catch but little of what the Indian said, strain as he might to arrange the few words that he recognized into thought. The combination words tricked him, leading him astray with names of things that had a bearing on the thought only in conjunction with the words to which they were joined, so that the Coyote seemed to be speaking in a disjointed code. [P. 115]

In time, the hero becomes obsessed with cryptic messages, interpreting everything in terms of written codes. Thus, at his lowest point, he sits in a saloon, listening to the "jargon of a clock":

> It was reading the story of his life. Meaninglessly, cryptically, it was naming the innumerable episodes of his days, incidents that were meaningless and cryptic too. Presently, after a long time, the clock would catch up with him; then there would be nothing more for it to tell, and it must stop. [P. 238]

In the end, he pulls himself out of his nadir, faces up to a shoot-out with the villain, and wins the girl, thus emulating the men around him "who wrote their own destinies" (p. 306).

The idea that these novels are centrally to do with coded systems is taken one step further in *Bug Eye* (1931), when the text of that novel admits the diagrammatic properties of language into its very structure. This is a comic story which consists of letters between Hank, the hero, and Bug Eye, his partner in the mines. The letters recount Hank's adventures, and they are all written in a kind of code, with idiosyncratic punctuation and phonetic spelling which converts words into figures: "forewarned is 4 armed."[6] The layout of the ending acknowledges that the syntax of the book and the action of the plot are part of the same system:

> *Hurry partner hurry.* How will this damn thing
> END.
> [P. 276]

With his repeated emphasis on language as some kind of code, Le May makes his questing characters in his mysteries seem very like the readers of a formulaic story. Both types read signs, try to understand their significance and place them in a pattern. Inevitably, the heroes begin to sound like their readers, in their reactions to the events in the plot: in *Winter Range*, Hughes "needed more of the missing fragments before he could piece that picture together,"[7] and in *Cattle Kingdom*, Wheeler says, "God knows where this thing leads to; but it ought to lead some place pretty soon" (pp. 239–40). The linguistic sign systems also have a self-reflexive effect: in *Bug Eye*, the last sentence of the last letter recognizes its narrative function, which is to end the book.

This accumulation of sign systems which suggest a self-reflexive narrative seems to be no more than a straightforward inheritance from the dime novelists. Le May writes more artistically than any of his predecessors, and he sets his formulaic devices within more credible and coherent plots, but he achieves an equivalent effect. He pays so much attention to elaborate sign reading that a parallel is inevitably suggested between the codified formulas with which the characters work and those which the reader is encountering. Yet the parallel is not overt. Despite all the pointers and hints and subtle reflections, the author, like the dime novelist, never admits that he is writing in code. The many formulaic devices finally remain functional; they are still the equipment necessary to the progress of the plot.

After working for some years in the movie industry, however, Le May returned to the same set of narrative conventions with a very different perspective. After 1939, he stopped writing for *Collier's* and went to Hollywood, where he was involved in the writing of seventeen screenplays and did a little directing and producing.[8] His work with the cinema brought him into contact with all the devices of the film industry which lie behind the fictive illusions and involved him in what Arthur Miller has called (in introducing his own version of the Western) "the telegraphic, diagrammatic manner of screenplay writing."[9] This experience may well account for the change in Le May's technique. Although he still wrote about heroes discovering and solving mysteries, he began to treat the sign systems and codes by which the mysteries operate as the most important part of his fiction. In three important Westerns, he makes it clear that the familiar narrative devices are now the raison d'être of his fiction and not just the method of its telling.

Useless Cowboy (1943), his first novel of this later phase, is a humorous Western which tells the usual Le May story, but inverts all the conventions associated with the Western hero and scene. It is the story of Melody Jones and his sidekick, George Fury, a pair of incompetent drifters who are mistaken for vicious outlaws. In the course of untangling the mystery of strangers' reactions to them, they encounter the real outlaw, Monte Jarrad, and his fiancée, Cherry. With the help of the girl, who falls in love with him, Melody recovers the gold which Monte has stolen and protects the girl and her father against the outlaw's wrath, although it is Cherry who finally kills the outlaw and proposes to Melody. The outlines of the mystery and the love story conform to Le May's usual pattern, but the details of the action are significantly different.

The jokes all arise from the fact that Melody realizes that there is a code attached to his role as hero but consistently fails in his attempts to live up to it. The rules of the code seem to derive from the cinema. Melody is described as a Roy Rogers look-alike: "Melody's face was smooth leather from perpetual wind and sun . . . it was lopped over by a broncho [*sic*] mop of sandy hair. . . . His idly wandering eyes were slit-squinted from the desert glare, but in the shade were uncommonly mild, and brightly blue, as if lighted by an unjustified inner hope."[10] Like Rogers, he sings from the back of his horse, but his reception is less favorable: Fury grumbles, "don't start in with that Gar' damn singing again, neither" (p. 6). Melody tries hard to emulate the kind of heroic image produced on the screen. He has a secret ambition to be called "Unsmiling Jones" and tries desperately to remember to ride "looking neither to right nor left" (p. 7) and to swagger with his hands in a "gun-fighter's hook" (p. 19). Needless to say, these self-conscious attempts to fit himself into a formulaic pattern fail utterly. He remains an unconvincing cowboy who cannot shoot or ride well or even roll a cigarette. At times, he even confuses different myths of the West, mistaking the agricultural West of the settler for the wild West of the cowboy: "He couldn't see why his life should not be romantic and fascinating, like a farmer's life" (p. 104).

The gap between a figure and the meanings conventionally ascribed to it is a recurrent topic in the book, as dreamlike confusions and inaccurate sign systems proliferate. When Melody and George enter the town of Payneville, where the case of mistaken identity begins, they encounter numerous puzzling symbols. The townsmen derive much fun from puns about "painful" and "in pain," which thoroughly bamboozle Fury, who has not seen the town sign. The old-fashioned type on Payneville's newspaper is almost as puzzling—"What the heck is a horfe?' Melody said" (p. 26)—and the initials burned into Melody's saddle wrongly identify him as Monte Jarrad. The most askew signifier is the brand belonging to the heroine's ranch: it should have been a Flying W, but the branding iron was bent in a fall and the mark turned into the Busted Nose brand.

Le May is making fun of the false, rigid expectations involved in the heroic Western code and, more generally, pointing out the arbitrariness of the relationship between signifiers and that which they are assumed to signify. Melody is doubly playing a part and therefore he is twice as big a failure; he is unconvincing as Monte and as a cowboy. He exists in a Western milieu which is populated with symbols which are fraudulent, too, in that they bear no clear, direct relation to their referents. The jokes which arise from the lack of fit between hero and code or between signifier and signified are the real point of *Useless Cowboy*. The mystery story, which is much less intricate than in the earlier fiction, is only the device to create opportunity for the continual joking.

The Searchers (1954) concentrates on sign systems also, but it is much more ambitious and serious in its treatment. The interpretation of signs is absolutely at the center of this text, for the plot is made up of a series of sign readings. When a young girl is captured by Indians on the Texas frontier, her uncle, Amos, and her friend, Martin Paul, set out to find her. Their search lasts for six years, and it constitutes the body of the book, with Debbie's captivity and her eventual rescue by Martin figuring only as brief scenes at either end of the novel. The search consists of Martin and Amos doggedly following a stream of clues and signs, moving from one piece of evidence to the next. They "read sign" in the usual Western meaning when they follow the tracks of the attackers early in the story, but they also have to decipher more complex and more specifically linguistic signifiers. For example, they have to work out the Comanche system of multiple names and the way in which Indian symbols relate to individual members of a tribe. One of their many detours occurs when Martin connects the words "scar" and "sheep" through the similarity of the Indian signs for them, and, instead of searching for an Indian with a scar, they investigate the warriors in the Kiowa Sheep Society. The whole process of deduction is detailed by Martin in the text, so not only most of the action but much of the dialogue, too, is taken up with the reading of coded signs.

If the plot proceeds by signs, so do the character studies, since there are many symbols which appear as tokens of considerable personal significance in the characters' lives. Martin is haunted by all sorts of emblems. He is spurred on in his search for Debbie by the memory of a flawed calendar which she made for him, by the fake locket which he once bought her, and by his recurrent dream of her as a living statue. He is more literally tormented by the more private images which appear in his nightmares. By the end of the book, he has learned that the sounds, shapes and smells of his dreams were those which surrounded him during the wagon train attack from which he, as a baby, was the only survivor. He identifies the focus of his fear as a warped juniper stump which was in his sight during the massacre, and he destroys the power of the image when he eliminates its origin: "An elongated knot at the top no longer looked like a distorted head, but only a symbol representing the hideous thing he had imagined there. He lashed out and struck it . . . and a twisted old stump tottered, splashed in the creek, and went spinning away."[11] Martin obviously undergoes a process of self-discovery, alongside his search for the captured girl, which also has to do with the reading and interpretation of images. When the images are understood and eliminated, the process ends.

What finally elevates all these symbols from the level of mere evidence or private memories is their potential for autonomy. Whereas *Useless Cowboy* exploits the arbitrary relationship between sign and referent, *The Searchers* goes further, detaching the signifier from its signification and showing how it can have power in its own right. Creating unattached signifiers is what, at one level, Amos does when, to protect himself and Martin from Comanches, he makes smoke signals which actually mean nothing at all. They are made simply to frighten off the Comanches, who will interpret them as signs of an alien tribe, so their meaning is in their existence, not in any genuine correlation between image and message. The climax to the story depends, too, on the intrinsic power of signs, in this case, in the form of letters. When Amos and Martin find Debbie, they discover that she is reluctant to leave the Indians, who have inculcated her in their ways. She will not believe Amos's stories of Indian depredations, so he tells her that her captor, Scar, wears a brooch which belonged to Martin's mother and was removed from her body during the Indian attack in which she died. He tells her that the brooch's origin is proved by the words on its back, "From Ethan to Judith." The story stays in Debbie's mind and it eventually leads her to run away:

> [The Indians] hadn't done anything to her. It wasn't that. It was the medicine buckle—the ornament, like a gold ribbon tied in a bow, that Scar always wore, and that had given him his change of name. She had believed Amos lied about its having belonged to Mart Pauley's mother. But the words that he had said were written on the back stayed in her mind. Ethan to Judith. . . . The words were there or they weren't. If they were there, then Amos' whole story was true, and Scar had taken the medicine buckle from Mart's mother as she died under his knife. [P. 254]

Debbie creeps to the chief in the middle of the night and turns the buckle over. Although she has been so long separated from whites that she finds she can no longer read, the signs have a meaning for her:

> she could see the writing on the back of the medicine buckle. And then— she couldn't read it. . . . But Amos had told her what the words were; so that presently the words seemed to fit the scratches on the gold: "Ethan to Judith. . . ." Actually, the Rangers were able to tell Mart later, Amos had lied. The inscription said, "Made in England."[P. 255]

It is entirely possible to read *The Searchers* as an extended analogy to the reading of a Western. For both the searchers and the reader, the novel is the story which results from the reading of one sign after another and the language of the story is made up of these signs. The climax shows Debbie behaving like a habitual reader of formulas: she reads words as if they are a code to which she already has the meaning. Whereas Le May earlier suggested a parallel between reader and character, he now dovetails their activities precisely. He enacts openly the message which dime novelists like Ellis and Ingraham convey subliminally—that the Western story is predominantly a sign system.

The notion that signs and symbols can be determining in themselves, and not just as functional pointers to further meanings, is underlined in Le May's final Western novel, *The Unforgiven* (1957). The story reads like a rewriting of his first Western, *Painted Ponies*, since it concerns, now much more centrally, the possible Indian blood of the main character. In this case, the story revolves around a girl, Rachel, who is the adopted daughter of a frontier ranching family. They are harassed incessantly by an old madman, vilified by their neighbors, and finally attacked by Indians, all because of the suspicion that Rachel is an Indian.

Sign systems do not dominate the whole story, as they do in *The Searchers*, but they do cluster around the mystery of Rachel's origins. She first sets the story in motion by saying a name out of her past which, she realizes, has "pulled a trigger."[12] "That mysteriously powerful name" (p.

23) haunts her throughout the action, while she encounters various rid-
dles in her attempts to understand what is happening. She is particularly
baffled by communications between her supposed brother and the Indians, which are conducted in a language unknown to her. When the
meaning of all the different signals dawns on her and she understands
that her life has not been what she thought it, she says that she has lost
all her familiar compass points. It turns out that the secret to her birth
is answered in a Comanche "history calendar." This is a piece of hide
on which are marked pictorial symbols for the events of each year, and
it will reveal whether or not an Indian baby was born and lost in the
year that Rachel was discovered. This document is crucial to the action:
one brother dies in his search for it, and his queries about it bring down
a Comanche attack on the whole family. After the attack, which only
Rachel and two of her brothers survive, an old Comanche delivers the
deerskin, wrapped round the handle of a lance. The older brother discovers the lance and, after some consideration, puzzles out its purpose.
However, he decides to burn the pictograph intact, without ever opening
or reading it, since it seems to him irrelevant whether or not Rachel is
an Indian. Thus, the secret which is central to the plot is never revealed,
and the semiology surrounding the mystery functions in the text as a
code which is never deciphered. All the different clues about Rachel's
origins, in the end, work as elements of the narrative in their own right
and not just as reference points leading toward a more interesting meaning. The code is an important narrative device in itself.

In Le May's Westerns, codes replace East-West debates as the main
subject matter. In the later books, particularly, he draws his reader's
attention to the conventions and sign systems which operate in his earliest
works and are an important part of all formula Westerns. *The Searchers*
is the cleverest conventional Western I have read, because it both embodies and exposes the mechanism which is central to the genre's survival. The novel qualifies as popular fiction because it is composed of
utterly standard materials, but it makes a subject of the process by which
each story accommodates itself to the formulas of the genre. The ritual
stages of the plot and the interplay between the characters, which is so
often to do with the passing of coded messages, are to be read as signals
that the story is adhering to a predetermined pattern. The whole point
of *The Searchers* is that signs can be interpreted in such a way that they
form a coherent pattern and provide a final solution. *Useless Cowboy*
demonstrates the confusion which results when signs are read wrongly,
and *The Unforgiven* shows how the diagrammatic quality of language can
become its primary meaning in the formulaic text.

Le May does not work up the thematic, historical, or social concerns
in his adventure stories; instead, he capitalizes on their programmatic
nature to create his subject. He exposes the diagrammatic nature of

formularized language and tells the reader that the predominance of convention in Western fiction is a subject in itself—a message conveyed by the dime novelists, much more covertly, almost a hundred years earlier.

JACK SCHAEFER

If Le May seems a descendant of the dime novelists, Schaefer is just as clearly related to Owen Wister. Schaefer's first concern is not the convention of the Western story, but its relevance to the history of the West. Like Wister, he wants to make his fictional West part of America's history; but, unlike Wister, he does not propose to revise the historical record. While Wister and Remington structure their fictions as alternatives to the process of historical change, Schaefer represents himself as simply providing some unknown details which supplement, but do not overturn, the historical account.

Schaefer has developed into a much less formulaic writer than either Le May or L'Amour. In the 1940s he began publishing in the slick magazines, and *Shane*, his most famous piece of fiction, appeared in an earlier form in *Argosy* in 1946. After the success of *Shane*, however, Schaefer made a decision not to write commercially, but to continue exploring the subject of the West in different ways.[13] This attitude is reflected in the development of his fiction. His theme is always the same: it concerns a transitional period when the wild West was changing into a more domesticated country, and the reactions of the inhabitants to this change. His cast is made up of the heroic frontiersman who helps effect the transition but is simultaneously eliminated by it and the settlers who survive to enjoy the benefits of civilization, with particular emphasis on one young, naive settler who is educated by the hero. However, Schaefer's presentation of this material develops in two significant ways: in time, he imposes a less and less schematic organization on his fiction, and he develops notions about space as the context and justification for his work.

Shane (1949) was Schaefer's first version of his perennial story, and it is the most neatly patterned work he ever produced. The main characters are a big rancher, the nesters who oppose him, and the mysterious gunfighter, Shane, who kills the villain, simultaneously saving the nesters and outlawing himself from their community. The narrator, Bob Starrett, is the son of the leading nester family, and, since he figures in the plot as a young boy but tells the story as a grown man, his narrative demonstrates the maturation of the naive youngster. The action takes place in the interval between Shane's riding into the valley out of the plains, with his black clothes and guns, and his leaving in the same way, in the same dress. In between, he changes into farmer's clothes and leads a domestic life within the Starrett family. The events of this period are constructed around reflecting pairs of images, which suggest a circular structure: various "two plus one" groupings take place within the triad of Shane, Joe Starrett, and Marian Starrett, and scenes which occur early in the novella reappear in different guise toward the end. For example, when Joe and Shane together attack the tree stump which is the one blot on Joe's pasture, their work with the axes is described as "the steady rhythm of double blows, so together they sounded almost as one."[14] This pattern prefigures the gunfight scene, in which Shane eliminates a much greater threat to Joe's life; when he and the villain fire at each other, "the roar of their guns was a single sustained blast" (p. 147). Again, during the stump episode, Joe "straightened and stretched his arms high and wide. He seemed to stretch and stretch until he was a tremendous tower of strength reaching up into the late afternoon sun" (p. 34). Before Shane rides into town for the showdown, the narrator sees him against the sunset: "he stretched his arms up, the fingers reaching to their utmost limits, grasping and grasping, it seemed, at the glory glowing in the sky" (p. 135). The characters themselves point out analogies (such as that between the stump and Marian's pie), and the final effect is a neat patterning of imagery which complements the closely worked plot.

As well as being Schaefer's most schematic fiction, *Shane* is also his most formulaic. With the figure of the mysterious gunman and the pattern of mounting tension which results in a dramatic shoot-out, Schaefer is conforming to the formulaic action developed in the dime novels and *The Virginian* and copied in hundreds of popular books and films in the first half of the twentieth century. He does not seek to hide this fact: much of the dialogue, especially in confrontations, exploits the hackneyed phrases of pulp writing, and metaphors from poker abound. The narrator actually reminds the reader that Shane can be regarded as the stereotyped Western hero: "I conjured up all manner of adventures for him, not tied to any particular time or place, seeing him as a slim and dark and dashing figure coolly passing through perils that would overcome a lesser man" (p. 58). In the shoot-out, particularly, Shane fits this role: "This was the Shane of the adventures I had dreamed for him" (p. 144). The narrator and other adult characters repeatedly assert Shane's indestructibility and characterize him as the hero who can vanquish all enemies with his lightning-fast draw. He represents Schaefer's closest approach to the incredible, dime novel kind of hero.

After *Shane*, the short stories, novellas, and novels become less and less patterned or plotted. Either they are undeveloped anecdotes or they emphasize sequence more than causality, and none of them is endowed with such an elaborate system of imagery as *Shane*. The reason why Schaefer moved away from the complex organization of fictive material is suggested in his first full-length novel, *Company of Cowards* (1957), when it describes fighting in the Civil War. The anonymous narrator declares that too carefully plotted an account can only falsify experience:

> You can follow the battle on the maps and in the accounts written in the serene perspective of hindsight, piecing together a coherent whole out of the scattered data. . . . To the men themselves who wrenched that data out of the bitterest fighting of a long bitter war . . . there was no pattern, no real sense of taking part in co-ordinated battle movements.[15]

This criticism of the limitations of formularized description can obviously be extended to all formulaic writing; and, indeed, the disavowal of neat patterning is directly connected with storytelling in a host of first-person narratives which come after *Company of Cowards*. Again and again, as narrators begin their stories of frontiersmen who cannot adapt to changing conditions, they preface their tales with disclaimers about organization. One old narrator tells an Eastern writer, "you can fix the words up some, unravel them out where I get tangled. But don't you go doctoring what happened any. The trouble with you writing men is you like to have things go along neat and fitting in together the way they don't in real living."[16] Another narrator begins his tale by defining it as "not a story, nor anything like that, because it doesn't have any form and hasn't any action and doesn't get anywhere. Just an account of what we saw of him and learned about him."[17]

Schaefer is not making any great claims for his fiction. More and more, he presents it as writing which can only approximately describe past events; it cannot reconstruct them in detail or convey the sensations of the actual experience. His comments imply that fiction is a limited form which is most truthful when it is least elaborate.

However, at the same time that the author dismantles pattern and form, because of their fraudulent effect, he builds up another context for his fiction, away from ideas of formula or literary tradition, by developing his treatment of two different kinds of space—geographic and historical. From the first, Schaefer pays a great deal of attention to the big spaces of the Far West, in the numerous landscape descriptions in his fiction and in the ideas about the West which he develops in forewords to the narratives. In prefaces like those to *The Big Range* (1953) and *Out West* (1955), he declares outright his priority: "First, and the basic conditioning quality: space, bigness, open bigness."[18] He believes that the bigness crucially affects the makeup of the land and its inhabitants. This is the space out of which Shane rides when he enters the valley, and into which he returns after the shoot-out. It is also the space, in a later novel, from which Monte Walsh recurrently materializes and into which he vanishes: "They came out of distance, going into distance, Monte Walsh and an old leggy dun."[19] The action of the stories, especially the more episodic ones, seems like an interlude between the hero's everlasting, uncharted wanderings in space.

Company of Cowards, again, makes it clear that another kind of space is at work in the fiction, contributing to the context of the action. This novel is not strictly a Western, but it is a key text in Schaefer's career. It tells the story of eight Civil War soldiers who are demoted for being cowards, then regrouped as a company with Jared Heath in charge, which goes west to fight Indians. The events are presented as authentic, purportedly reconstructed from Heath's journal and one or two other documents. It is claimed that the company's history cannot be traced from more official sources because the group was never recognized officially and so "it never became more than a beginning, was thwarted, tossed aside, soon all but forgotten and eventually erased from whatever records there might have been" (p. 68).

The narrator claims that he is filling the gap left by this deletion and, as he tells of the different events, he repeatedly reminds the reader that his account is conditioned by the lacks in the material available to him. As usual, the narrator does not feel that he can expand the events on his own authority: "Heath never spoke of what these events had meant to him. . . . All that can be done is to tell what happened there in the Wilderness and what followed" (p. 16). Sometimes he faces a complete blank: "Here is a loss that hurts. What did Major Pattison say in that note? . . . What the major wrote beyond the bare certain information he must have included is gone beyond recovery" (p. 132). At one point, the narrator reconstructs an erasure, as if to show the possibility of such an act and the impenetrability which results. He describes Heath blotting out the name of a deserter in his own official record book:

> Silence. He looked down at the open page with the one name written on it. He took a small slate pencil from a pocket and drew a line through the name. He stared down at it and with careful strokes drew more lines through it and rubbed the pencil point back and forth over it, marking it out, unreadable. [P. 35]

In his foreword and afterword to the novel, Schaefer makes it clear that he feels both that his work is filling a gap in the records of the Civil War and that it is not meant to overturn the accepted versions of the event. He explains that his novel simply amplifies the historical accounts with its concentration on forgotten individuals:

> All that is nailed down in history, described and redescribed and argued and analysed in volumes enough to fill a large library. Why worry it again and in words that can never recapture the harsh stinging reality of the bitterest bloodiest fighting ever to torment American soil?
> Because this is not a story of the Civil War. It is the story of a man who

followed his own peculiar trail out of that war and on to his own peculiar victory. And of the queer crippled unrecorded company that went with him. [Pp. 9–10]

At the end, in an epilogue, he also explains that the book really did come about because of supposed omissions in historical records. He first saw mention of a company of cowards, Company Q, in a history book by Bruce Catton. Fascinated by the idea of such a group, he searched the Library of Congress records exhaustively but found no further reference to it. In the end, he decided that there was no omission in the records and that the company was simply apocryphal. Nevertheless, he presents the story as if it fills a space in the official documents, and, thereby, he gives the novel an air of authenticity and indispensability.

Schaefer not only shows that there is a profusion of spaces in the Western landscape and in historical texts; sometimes he also brings both kinds together. One example of this happened in 1953. In the preface to one collection of stories that year, the author suggests that his tales supplement factual accounts. He quotes Harold E. Briggs, a historian who, at the end of his "sound, thorough, authoritative" history book, suggests that his own factual method is not the best: "The true story of western settlement . . . is best told when the broken lives it exacted are recorded, when romanticism and realism run hand-in-hand through the narrative."[20] Schaefer maintains that his stories are exactly this compound of realism and romance. What that means in practice is demonstrated graphically in the opening to a 1953 short story in another collection, "The Canyon." It begins with precise geographical coordinates, directing the reader to a certain area of the map, then to a mountain range, then to a river valley and one particular confluence of streams. Just at the end, the directions become much vaguer: "If you could follow the right one of these streams . . . and take the right one of its branches . . . you would come at last to a wall of stone. . . . You are looking at the lost canyon of Little Bear."[21] This is, exactly, the romantic, imaginary setting within the coordinates of documentary realism. Up to a point, the author plots out accurately a Western landscape. Within that area, with his pun on *right*, he changes from the literal to the metaphoric level. He creates an imaginary space (the lost canyon) which he proceeds to people with the creations of his own imagination. His claim is that, in supplying the lost details of this geographical space, he is also filling in spaces in the historical records.

Like Wister, Schaefer moves from the space of a landscape to the formal properties of space itself. From justifying his fiction on the basis that it fills in gaps in geography and history, he goes on to suggest, tentatively, that the real pattern governing his work is not a literary one, but a spatial one. This pattern first appears in *First Blood* (1953). All the characters and events in this novel make up one "vast interlocking web,"[22] in which an act by any one figure affects the arrangement of the whole design. By the time of "The Fifth Man" (1959), the pattern is extended so that the effect of an event or a piece of information in the fiction is felt both by participants in the story and by those in the outside world. The theory of interconnecting elements is given a scientific gloss:

> Is not all matter composed of atoms, themselves of whirling mites of energy, and some simple in organization, as hydrogen, and others complex, as uranium, with all shadings from simple to complex between? Do not these atoms, restless as in gases, more serene as in solids, impinge upon one another, touch and meet and often mingle, all through any cluster of matter, star or planet or moon or meteorite, out to the edges where what is discoverable, verifiable, merges into the mystery of space? And does not a movement, a convulsion, among these atoms anywhere send impulse radiating outward, producing effects according to the character of the ever adjoining atoms?[23]

The point of all this is an analogy which the narrator constructs, between atoms and human beings: "What one, or a group of ones does, sends impulse radiating out, communicating atom to atom, person to person, in the wondrous involved web of existence" (p. 191). After telling his story, of an old Westerner who is trying to atone for a misdeed of his past, the narrator returns to his atomic theory. He explains that the old man has communicated an impulse to him, which now colors his attitude toward all other atoms of humanity. "And it still radiates outward. If you have followed me this far, it has been communicated, if only in another brief wondering, a brief pondering, to you" (p. 221).

The action of the story is presented as some kind of spatial movement, spreading outward to affect all who come in contact with it; and, at a further level, the story is shown to make an indelible impact on the entire body of extant knowledge. The narrator comments that he sees "glimmers of a possible pattern" (p. 192) in all this activity, an interesting observation, which is immediately followed by Schaefer's standard disclaimer: this is "not really a story, simply an account and a wondering." He seems to be suggesting, tentatively, that his tales embody a different, more organic pattern than that of the usual fictional forms. The organization connects his fiction to the real world instead of separating it off as an artificial construct.

But if Schaefer sets up a design whereby his fiction can alter the perception of space in the real world, he also recognizes that the relationship can be reversed. The real world can impose its temporal qualities on his narrative. Because Schaefer accepts the course of history in outline and because he regularly uses a first-person narrator, his stories are subject to the rules of aging. Clearly, the central complication in all his fiction is caused by the effect of time on the land and its hero. The young naif who is educated by the hero certainly represents regeneration, but, because he figures as an adult narrator, he too is encompassed by the general passing of time and dying of the wild West. It seems significant that moments of climax in the fiction, such as the duel in *Shane* or the stagecoach attack in *First Blood*, are invariably introduced with the phrase, "Time stopped." It is significant, too, that in the same collection as "The Fifth Man," with its theory of atomic movement, appears "The Kean Land," in which the old Westerner admits that the old West is dead and so is his usefulness: "you can't turn time back. . . . Maybe I've just lived too long" (p. 59). The spatial theory seems to be brought in to counterbalance these impressions of aging and death, for the theory maintains that nothing ever really disappears, because it leaves an indelible impact. Of course, in the final count, the effects of space do not balance those of time: none of the arguments about the indispensability of these adventures (that they fill a space, or that they are part of an everlasting spatial organization) really outweighs, or even weighs evenly with, the acknowledgment of the inexorable effect of time. Schaefer does not, like Wister, construct a pattern which can halt the processes of time and history; he, much more tentatively, suggests only the "glimmers" of a pattern while fundamentally accepting the fact of the passing of the West.

His acceptance of temporal change brings its consequences after 1960, when his imagination seems to be overwhelmed by the ultimate implications of fiction's limitations. He has written only two novels in the last twenty-five years, *Monte Walsh* (1963) and *Mavericks* (1967), both of which are very detailed, but much less plotted than *Shane*. They are also entirely without the regenerative element, and they suggest, finally, that the wild West is not to be recovered.

Monte Walsh is like Shane in many ways, but in one respect he is crucially different: he is a mortal hero. The whole course of his life, from boyhood to middle age to death, is charted, chapter by chapter, with dates and places. There is no plot, just a detailed chronology of incidents. There is no naive narrator or actor, either. Monte himself functions as the naive youngster early in the book, but his maturation is charted in the course of the story. Although Schaefer borrows some phrases from *The Virginian* about the eternal youth of the cowboy, he also ends by dismissing the idea: in one of the final chapters, a landlady says to Monte, "You're the first cowboy I've had. But I think that's a silly word because you certainly aren't a boy" (p. 437). So, while Monte's aging is emphasized, there is no accompanying regenerative movement, since he leaves no heir. (Instead of educating a boy, as Shane does, Monte is banished from his partner's family circle because the wife believes him to be a bad influence on her young son.)

Despite the plenitude of details, the impression is that, instead of the story filling a space, the spaces have now invaded the text. Monte's life is made up of many "nothings": there is the "nothingness of distance" (p. 193) which is his natural habitat, his recurrent movement "out of seeming nowhere and on into the same" (p. 422), and his periodic chorus,

"Nothing and nobody. . . . *That's what I've got like before. Nothing and nobody"* (p. 38). The vacancies in the novel are underlined by the ending, especially when it is contrasted with the last pages of *Shane.* When Joe Starrett is sad because Shane has gone, Marian tells him, "He's not gone. He's here, in this place, in this place he gave us. He's all around us and in us, and he always will be" (p. 157). When Monte dies, he too is mourned by his closest male friend. However, there is no one to comfort Chet or contradict his sense of emptiness, and the book ends with his elegy beside Monte's grave. " 'Yes,' he said softly. 'Yes. It's a lonesome lonesome world' " (p. 501). This conclusion accepts the destructiveness of time and the death of the cowboy.

Mavericks, Schaefer's last piece of fiction, confirms that the wild West has died and cannot be revived, except as a memory. The storyteller cannot recreate; he can only commemorate. The novel begins where *Monte* ends, with an old man, Jake Hanlon. He sits in a deserted, ramshackle farm, waiting to die and remembering events from his past. The contrast between the stasis of his old age and the activity of his youth is vivid. The two periods do not feed into each other, as they do in the regenerative cycle of storytelling demonstrated in Frederic Remington's *Sundown Leflare.* In Hanlon's case, both periods lead toward death: his reminiscences move from youth to old age, and at the end of the book he dies. Here it is made clear that not just the frontier Westerner but the wild West itself is gone. Furthermore, the Westerner has contributed to the vanishing process, as Jake realizes near the end:

> He was facing the fact at last that he had outlived his time . . . the realization sank into him that he too, in his time, all unknowing and unthinking, had been a part of that deadly creeping conquest called the advance of civilization. . . . Its beginnings here in the big land had been made in his own time and he had been a part of them and once begun what was happening now was inevitable.[24]

The Westerner has contributed to the disappearance of the old West, and there is now no bulwark he can build against that process.

Of course, the passing of the West has often been part of the formulaic theme. However, other authors of popular Westerns (excepting Remington in *John Ermine*) have invented formal structures to counterbalance their admission of the death of the wild West. Fenimore Cooper, both in the mythic time scheme created by the order of the Leatherstocking tales' composition and in his imagery of the setting and rising sun, suggests Natty's immortality. Wister erases time with his metaphors of space. And the pulp authors' successful wedding of East and West implies that the effects of the West will live on forever. These artificial structures are the very thing that Schaefer rejects when he condemns stylization. Thus, he is left in the same predicament as his last hero, Jake Hanlon. The author, too, is left without a wild West, because he accepts its destruction by time. He does not use his spatial formulations to block the temporal process: at no level does he allow his fiction to perpetuate falsely that which no longer exists. Jake articulates the only possible relationship either he or the author can have with the days of the old West: "I'll tell you what we can do. We can remember 'em. I reckon that's all we've left ourselves able to do. We can remember 'em like they once was" (p. 170).[25]

What Schaefer loses, in admitting the temporary nature of his subject, is the permanence which a novel like *The Virginian* claims for itself, at least within its own covers. By eschewing manufactured timelessness and artificial formulations, Schaefer rejects the superficial immortality of the formulaic Western in favor of what seems to him a more authentic depiction of a West in the process of vanishing. At the same time, he forfeits the staying power of formulaic writing, for his treatment does not bear eternal repetition, since, ultimately, it must be overtaken by the process of aging with which it is centrally concerned if it is to remain an authentic treatment. This is one reason why, after 1960, death and elegy are so prominent in his work. Schaefer has written literature which is much superior to that of the hack writer, but is certainly not as self-regenerating.[26]

LOUIS L'AMOUR

> So too does the hungry Grub Street hack wish to write in order to prevent other writing from first occupying the space he hopes to find for his own. Every bit of writing is imagined as mass which occupies scarce space. It is the duty of writing, therefore, to admit no other writing, to keep all other writing out.
>
> Edward Said[27]

As the archetypal producer of if-you've-read-one-you've-read-them-all Westerns, Louis L'Amour has all the problems associated with mass production. He has written (and sold) more books than any of his contemporaries in the field, and yet his repertoire of plots and character types is among the smallest. Somehow, while churning out fast, repetitive material, the author has to make each book seem desirable as merchandise; somehow each text has to assert its superiority to and difference from all its competitors, although it is virtually indistinguishable from them. The methods by which this author has survived that competition can be witnessed both in his own attitude toward the marketplace and in the details of his fiction.

L'Amour has always been involved in the most blatantly commercial end of the publishing business. He began publishing Westerns in the pulp magazines in the late 1930s, thereby placing his fiction within the scaffolding of selling apparatus created by editor's departments, advance notices, quizzes, and advertisements. But he entered the pulps toward the end of their life and after the Second World War, he moved into the slicks and then into the mass-market paperback, with its cheap format, high-pressure promotion methods, and reliance on huge sales to a wide spectrum of purchasers for its survival.

In making the latter move, L'Amour became much more closely involved in the economics of book publishing than his predecessors in the twentieth century. Book publication was always a consideration for Western authors, but it tended to occur after magazine serialization and, until the late 1930s, in hardcover format. Even once the "paperback revolution" was underway, most novels became paperbacks only in reprint editions, after hardcover publication—thus at several stages', and often several years', remove from the author's manuscript. L'Amour, however, was one of the generation who experienced the introduction of paperback "originals"—that is, books issued only in cheap pocket-sized paper covers at very low prices. This format has come to be L'Amour's major mode of publishing and the way in which he has made his millions.[28]

It has also put him in direct contact with heightened commercial pressures. The mass-market paperback borrowed its production techniques and circulation channels from the magazine industry, setting itself up in direct competition with the magazine's eye-catching packaging and periodical installments. In the economics of cheap paperback publishing, effective merchandising has become paramount: there is a premium on aggressive salesmanship, a ruthlessly quick turnover of titles, and saturation methods of display in all sorts of outlets beyond bookstores, such as drugstores, supermarkets, and newsstands, in plain view of all potential consumers. Retail outlets accept paperbacks on the same sale-or-return system as magazines; thus, this kind of book is under unusually high pressure to sell quickly and in large numbers. William Jovanovich has said that "each competes desperately for display space at the newsstand or drugstore, and each is held in stock only briefly with a life cycle scarcely greater than that of a fruit fly"; more succinctly, John Sutherland has said that the pressure is on to "sell out or get out."[29] So L'Amour has tied himself into a system of speed and profitability; his contract with Bantam, the largest paperback company in the world, requires him to produce three novels a year.[30]

The immediacy of these commercial pressures is further heightened by L'Amour's own willing involvement in the merchandising process. He does not use an agent, since he prefers to negotiate directly with his publisher, and he is well known for his aggressive promotion of his own books. Bantam's sales director has said that "Louis is a book salesman's dream": he works both with his publisher's sales people and with book wholesalers.[31] With such an attitude, L'Amour has not only survived the ruthless competition, he has won exceptionally high sales (Bantam claims at least 500,000 sales for each novel in a market where 100,000 is the norm) and unusually long shelf life (because Bantam rereleases his titles every three or four years, their overall display time is considerably longer than the average fifteen days).[32] Not surprisingly, the commercial pressures show not just in L'Amour's activities but in his writing. He claims that he has never experienced any specific editorial direction: "No editor has ever given me advice or suggestions. They just ask when they will get the next book." Nevertheless, he has tailored his writing method to his requirements, producing his novels in just one draft, at the rate of five pages per day.[33] Moreover, when he moved out of the network of puffery provided by the pulps and into the high-pressure methods of the mass-market paperback, his fiction itself began to take on the features of salesmanship.

The general conservatism of commercial publishing makes itself felt in L'Amour's fictional formula. He established his literary conventions when he began his career, in Leo Margulies' *Thrilling West* pulp magazine, and he has adhered to them with an unusual degree of consistency. Through time, he has refined his treatment of women and cultural minorities to some extent and from time to time he moves his setting away from the Far West of the late nineteenth century; in all other respects, however, the ninety-six novels he has written to date conform to the familiar pulp formula: they tell of range wars, gold thefts, or Indian attacks in which the heroes intervene to eliminate the villains and save the, often Eastern, heroines, whom they sometimes marry. The action always proceeds by ritual scenes: L'Amour's favorite is a chase sequence in which the hero is alone in the wilderness, being hunted by a posse. Nearly all the attention is, of course, on the hero, who is always a man of contradictions: famous as a gunfighter, he thinks of himself more as a cowman; he is a rough Western drifter, yet well educated; he is poetic and philosophical but goes berserk in battle. From the first book to the most recent, the hero has a name which stops people in their tracks, and his appearance never changes, down to his black, flat-crowned hat, which eventually acquires a bullet hole as the only evidence of the passage of time.

Like all pulp authors, L'Amour portrays an easy marriage of civilization and wilderness. Although the setting is the wild West, the hope for a domesticated West invariably figures as the justification for all the violent activity. More emphatically than in many Westerns, L'Amour's plots function as only the preliminary action necessary to a more desirable state. Even the heroes see the action in this light: they consider themselves anachronisms and want to give up the life of wandering and gunfighting for a home, a wife, and some security. They believe in the value of government and the possibility of coexistence between traditional enemies, and consider the violence which they perpetrate necessary only as a way of ending the general violence forever. It is not only the hero who is adaptable and desirous of harmony; the heroine, too, fits into the West unusually easily and her desires coincide with the hero's exactly. Despite the ritualistic romantic confusions and physical dangers, the stories convey an unusually high degree of harmony and a relatively easy transition from wilderness to civilization.

If L'Amour's plot remained much the same through the years, one crucial change in his writing did occur when he moved away from the pulps: his use of factual material. In the slicks and, especially, his paperbacks, L'Amour began to include many allusions to facts about the West, romantic literature, and his own works, mixed in with the repetitive adventures, or accompanying them in footnotes, forewords, and afterwords. This profusion of references also distinguishes his work from the general run of pulp fiction. There are many strands to this material. When they interweave, they do the work previously carried out by the paraphernalia of the pulp magazines: they puff L'Amour's work, and thus create a space for it in the market.

In all the novels he has written since leaving the pulps, L'Amour has included some quota of facts, but over the years he has increased the quantity to the point that, for both him and his publishers, his attention to fact has become his trademark. L'Amour always emphasizes this facet of his work in interviews, and the book covers have come to announce his novels as being "from the foremost story-teller of the authentic West."[34] The author and characters convey a great deal of information in observations and dialogue in the text itself. The hero always has an educative function, from the earliest novels like *Westward the Tide* (1950) and *Hondo* (1953), in which the hero teaches a young boy (and thereby the reader) about plainscraft, to the later works, in which the hero is the first-person narrator and thus talks directly to his audience, explaining Western phrases and customs. In *Galloway* (1970), the hero, Flagan, has escaped from his Apache captors and has to survive in the wilderness, naked and unarmed, until he can reach civilization. His account of his journey is so detailed that it almost functions like a practical aid: for example, he describes how to make moccasins from animal skin, with instructions for each step of the procedure, including which kind of rock is sharp enough to cut hide. The footnotes and the appendices concentrate on information about geography, correlating exactly the points in the fictional scenes with their present-day names.

Of course, there is a long tradition of inserting factual references into romances; in Western fiction, the precedent is set by Fenimore Cooper. The practice has been analyzed by Stephen Fender as the alienation of romance by history; that is, authors employ facts to point up the romantic content and emphasize its separateness from real life.[35] Thus, both Natty, in *The Last of the Mohicans*, and Tom Kendrick in *Showdown at Yellow Butte* (1953), discuss the merits of their firearms ("the long barrelled, true grooved, soft metalled rifle" in one case;[36] the Watch 12-shot .36 Navy pistol in the other) in the midst of fierce fighting. In both instances, the factual content is accurate and verifiable while the action, including the hero's capacity for slaughter and survival, is fantastic. Although the details of a L'Amour plot are a little different, his attention to Indian customs, the habits of wild animals and other data is in a direct line from Cooper's.

It seems to me that, whether or not L'Amour includes factual material in greater quantities than Cooper, he certainly makes more fuss about the practice, using his appendices not only to convey information but to trumpet the fact that he does so. For example, at the end of *Mojave Crossing* (1964), he adds in a "Note": "Although a writer of fiction is under no compulsion to be as exact as I have chosen to be as to locale, I regard each of my novels as, in a sense, historical. Each water hole or spring, each valley, canyon creek or mountain, each store, gambling house, or hotel exists now or did exist at the time."[37] His phrase, "When I write about a spring, that spring is there, and the water is good to drink"[38] has become his clarion call, in the endnotes and in the publicity material which now surrounds his work. His readers obviously care about the accuracy of his references as much as he does: one of his favorite interview stories is of the time when an editor omitted one of the author's footnotes about a test model gun, and L'Amour received thousands of letters from frontier buffs and gun experts who thought that he had made a mistake.[39]

There is a life in L'Amour's textual "asides" which, to my mind, is more vivid than that in Cooper's. L'Amour has many more different kinds of allusions than his predecessor, and they interact more, with each other and with the narrative. L'Amour goes well beyond the historical or geographical framework of the nineteenth century. For instance, Flagan Sackett, while fighting his battles against Indians and rustlers, manages to bring a bumper sticker slogan of the National Rifle Association and the language of the Cuban Missile Crisis into 1870s New Mexico: he believes both that "when guns are outlawed, only the outlaws will have guns" and, in the same vein, that "when feeding time comes around there's nothing a hawk likes better than a nice fat, peaceful dove."[40] Without open acknowledgment, L'Amour brings into his unreal adventures the weight of modern political debate.

More explicitly, he brings into play the whole panoply of writings that constitute the literary heritage of the Western, as if to add authority and erudition to his own contribution to the field. In his first book, *Westward the Tide*, he declares the level at which he is aiming—"It was an epic of strength, of heroism, and of greed"[41]—and from then on he piles on references to Homer, Scott, Cooper, and many more writers of heroic romance. He is aware of the Western's heritage and willing to make it part of his text. For example, in *Shalako* (1962), there is an argument between the European nobleman and the Eastern heroine over the Western hero, Shalako. Von Halstatt says, " 'I am afraid he impressed you too much. Did you not tell me you had read the novels of Fenimore Cooper? I am afraid you see your man from the desert as another Leatherstocking.' Irina smiled. 'And he may be. I think we could use one now.' "[42] There are many analogies with medieval knights, Scottish border heroes, and Elizabethan adventurers. L'Amour's heroes are compared to Hickok, Hardin, Holliday, and Earp, while figures like Clay Allison make silent appearances and in *The Sky-Liners* (1967), Wyatt Earp and Bat Masterson come into the story for three chapters, helping the heroes to find the villains. There is much more of this kind of thing: references to trappers' journals, emigrants' diaries, Lewis and Clark, and Mark Twain. The author even drags in whole bookshelves of erudite reading—Schopenhauer, Shakespeare, Plutarch (the last, his gunfighters' favorite)—and rather inappropriate figures—Shalako has mixed with Manet, Degas, and Zola in Paris, but disliked them because they argued too much. The final impression is that no possible element of the Western tradition has been omitted. All the literary baggage that has ever collected around the subject of the West seems to have been brought on board with these formulaic plots.

Along with all these allusions to works by other authors, L'Amour creates a web of cross-references back and forth among his own books. This set of references begins after 1960 and relates to a new venture he began at that time: a multivolume saga about three families, the Chantrys, the Talons and, most famously, the Sacketts. The Sackett story begins with *The Daybreakers* (1960), which tells of two Sackett brothers traveling from Tennessee to New Mexico in 1867, becoming involved in the usual battles, and finally establishing their own ranch. There have been eighteen volumes so far, each dealing with a Sackett brother, father or cousin and mostly set at different points in the nineteenth century—though three recent novels have gone back to the first Sackett to arrive in America, telling of his adventures in England and then in Virginia in 1599. There are very many references from one book to another in the series, and to other L'Amour novels, at first conveyed in footnotes, but now absorbed into the texts through the author or characters mentioning names and scenes from other books.

The habit of cross-reference becomes obsessive as the details of the family tree and the sequence of events are filled in. The author sketches in the pasts of even the most incidental characters, and the Sacketts themselves begin to be compelled by a desire to know about their ancestry. *Treasure Mountain* (1972) is entirely composed of the search by three Sackett brothers to discover how their long-gone father died. It involves the detailed unraveling of a twenty-year-old trail, and thus a twenty-year-old story is reconstructed within that enacted by the present members of the family. The next Sackett novel goes even farther back. It is *Sackett's Land* (1974), the first book to return to 1599 and the original American Sackett. It begins with a preface by L'Amour, explaining that, "in writing my stories I have found myself looking back again and again to origins, to find and clearly see the ancestors of the pioneers."[43] He then opens the story proper with Barnabas Sackett, the Englishman, discussing his own ancestors, the Iceni of "the long ago." The apparent authorial desire to construct, or reconstruct, an entire epoch results in a heavy load of repetition. Each book carries both its own, internal repetitions and the references which remind the reader of those in its companion volumes. Far from covering up the repetitious nature of his work, or keeping other writing out of his own, L'Amour deliberately invokes the similarities and connections within his own accumulating volumes and with those by other writers.

All these allusions, cross-references, and family connections, while adding weight to the stories, also, unfortunately, end up giving an impression of an overcrowded stage. Every time a hero acts out a ritual movement, echoes of other L'Amour heroes and of those created by other authors, rush in upon the scene.[44] Occasionally the characters themselves bear witness to this profusion. In *Mustang Man* (1966), Nolan Sackett, one of the less law-abiding and literate cousins of the main branch, becomes involved in a fight over buried gold. Riding through the vast desert, he repeatedly comes upon plotters who are trying to find the money first. Eventually he exclaims, "Looks to me as if ever'body on the Staked Plains is related . . . and all of them after Nathan Hume's gold."[45] The accumulative effect of this kind of overpopulation is, of course, fatal for the Western: L'Amour depends on vast empty wildernesses both for the excitement of his hero's lonely flight and survival and for his philosophizing about the regenerative effects of an open, untamed, lonely land. At another level, the densely populated scene also puts the reader in mind of the hundreds of other Westerns, with many of which L'Amour's texts are competing in the bookshop and supermarket. The danger is that each L'Amour story will lose its proclaimed uniqueness.

To counteract this impression of overcrowding, L'Amour introduces yet another set of references in his "asides." These are comments which, instead of adding other Western writing to the text, take it away by discounting its authenticity. This kind of subtractive strategy helps L'Amour's fiction to displace earlier and current work, much of which it closely resembles. This concern for deletion seems to me, again, not to exist in Cooper's fiction; it is a modern obsession in the Western, necessitated by the thousands of Western works which have piled up since Cooper's time. There are very many revisionist statements in L'Amour's fiction, usually delivered by his heroes, which discount the contents of adventure stories. Sometimes, an earlier version of the genre is criticized. In *Heller with a Gun* (1955), one character articulates the worthlessness of dime fiction: "His years began to seem woefully wasted, for in this emergency he had nothing on which to base his plans but remembered sequences of old melodramas or the stories of Ned Buntline."[46] More often, heroes make general disparaging observations, like "so many things that are so dramatic or exciting when you read about them actually happen so simply and quietly" (*Westward the Tide*, p. 78) and "they were always telling the foolish romantic stories of outlaws and men on the run . . . the writers of such stories should try it some time; they should try living in swamps, living with sweat, dirt and death."[47] Not only does L'Amour imply that other Western writers are too romantic, but also very often he corrects other authors' misinformation about the details of Western life.[48]

The clearest case of deletion takes place completely within the boundaries of L'Amour's own fiction; his concern with correcting statements in his own work has developed in accordance with changes in his career. Early in his writing, he took on a commission to write "Hopalong Cassidy" novels under the pseudonym "Tex Burns." He wrote four novels which clearly take the original Cassidy books as their model, conforming to all the hero's biographical details, but they are even more extreme than the originals in their portrayal of an incredible stereotype. L'Amour may well have been more influenced by William Boyd's cinematic depiction of Cassidy than by the figure in Mulford's novels; certainly, his hero is both unbelievably invincible and showily dressed: "Clad entirely in black, from his sombrero to his ebony-hued boots, he was a striking figure— a man to attract attention anywhere. In marked contrast to his dark range clothes were his white hair, his silver spurs, and the two white bone-handled silver six guns which he wore against his thighs."[49] He also rides a gleaming white horse called Topper. The action in these books is routinely formulaic, melodramatic, and incredible, with a great deal of hackneyed dialogue and improbable characterizations. Cassidy is "actually a living legend,"[50] one who relishes danger, perhaps because he always comes through unscathed. He says, "I got to see . . . what Mesquite's doing. That kid'll sure be in trouble, and he has no right to grab it all. If there's trouble, we'll have it together!"[51] Nor is he averse to doling out the kind of advice Roy Rogers and William Boyd busily dispensed on the screen and in magazines throughout the forties: " 'Food worth eating,' Hopalong said seriously, 'is too good to throw away. Then every time I sit down to eat I think of all the folks that don't have anything to eat, or not nearly as much as I do' " and so on.[52] This early work is stereotyped through and through and not unlike the dime novels which L'Amour later deplores.

When L'Amour finished these novels, he returned to his own name and immediately created Hondo, a much rougher hero. Hondo believes that "people learn by gettin' bit,"[53] he is tortured savagely by Indians, and he has to be rescued by the woman whose husband he has killed. The contrast between Hondo and Hopalong is not left wholly implicit; Hondo says, "Nobody but a fool or a tenderfoot wears bright shiny stuff on his clothes. Only a fool would ride a white horse. You can see it too far off. That bright, shiny stuff is for sissies, townfolk" (p. 141). This specific criticism arises repeatedly, in *Kilkenny* (1954), *Shalako*, and elsewhere. People who welcome trouble are also labeled fools by the L'Amour heroes: "Nobody but a fool or some crazy kid goes hunting trouble. It's different when you meet it face to face on a dark night than when you read of it in a book. All this talk of people who look for adventure is from people who've had no experience."[54] These comments are habitual, and it seems obvious that one of their functions is to erase the unreal formulations that L'Amour previously created in the Hopalong books. He wants to wipe out some of his own writing, as well as other people's.

Given all this evidence of an impulse toward deletion, it seems permissible to consider a last, more literal kind of recurring emptiness as part of this strategy whereby the author wipes clean his stage in each text, removing all that has gone before. The emptying-out process has to do, in this case, with the actual landscape in which the adventures take place. Although L'Amour gives the impression of filling up his deserts and ranges with clone-like heroes, villains, Indians, rustlers, relations, and long-lost friends (not to mention the famous gunfighters and the adventurers from bygone days who are brought in as analogies), he just as quickly empties them out with sweeping descriptions which rub the scene clean of all humans, near the start of every book. The process is accumulative: the more L'Amour fills up his Western milieu with references to people, weapons, customs, books, and philosophical theories, the more often he insists on the emptiness of his scene.

The emphasis on an empty landscape begins in *Hondo*, the first novel after the Cassidy tetralogy. It sets its scene early: "Nothing moved. It was a far, lost land, a land of beige-gray silences and distance where the eye reached out farther and farther to lose itself finally against the sky and where the only movement was the lazy swing of a remote buzzard" (p. 6). The emptiness of the land is a constant note: "Not a tree, not a bush, just the low, dusty grass, and the wide milky-blue sky above" (*Mustang Man*, p. 4). Fighting Indians is almost impossible, for even when it is full of Apaches, the land still looks empty: Tell "searched the terrain for something at which to shoot."[55] As one soldier, waiting for an Indian attack in *Last Stand at Papago Wells*, says, "nothin' . . . just nothin' at all. I never seen so much of nothin' " (p. 79). Again and again the word "nothing" appears in the text, adding suspense to chase and survival scenes, until, by the time of *How the West Was Won* (1962), to go west is to "step off into the nothingness of the unknown."[56] The hero himself is more and more often "a man with nothing," "a man alone," "a naked man with enemies behind me and nothing before me but hope," "alone upon this land."[57] In *Flint* (1960), the hero returns west at the beginning of the book, believing himself about to die: "This was the end of everything and the beginning of nothing."[58] Going under an assumed name, he can answer the heroine's question about his identity only with, "I am nobody . . . I am nobody at all" (p. 91), all the time vividly aware that he will soon be less, only lifeless bones and dust. There are many more of these descriptions and they are interpolated into the action so frequently that, instead of the scene being overcrowded, at one level the impression is of bursts of action by isolated figures occurring between moments of silence in an empty landscape.

Because it has been established that the content of formulaic or popular fiction is perceptibly affected by commercial conditions, it seems justifiable to extrapolate from the level of action in the plot to the workings of the novel within the marketplace. The economics of mass-market paperback publishing—cheap production necessitating a low retail price which in turn requires huge sales for profit—have created aggressively competitive displays in which each book, gaudy cover forward, fights for attention. The contents of L'Amour's novels seem to reflect some of this salesmanship: all the adding and subtracting of material exemplify what Edward Said describes in *Beginnings* as texts vying for scarce commercial space. In different ways in his fiction, L'Amour sets up deletion devices which clear a space, free of other people's creations or his own previous writings. In a recent Sackett novel, *Lonely on the Mountain* (1980), the characters seem to recognize even more directly that each novel must establish itself as a new beginning. The story opens with William Tell Sackett speaking: *"There will come a time when you believe everything is finished. That will be the beginning.* Pa said that when I was a boy" (p. 1).

In a way, L'Amour tries to go one better than Said's Grub Street hacks, for he attempts to have it both ways. He wants both to profit from the weight of other sources and to clear them out of the way, to make room for his own work. This is why he has two different kinds of allusions, those which cite other works and those which dismiss them. The balance is a precarious one to maintain: he is simultaneously using and opposing other writers' formulas in order to clear space for more of the same. Moreover, he is torn between filling the space with his own burgeoning family sagas and leaving it empty for each succeeding story. In such an overwritten genre, his writing must be in constant danger of merging into the general mass.

I said at the beginning that there is little tension between wilderness and civilization in L'Amour's adventures. It now seems that, with this contemporary pulp author as with the earlier ones, the tension is located, not in the ever-repeated and little-changing plots, but in all the information and comment which frame the story. The interplay between the different kinds of material involved throws up a host of contradictions: his revisionist statements about adventure stories sit uneasily beside his formulaic melodramas; he constantly insists on the variety of people in the West while consistently dealing in a limited cast of repetitive types; and his heroes assert that the only true education is that conferred by raw experience in the West, yet they are quick to claim familiarity with a vast array of erudite sources. These disparities help to prove that the real action in L'Amour's work occurs in the operation of his verifiable, factual references, more than in his fantastical adventures; his presentation of facts develops more than his telling of stories. The tension involved in the use of this material filters down from conditions in the marketplace. In his stories, L'Amour is doing little that is new or different; therefore, each time he creates another repetition he has to bring into play the checks and balances which create the conditions necessary for the success of his fiction. On each occasion, he has to clear the stage anew.

Here, then, are three writers who have found strategies for distinguishing their work, even though it comes at the end of a long line of fiction very similar to their own. They do not obscure the existence of their predecessors; instead, they exploit the existence of a tradition to which they are late contributors.

Le May concentrates on the artifice of formulaic stylization. He identifies the main devices which govern the action in the Western and utilizes them as the one area of unworked material out of which he can create a new subject. His fiction approaches a point at which everything becomes a sign which can be interpreted verbally.

Schaefer, who sees the real, historical West as the justification for the Western story, places his work in the tradition of historical writing, rather than of fiction. He finds new spaces in the Western landscape and in the records about the West and maintains that his stories can fill in those spaces. That is not a permanent or everlastingly repeatable method because, in time, Schaefer, whose standards are truth and authenticity, has to face up to the fact that he has filled in the space. Not only has the West gone, but its potential as a subject for fiction is vanishing too.

However, if Schaefer seems caught in a dilemma by addressing himself

to a space which is fast running out, L'Amour is in an even more precarious position. As he is the most commercial of these writers, his work
is the most directly subject to the competition of the marketplace. Once
his fiction is no longer embedded in the apparatus of the pulp magazine,
with all its strategies for puffing authors, he sets himself to create his
own selling apparatus, within each novel. First of all, he wants to reinforce the existence of a Western tradition and so make his work the more
weighty as a contribution to it. Thus, he peppers his novels with references to other literary and historical works. But these references also
gesture toward the crowd of writers who have covered the ground before
him. He has to clear a space for himself, both in terms of his predecessors
in the genre and his competitors in the contemporary marketplace. On
the supermarket shelves, even his own earlier work constitutes competition for his newest volumes. He establishes the supremacy of his work
by discounting the authenticity of any other. The message is that the
account the reader is presently reading is the only one worth attending
to. But this most temporary kind of space is, of course, filled up by the
end of every novel. Therefore, at the beginning of the next, L'Amour
must begin the process all over again. His first priority must be to give
an impression of space and unique happenings; at every level of his text
he emphasizes emptiness and isolation.

And the strategies have paid off. Each of these authors, in his different
way, has shown that it is possible to achieve distinction in an overwritten
genre, even when conforming to conventional materials. Their achievement has exhausted the material, however. The strategies which they
have discovered are not self-generating or repeatable. Even L'Amour
has been driven into Siberia in a recent book in his desperate search for
convincingly unpopulated spaces. These three writers really do seem to
have used up the last room available for genuinely new contributions to
the form.

FIVE

Anti-Western Westerns

Among all the distinctive literary developments of the 1960s, something happened to the formulaic Western. Around 1960, Jack Schaefer, for one, lost hope for the Western as a living genre. One sign of this is the change in his fiction. In 1959, in "The Fifth Man," he used spatial formulations to demonstrate the immortality of the West. By 1963, *Monte Walsh* shows that the old West is dead, and *Mavericks*, that it can be revived only as a memory. Schaefer declared the death of Western writing more explicitly in the introduction to his anthology of Western stories, *Out West*. In 1955, when he introduced the first volume of the collection, he spoke of the inherent vitality of the Western and its continuing potential: "Despite the long past of the western story and the millions upon millions of words that have been written in the field, the dramatic and significant possibilities of that material have as yet scarcely been touched."[1] By 1961, when he introduced the second volume, he was pessimistic about the form. In the six years since the first volume of the anthology, no memorable writer had appeared, and Western writing was deteriorating badly:

> because of the increased demand for such stories, they can get by, and most of them do, with even less competence in the writing and even greater reliance on hackneyed repetition. There must be almost twice as many writers tossing out Western stuff as there were six years ago—and the general level of achievement, even for those who do have obvious technical competence, is distinctly lower.[2]

After about 1960, there also seem to have been few new novelists of the kind in whom I am interested: authors who produce formulaic fictions, but also write their individual reactions into their texts in some way. Perhaps writers felt that the genre had become so oversubscribed that there was little room for individual authorial engagement at any level. After all, in 1960 L'Amour—who still remains far and away the most popular and most prolific Western author—began his family sagas which, with their indefatigable spread backward and forward through history and their myriad cross-references and allusions, threaten to plot out every possible combination of time, place, and character in the

American West. Other big sellers who began to compete with L'Amour in the sixties and seventies—like George Gilman and J. T. Edson—seem to trade on the impersonality of their products, if anything. Both repeat wholly familiar scenes, characters, and plots. Gilman's one distinguishing mark is his detailed attention to pornographic violence and sex, which serves to cut the reader off from identification with any of the characters. Edson does not have an original trademark. He strings together stereotypes and clichés with a grammar which cannot even sustain itself, far less convey any level of creativity. The trend against individual input continues. Playboy Westerns, one of the few additions to the Western genre in recent years, have returned to pulp assembly-line methods. Each series of these novels is composed by a team of cowriters, orchestrated by a central editor.[3]

But the 1960s also saw the beginning of a new type of fiction which uses the stereotyped images and plots of the formulaic Western toward different ends. This is the New Western, which Leslie Fiedler discusses in *The Return of the Vanishing American* (1968). This kind of novel seems to be directed at a more sophisticated audience than the formulaic Western, and it is marketed in a more expensive format. In fact, Fiedler's term can cover three different categories of novels. The first type constitutes an elegy for the rituals of the old West and Western. Novels like Edward Abbey's *The Brave Cowboy* (1956) and Arthur Miller's *The Misfits* (1961) show typical Western heroes acting out their conventional existences, but in a modern world where their skills are redundant. The plots of these novels demonstrate that the heroic cowboy cannot survive in the twentieth century, but also that his rituals are superior to the behavior of modern, technological society. The second kind of New Western overturns the conventional attributes of the Western hero to chart and even celebrate the new, unheroic West. This fiction is epitomized in Larry McMurtry's *Horseman, Pass By* (1961), in which the young antihero, Hud, deposes his stepfather, avatar of the old West, by killing him. Hud is the reverse image of the conventional wild West hero: not a stoical, reluctant executioner of villains who is awkward with women and close to the land, but a brutal killer who rapes the black maid and exploits the land's resources by ruthless strip-mining.

The last category is the anti-Western Western, which gives new life and new significance to the old formula. This form grew up as part of the general rebellion against conventional patterning in fiction that took off in the sixties and seventies. The most extreme example of both convention and patterning is, of course, popular formulaic fiction and, thus, versions of various popular genres—such as the fairy tale, science fiction, and the Gothic, as well as the Western—came to be incorporated into experimental works. Repeatedly, the two-dimensional characters and predictable plot outlines of the adventure story are played out and ultimately parodied in these works. The consequences for the Western are described by Fiedler: "a kind of anti-Western Western . . . begins by assuming the clichés and stereotypes of all the popular books which precede it, and aims not at redeeming but at *exploiting* them, bringing the full weight of their accumulated absurdities to bear in every casual quip."[4] Thus, the anti-Western novel makes an explicit subject of the illusoriness and two-dimensionality of the Western formula, which was hinted at, increasingly strongly, by some Beadle dime novelists, and by Frederick Faust and Alan Le May.

There were two forerunners to this kind of novel in the Western field before 1960, both holding up the image of the heroic West to comment on its insubstantiality. The first was Nathanael West's *The Day of the Locust* (1939). Among the many illusions in the Hollywood of this novel is the cowboy dandy from Arizona. Earle Shoop is, literally, as lacking in depth as his screen image: he is so thin that his trousers

> hung down without a wrinkle, as though they were empty. . . . He had a two-dimensional face that a talented child might have drawn with a ruler and a compass. . . . His reddish tan complexion was the same color from hairline to throat, as though washed in by an expert, and it completed his resemblance to a mechanical drawing.[5]

In *The Ox-Bow Incident* (1940), Walter Van Tilburg Clark exposes the unreality of the heroic Western image in a serious tale about a lynching. Clark portrays familiar enough cowboys, but he shows that the codes by which they operate—which are those of *The Virginian*—are empty and dangerous.

After 1960, the illusions surrounding the heroic Westerner become a joke, as authors start to parody the formula in both conventional and experimental novels. For example, David Markson's *The Ballad of Dingus Magee* (1965) portrays the pursuit of a feared outlaw by a lawman. The action is full of men disguised as women and vice versa, and ends with the hero's identity being revealed by a locket (a scene straight out of the dime novels), followed by a classic retreat from the white woman by these late descendants of Leatherstocking and Chingachgook. But the tale also unravels all the fraudulent events which lead to the hero's reputation. In the course of this exposure, which is the point of the novel, Markson burlesques stereotypes like the tenderfoot, the cavalry officer, the virginal schoolmarm, and the Indian maiden, rituals like the shoot-out, and historical figures like Billy the Kid and Wyatt Earp. Robert Flynn's *North to Yesterday* (1967) tells of a cattle drive, only to make fun of all the illusions necessary to its romanticization. Very different from these stylistically traditional narratives is *Yellow Back Radio Broke-Down* (1969) by the black postmodernist, Ishmael Reed. This is a discontinuous, fabulous, dadaist tale which thwarts all expectations of causality or plot links. In it, the

Loop Garoo Kid fights for the children of a town against an evil rancher. But, in this most fantastical version of the Western stereotype, the hero has highly unconventional racial and mythic associations: like the Virginian, he comes from the South, but he is a black, not a white, Southerner; and whereas the Virginian represents Adam, this "Hoo Doo cowboy" embodies Satan, practising Voo Doo magic with the aid of a white snake. During Loop Garoo's adventures, he is saved from a desert trial by an Indian in a helicopter who restrains himself from criticizing white tradition too openly, out of concern for the impact of the Western on the East: "If I run down that shit, Loop, the book won't be reviewed in Manhattan."[6]

In the 1970s, the literary allusions accumulate. John Seelye's *The Kid* (1972), a complicated parody which explodes the harmony in the union of blonde heroine and black hero, is dedicated to Fiedler and its epigraph quotes him: "To understand the West as somehow a joke comes a little closer to getting it straight."[7] The climax of *The Return of the Virginian* (1974) by H. Allen Smith is a confrontation between the Virginian's grandson and Trampas's son, in which the latter reveals that the Virginian was an alcoholic and was drunk at Steve's hanging. In George L. Voss's *The Man who Believed in the Code of the West* (1975), the narrator is a tenderfoot from Harvard who quotes Zane Grey axioms at bewildered Westerners. Finally, the ritualistic trail drive of *The Last Cattle Drive* (1977) by Robert Day involves a viewing of *Hud* (the film of *Horseman, Pass By*) and *Midnight Cowboy*. By implanting these references within the parodic action, these works simultaneously retain and explode the Western formula.

These post-1960 novels parody, in a general way, the plot conventions followed by the formulaic writings which I have discussed. However, there are some anti-Western Westerns which relate to the patterns in conventional Westerns in a more specific way than this. I have said that the vigor in the formulaic pieces repeatedly derives from the friction between the authors' individual visions and the conventions of their genre. This tension is expressed in the narrative methods: authors either weave their personal commentaries in and out of the action of their fiction, or they use their individual reactions to shape their texts at different levels. Typical of the first type are the dime novelists, Frederick Faust, Ernest Haycox, and Louis L'Amour, who gesture toward the artificiality and commercialism of their products. The second type consists of writers like Owen Wister, Zane Grey, Alan Le May, and Jack Schaefer, who try to do something more creative with their form. While this struggle can be seen as paralleling that between nature and culture in the plot, it never overtly takes over as the main theme of the work. Nor do any of these formulists ever foreground their individual responses enough to interfere with the predictable course of their plots. To that extent, the two strands I have discussed—the formula and the authorial commentary on it—remain separate.

There are three anti-Western Westerns which bring together plot and commentary, by making explicit, in the course of their adventure tales, some of the authorial concerns which remain partly submerged in the formula Western. These three novels—*Welcome to Hard Times* (1960), *Midnight Cowboy* (1965), and *Cattle Annie and Little Britches* (1977)—show that, eventually, the formulists' obsessions can subvert the formulaic action. They focus on different issues: one novel deals with problems of repetition similar to those experienced by the pulp stars, one takes further Wister's attempt to erase time, and one explores the dime novel convention which linked characters directly to their audience and downgraded the authors' role.

In the pulp Western, from Zane Grey, through Frederick Faust, to Ernest Haycox, there is increasingly clear evidence of the authors'—and, in time, the characters'—obsession with the repetitiveness of the Western formula. None of these authors actually disrupts the formula on account of that concern; even Haycox slides into another genre, naturalism, rather than make radical changes to the standard Western plot. The foregrounding of the problem of repetition happens only in the anti-Western novel, *Welcome to Hard Times*, which was written by E. L. Doctorow as a direct counterpoint to all the very conventional, repetitive Westerns he encountered as a script reader for the movie companies in the 1950s.[8]

The novel begins in a conventional enough way for a modern, violent Western, when an evil stranger, the Bad Man from Bodie, rides his horse into the saloon in Hard Times and begins to shoot up the town. He rapes women, kills townsmen, then razes the whole settlement. The only survivors are Blue, the narrator, who has been too cowardly to challenge the Bad Man; Molly, a prostitute who has been raped and badly burned; and Jimmy, an eleven-year-old who has been left an orphan. These three set up house together in a dugout at the edge of the ruins, and Blue begins to rebuild the town. Various figures arrive out of the desert to join them, the most important being "Dead-Eye" Jenks, an ugly, stupid youth who is a crack marksman. When he begins to teach Jimmy how to shoot, it becomes clear that this quartet is a parodic version of the family in *Shane*. Husband, wife, and son are trying to settle in a land which is threatened by an evil, powerful man. But here the husband is a coward, the wife—married to him symbolically by the torn wedding dress she wears throughout the action—is a prostitute (and namesake of the Virginian's sweetheart), and the boy, born to them through violence, is being turned into a rabid hater of all men by his "mother." The gunman who rides out of the desert to join them is ugly, unkempt, stupid, and garrulous. These characters live in peaceful domesticity for a time, building up defenses to protect them from the Bad Man, should he return. The town prospers, and it begins to look as if, through mutual cooperation, the settlers have established a permanent civilization. At this point, however, the Bad Man returns and events repeat themselves. Again he kills and rapes and sets fire to the town, and again the towns-people run off. Emboldened by Molly's sexual promises, Dead-Eye goes to challenge the Bad Man to a duel, "trotting like a hero,"[9] but is summarily shot down. The Bad Man attacks Molly again. Jimmy shoots at him, but accidently kills them both and wounds the narrator. The boy then rides off into the desert, to become another bad man.

By the end of the action, the reader realizes that the narrator is writing the tale amid the smoking ruins of the town, as he lies dying from his gunshot wound. There are two important things about this figure: first, he is an author of diagrammatic writings with which he tries to control reality, and, second, he is defeated by the inevitable repetition of events.

This book, the narrator's story, is divided into "ledgers" instead of chapters. The narrator tells us near the beginning that he has a weakness for documents, since he believes that they enable man to control past and present; this document, his novel, is also intended to control the events it describes. Writing of this order conforms to Cawelti's definition of formula, cited earlier: "the formulaic element reflects the construction of an ideal world without the disorder, the ambiguity, the uncertainty, and the limitations of the world of our experience."[10] The problem, as the narrator comes to realize, is that his kind of tale has a predetermined ending: "now I put it down I can see that we were finished before we ever got started, our end was in our beginning" (p. 156). He begins to realize that he is locked into a pattern of repetition: "the Trick, I couldn't tolerate it, what other name is there for the mockery that puts us back in our own steps?" (p. 166). Writing down these repetitions does not change them; it only makes them more obvious. And yet, even as he feels himself trapped in the pattern, the narrator continues to write: "I scorn myself for a fool for all the bookkeeping I've done; as if notations in a ledger can fix life, as if some marks in a book can control things. . . . The only hope I have now is that it will be read—and isn't that a final curse on me, that I still have hope?" (pp. 156–57). In the end, he suspects that his writing is neither powerful nor meaningful: "Does the truth come out in such scrawls, so bound by my limits?" (p. 178).

At the beginning, Blue identifies the Bad Man as an intrinsic part of the Western scene: "Bad Men from Bodie weren't ordinary scoundrels, they came with the land, and you could no more cope with them than you could with dust or hailstones" (p. 6). When, at the end, the narrator says the Bad Man can never be beaten, he is also saying that the Western scene can never be changed: "I told Molly we'd be ready for the Bad

Man but we can never be ready. Nothing is ever buried, the earth rolls in its tracks, it never goes anywhere, it never changes, only the hope changes like morning and night, only the expectations rise and set" (p. 179).

This character seems to take up where Haycox's heroes stop. They fret over the repetitiveness of their deeds for a time, but end in happy domesticity. Blue goes through that cycle and into the beginning of its second revolution. He concludes that any achievement of permanent harmony or elevation above this pattern of action is impossible, because these repetitions are endemic to the Western scene. This message from an impotent author is made the center of the obviously allegorical tale.

I have said that Owen Wister's two main aims were to unite West and East in his fiction, in order that the West could be seen to rejuvenate the East, and to create a fictional environment in which the spatial measurement was more important than the temporal one, so that his West would be immortalized. These designs are never quite articulated by Wister's hero; they are only hinted at by the author and the narrator. In James Leo Herlihy's *Midnight Cowboy*, the hero himself realizes the importance of these two goals.

Joe Buck believes, like Wister, that Western man has a special power to transmit to the East. But in Joe's case, the energy is purely sexual. Joe is a Texan who decides to dress up as a cowboy and go to New York City as a prostitute. He believes that he will make his fortune there because the cowboy's potency is unknown among degenerate Easterners. When Joe identifies the cowboy with sexual prowess, he is only exaggerating the animalism already hinted at in *The Virginian*. Wister's Eastern narrator first notices the Virginian when he lassoes a horse, "with the undulations of a tiger, smooth and easy, as if his muscles flowed beneath his skin" (p. 2). When Joe reaches Manhattan, his "hand moved to his crotch, and under his breath he said, 'I'm gonna take hold o' this thing and I'm gonna swing it like a lasso and I'm gonna rope in this whole fuckin' island.' "[11]

Joe caricatures other features of the Adamic Westerner. Where the Virginian is untutored, but naturally moral and wise, Joe is naive, gullible, and completely lacking in intellectual processes. Like the Virginian, Joe is a handsome dandy, but all Joe's power resides in his cowboy costume. Within it, the man is an empty shell who can think only when looking at himself, in his Western clothes, in a mirror.

In donning a cowboy costume, Joe hopes to gain control of time, as well as attract rich Eastern women. He first begins to see himself as a cowboy when he watches hundreds of television Westerns as a boy. In fact, in the course of his addictive viewing, he begins to look like a cowboy. Without these televised images of himself, his existence becomes unbearable. He remembers, later, "a period in his childhood when the TV set had been out of order. Time had been an actual burden under which he was unable to move. It surrounded him like a solid mass through which movement was not only impossible but inconceivable" (p. 47). In other words, time canceled out space. When he boards a bus for New York, in his new cowboy suit, he intends to change his relationship to time:

> knowing and savoring something he had no words for about destiny: that there is a certain way of climbing inside of time that gives a man ownership of the world and everything in it, and when this takes place there is a kind of *click*, and from then on when you hear a jukebox, for instance, it plays only what you need to hear, and everything, even Greyhound buses, operate for your convenience—you walk into the station and you say, "What time's a bus to New York City?" and the man says, "Right away," . . . you *are* the schedule, and that bus *moves*. [Pp. 20–21]

There are other signs in the novel that power over time is a major indication of a character's potency. One of the book's evil geniuses is Perry, a pusher of drugs and sex. Joe watches one of Perry's victims plead with him in a kind of code, which ends, " '*Please*, I said, Perry.' No answer. 'I just want to ask you if you know what time it is, that's all' " (p. 56). Near the end, Joe is picked up by a homosexual who uses prostitutes to assert his own power and escape from his mother's dominance: "He was listing the aspects of New York that delighted him most.' . . . the utter and total privacy, the sort of, I don't know, madly forward thrust of everything; do you understand that? I mean, how shall I put it? My sense of *time* here is completely altered. . . . Time is a Colossus, and he's marching up Broadway!' " (p. 213)

All Joe's experiences in New York show him only the impotence of himself and the cowboy image in the degenerate Eastern city. He stumbles through nightmarish experiences in New York's seedy underworld, barely surviving with the guidance of his new Italian-American sidekick. One night, he attends a gathering organized by the MacAlbertson twins, and "this waiting time ended altogether" (p. 174). The theme of the party is spelled out on a sign: "IT'S LATER THAN YOU THINK" (p. 186). The climax comes with the declaration, "Time is run out on us. They ain't no more of it!" (p. 196) At the party, Joe meets a woman who recognizes that he is "pure symbol" (p. 191). With her, he fulfills his only successful act of prostitution and, immediately after orgasm, sees the MacAlbertsons in his mind: "in this brief clarity Joe Buck had a sense of knowing just who the children were: his own. His own offspring, born full-grown from this very night's union" (p. 204). In terms of Joe's cowboy ambitions, this is his most potent act, and from it issues, directly, a declaration of the destruction of time.

By this stage (in the novel and the myth), however, the cowboy's achievement of his goals—the transference of his power and the destruction of time—are barren acts. Very soon after this, Joe discards his Western outfit and heads south, on a new search for happiness and power. In making this move, he retraces the Virginian's steps backward; the Virginian comes from the South, and, more generally, there is something of the Southern gentleman in every chivalrous cowboy. Herlihy's world, and its hero, are travesties of Wister's. Joe is a caricature of the Virginian, but one who agrees with the Virginian's author on the crucial requirements of the cowboy image.

One development I traced in dime novels was the way in which the negotiation between author or publisher and audience came to be acknowledged in the fiction through characters' direct comments. An author like Ellis causes his characters to recognize their roles in ritualistic adventure stories, while a Wheeler character can realize the commercialism of his existence. Robert Ward's *Cattle Annie and Little Britches* mentions the commercial contract only in passing, but it does develop the fiction of the character who reads, writes, and acts out dime novels into a full-blown subject. His heroine's main goal in acting out Western adventures, and the main cause of her downfall, is her desire to appear in a dime novel.

At the beginning of the novel, Cattle Annie and Little Britches set out to act their way into a dime novel. Annie says, "Don't you want some adventure? Riding the purple plains . . . running down vast shipments of gold on speeding trains? . . . Fighting off posses and stealing out of town in the dead of night."[12] They decide to join up with those already featured in dime fiction. Little Britches, who is the narrator, imagines the characters they will meet:

> The Doolin-Dalton Gang! Annie had been reading me stories about that bunch for a month and a half, all those good books by Ned Buntline. Whenever we had a break at Morgan's Hash House, she would get out the books, and start acting out the Gang's latest adventures . . . we would meet them, and we would *dance* with them . . . with Bill Doolin, Bill Dalton, Bittercreek Newcomb, that big handsome half-breed I'd half fallen for just from the pictures in Ned Buntline's books. [P. 11]

When they meet up with the gang, the action becomes increasingly identified with that in a dime novel. The outlaws turn out to conform to Buntline's description almost exactly. Annie and Little Britches themselves look very like Arietta in Wild West Weekly: they are fifteen-year-old horsewomen with long rippling hair, and they carry guns. Little Britches realizes, "I guess I felt jes like a character in one of Annie's books . . . and that was the beginning of the whole damned crazy thing" (p. 31). Annie shows the outlaws the books in which they appear, with their garish covers and cameo portraits. She coaches them in how to behave by quoting Buntline's descriptions to them whenever they fail to live up to their novelistic images.

Annie becomes increasingly immersed in her role as a dime novel heroine. When conditions become dangerous for the gang, and Little Britches wants them to disband, Annie opposes this plan, because she is intent on her goal to appear in a novel. Little Britches accuses her, " 'All you see, Annie, is a goddamned dime novel,' I said. 'A dime novel with you on the cover' " (p. 208). In fact, Annie is already inhabiting a fictional world. When Little Britches asks her, "Do you love Bill Dalton? . . . Is it him you are talking about or them dime store romances?" Annie explains, "It's one and the same. . . . You see the real Bill Dalton is the dream guy from the books" (pp. 218–19). Annie believes that even stories which are not factually correct, like a tale they hear about Jesse James, are true: "It'll be true as long as people got money to spend and stories to tell" (p. 222). She even plans her death so that it will make spectacular reading.

Because of Annie's determination that the gang continue their dramatic activities, all the men are caught and killed. Now they become increasingly fictionalized in the narrator's mind: "It was as if they were figures from some book I had once read. Even the character Little Britches was nothing more than someone I had heard about in the papers" (p. 240). And she and Annie become fictionalized in another way, in the fanciful newspaper reports of their exploits and the imaginings of the crowds who turn out to cheer them: "we had somehow become the very heroes Annie had imagined we would" (p. 241).

Little Britches develops more as a dime novel author than a character. At first, she and Annie write their own novels, by turning their deeds into literary material in the moment of acting them out. Others in the book join in the fantasy:

> Now the whole damned thing was really speeding up fer me. A change come over my voice . . . in fact, it didn't sound like my voice at all to me but the voice I woulda imagined it being if Ned Buntline was writing about me. I could hear his words:
>
>> Little Britches barked her commands at the terrified gamblers. Her soft child's voice had given way to a sharp metallic growl which sounded like a curse. After the robbery, those present said she was more terrifying than any of the older men.
>
> It might sound a little corny now, but that's how it was . . . I could feel it happening to me. The fever of being an outlaw was surging through me and what's more, it seemed to be a fever which spread to our victims as well. For as Bill Dalton went down a row of men with his hat in his hand, collecting their wallets, the last man on the line dropped in his cash, then produced a copy of *The Amazing Exploits of the Doolin-Dalton Gang* and a pen.
>
> "Please, sir," he said. "I want your autograph."
>
> Dalton promptly obliged him, and we began backing out. [P. 152]

Later, Little Britches becomes a "real" author: a fictional appendix by a schoolmistress tells us that Little Britches has sent her a manuscript, entitled *Cattle Annie and Little Britches*, explaining, "All the while we was with the Gang, Annie kept dreaming of the day Ned Buntline would do a book about us along the lines of *The Amazing Exploits of the Doolin-Dalton Gang*. It never occurred to either one of us that it might be me. . . . Perhaps, someday, I will even find a publisher for my book" (p. 249).

Little Britches also hints at the outermost layer of this whole design— that is, Robert Ward's book. She says, "It was like up till then we was actors in somebody else's book. Whose? Ned Buntline's maybe. But I had a feeling that even Ned Buntline wasn't to blame exactly. Because he was only borrowing something that was floating around" (p. 215). This layer is as fictional as all the rest. Although the novel is ostensibly based on real figures, its treatment of them is as fictional as any dime novel's. Furthermore, the Buntline novel which Annie imitates and reads from is purely Ward's invention: Buntline died five years before the Doolin-Dalton gang came into existence.

These layers upon layers of fictions, all centering on characters who know that they have appeared in books and expect to appear in more, are a more elaborate version of the narrative devices of Edward Ellis or Edward Wheeler. But while self-reflexive comments in the dime novelists' work remain somewhat ambiguous, here, characters' lengthy discussions about their treatment in dime novels provide the main theme of the novel.

It is not surprising that the Western should be parodied in the 1960s, along with all the other popular forms which were subverted during this period. Nor is it strange that the formula should be revived repeatedly, in this way, after each dismantling of it: the process fits exactly with Raymond Olderman's explanation that the new romance of sixties' America has "secret yearnings toward the comic book hero's control over human events."[13] Clearly, there is nothing unusual about characters discussing authors and fictions, heroes who are two-dimensional dummies in reificatory costumes, or impotent narrators who try to control events with language, in the post-1960 novel. That these conventions should be applied to the material of the Western formula means that, for the first time since Fenimore Cooper, characters, plots, and scenes from popular Western fiction have entered into the mainstream of American literature. The formula has been revived, with a new significance, in the new context of the anti-Western Western. What is interesting to me is that the results are not altogether unprecedented. The process of fitting the formulaic material into the new context has brought to the surface some of the concerns of the self-conscious formulists from their hundred years of literary obscurity.

Conclusion

This book reads popular Western fiction in a new way, revealing a dynamic of tension and forced creativity which hitherto has gone unremarked. The major treatments of formulaic Western fiction consider it as a collective product, written by more-or-less homogeneous image makers who have responded to different historical climates in etching the stereotyped Western deep into the popular imagination. Smaller-scale essays tend to examine the contents of specific writers' works, stressing the literary or cultural contributions of their plots and images. This study argues that the formal properties of individual authors' writings are important, because they tell distinctive stories about different authors' responses to their own fiction. These responses often concern the limitations of formulaic production, and they are perceptible in the literature as individual commentaries which run in counterpoint to the predictable plots.

What I have discussed here are authorial rebellions of different orders, against a variety of forces. The only completely successful rebellion against formulaic requirements occurs outside the realm of commercial publishing, at the hands of the sixties' and seventies' anti-Western writers. Working under different conditions from the formulists, with different literary notions and a different audience in mind, these novelists create a new literary genre by debunking the rituals which hold sway in thousands of popular Westerns.

Among the conventional authors, there is one major attempt at using the formula subversively, when Owen Wister, Frederic Remington, and Emerson Hough try to oppose the course of history. They employ conventional Western types and events, but rearrange the stock elements in order to deny the changes to the West which these authors themselves witnessed. The doomed nature of their attempt to reverse, symbolically, the dying out of the heroic West is indicated by the details of their fictions. Repeatedly, textual discordances undermine apparently harmonious developments in their plots and betray that this rebellion is not entirely successful.

Then there are those authors who adhere to some of the formula's requirements, but do not routinely accept the assumptions at the heart of the genre's survival. Alan Le May and Jack Schaefer both produce recognizably traditional Westerns, but they write into them commentaries on the weaknesses of the genre. Le May's works hint at the shallowness of the rigid formula, by emphasizing the mechanical ritualism with which the Western perpetuates itself endlessly. Schaefer aims not to falsify experience in his fiction, and his writings expose the fraudulence in the formula's pretense that the wild West constantly regenerates itself.

At a less defiant level again, Grey, Faust, and Haycox produce formulaic fictions for profitable returns, but rebel against the repetitiveness of their positions, according to conventional notions of artistry. They mount this qualified rebellion by tinkering with their narrative techniques, implanting in their stereotyped works hints of their aspirations toward autonomy, subtlety, and literary progress. These limited inventions never lead them away from the Western formula nor free them from the restraining supervision of commercial publishers. Nevertheless, they do create the illusion, at least temporarily, that these formulists have elevated themselves above the exigencies of the marketplace which affords them their living.

Finally, there are the out-and-out hacks who do not rebel against the commercialism of their task, but actively incorporate the methods of salesmanship into their Western fiction. Thus, the early dime novelists use the language of commerce to talk directly to their audience, the later dime novelists introduce the machinery of mass production into their fictional images of the wild West, and in the twentieth century Louis L'Amour constructs within his novels a selling apparatus designed to help his work compete successfully with other cheap publications. The precariousness of these strategies is indicated by their gradual suppression over the years. Although these writers' narrative methods arise out of the practices of mass production, they do not flourish with them. On the contrary: the more sophisticated and aggressive merchandising techniques become, the more covert and oblique is the authorial rhetoric.

In terms of conventional literary standards, the success of all these formulists' rebellions is severely limited. If these writers' artistry is evaluated according to their achievement of authorial individuality, they all clearly fail in some way. None of them ever completely escapes the constraints of formulaic production and none produces first-rate work of original conception or masterly execution. This failure may well have something to do with the genre's history: proliferating at the time when assembly-line techniques were invented, the Western was imbued with the mechanism of those devices. But there are some authors who succeed more than others in doing something distinctive in their writing. The most artistically successful authors are those who seem to identify the main characteristics of the formula and exploit them to demonstrate the potentialities or limitations of the genre. This practice can amount to Wister and Remington trying to show how the illusions in the Western can defy historical reality or Le May and Schaefer revealing that the Western's survival depends on a distinct set of conventions. Either way, these four authors attempt quite subtle literary effects and make unique contributions to the genre. In contrast, the writers who try to sneak an element of artistry into predominantly formulaic work or who embrace the practices of mass publishing suffer a very different fate. Ultimately, they find their individual narrative voices and their freedom to make autonomous artistic decisions disappearing beneath the weight of the commercial machinery to which they subscribe.

But what of the audience's response to these formulaic works? One thing is clear: my ordering of the works according to conventional notions of literary merit is almost entirely reversed when the yardstick is popularity. True, Wister's *Virginian* did sell a million copies in eighteen years and Schaefer's *Shane* has been a steady seller since it appeared.[1] However, these authors' figures are modest in comparison to the sales of L'Amour, Grey, or Faust, and none of Wister's or Schaefer's other works sold as well as these two novels. Similarly, neither Remington nor Le May ever produced a bestseller. Again and again, the reading public has failed to respond in largest numbers to those works which subvert the Western formula. In this respect, the readers themselves are versions of Walter Benjamin's hacks, refusing to rebel or respond to rebellion against the commercial practice of repetition and conformity. Consistently, the reading public has preferred those works which do not disrupt the formulaic outline. The dime novelists, Grey, Faust, and Haycox have all had massive sales of their collective writings, and Grey and Faust have produced several individual best-selling titles. Of all Western formulists, the most appreciated has been the reliable Louis L'Amour: not only have his sales outstripped all other Western authors', but in 1983 he was the first novelist to receive a congressional gold medal, and in 1984 he was awarded the Presidential Medal of Freedom.[2]

Given that the audience's perspective on these authors seems to be so different from the literary critic's, any comments on readers' responses to authorial rhetoric must remain speculative. However, there does appear to be a correspondence between the kinds of narrative gestures I have identified and the preferences shown by readers. Consumers of formulaic literature seem to enjoy being reminded of the workings of the marketplace, either by the dime novelists' overtures, or by the paraphernalia of the pulp magazines, or by L'Amour's asides. This preference is indicated partly by circulation figures: besides the dime novelists' and L'Amour's massive sales, there is the fact that the writings of Grey, Faust, and Haycox sold in much larger numbers when they were published in the blatantly commercial magazines than when they appeared as books.[3] Further evidence of the audience's interest in production details is provided by Robert Warshow in "Paul, the Horror Comics, and Dr. Wertham." In this essay, he describes his son's fascination with the details of the publishing house and its staff who produce the magazines he reads voraciously every week. Warshow speculates:

> I think that Paul's desire to put himself directly in touch with the processes by which the comic books are produced may be the expression of a fundamental detachment which helps to protect him from them; the comic books are not a "universe" to him, but simply objects produced for his entertainment.[4]

Although Warshow is here discussing comic books for a juvenile audience, his comments seem applicable to the Western, too, with its mixture of young and old readers. After all, the Western pulp magazine contributed a great deal to the pedigree of the comic book, in terms of story lines and images of heroism, and the fantasies perpetrated by both are very similar. Whatever the precise reasons or proofs, it is clear that the relationship between formulaic fiction and its audience is not a simple one. Readers seem to find complexity and interest not so much in variations or disruptions of the formula as in their maintenance of a double vision: simultaneously, they follow the formulaic plot and the workings behind its production.

From the detailed evidence presented in this book plus these speculations about the reading public, it is possible to construct a hypothesis about the interaction between best-selling authors and their audience. Some authors who become very popular through the repetition of a successful formula seem to try to escape from the monotony of their production, either by turning to self-reflexive discussion of the details of their task, or by creating evidence of artistic development which protects their own sense of their literary status. By exposing some of the thinking behind formulaic production, they seem to hit on the very mixture of fictional illusion and mechanical reality which appeals to regular readers of popular literature. This hypothesis implies that the responses of authors and audience run along parallel lines: both appear to sustain their enthusiasm for formulaic fiction by interesting themselves in the circumstances of its production.

The main import of my discussion is that creating formulaic literature is not an automatic or a neutral task. Again and again, the most famous Western authors try to inject something of their own visions into the formulaic design by developing individual methods of presenting their material. This attempt always involves some kind of rebellion against an established pattern. Most often, the popular author struggles to profit from the formula demanded by commercial publishers while simultaneously imprinting his individuality on his text. Occasionally, however, an author seeks to create in his fictional form an alternative to the pattern of Western history itself. In either case, the friction which results from individual initiatives being applied to conventional material is the real locus of creativity and development in the formulaic Western story.

Notes

INTRODUCTION

1. Henry Nash Smith, *Virgin Land* (Cambridge, Mass.: Harvard University Press, 1950), p. 64; John G. Cawelti, *Adventure, Mystery, and Romance* (Chicago: The University of Chicago Press, 1976), p. 206; Richard Slotkin, *Regeneration through Violence* (Middletown, Conn.: Wesleyan University Press, 1973), pp. 467–68.

2. Cawelti discusses his theories of formulaic production and the features of the Western in *Adventure* and in *The Six-Gun Mystique* (Bowling Green, Ohio: Bowling Green University Popular Press, 1971).

3. Two works which follow from Smith and Cawelti are Daryl Jones, *The Dime Novel Western* (Bowling Green, Ohio: Bowling Green University Popular Press, 1978) and Russel Nye, *The Unembarrassed Muse* (New York: The Dial Press, 1970).

4. Philip Durham, in the introduction to *"Seth Jones" Edward S. Ellis and "Deadwood Dick on Deck" Edward L. Wheeler* (New York: Odyssey, 1966), p. v, says that more than half of Beadle & Adams's 3,158 dime novels concerned life in the trans-Mississippi West; Nye, *Unembarrassed Muse*, p. 210, records that the most popular kind of pulp magazine in the 1930s was the Western; and Clarence Petersen, *The Bantam Story*, 2nd ed. (New York: Bantam, 1975), p. 14, notes that in the 1940s Westerns were the strongest category of paperback publication.

5. Paul S. Nathan, "Books into Films," *Publishers' Weekly*, 19 April 1947, p. 2130, quotes the story editor of Universal-International: "Mr. Poling described the story conference as a 'literary striptease' in which a book, reduced to bare outline, stands or falls on its narrative values. . . . producers . . . select material on the basis of simple plot interest, since it is the main plot which gets carried over to the screen."

6. Ron Chernow describes the "committee method" in "John Ford: The Last Frontiersman," *Ramparts*, vol. 12 (April 1974), p. 46.

7. This is not to suggest that the market never affected the pre-1860 novelist. Wayne Franklin shows, for example, that Cooper could discuss his novels as commodities. *The New World of James Fenimore Cooper* (Chicago: University of Chicago Press, 1982), p. 84. However, the commercial aspect was not the main stimulus for Cooper's writing and, Franklin argues, it did not inform his literary technique. The opposite is true of the dime novelists.

ONE: THE VOICE OF THE FICTION FACTORY IN DIME AND PULP WESTERNS

1. "The Author as Producer," in *Understanding Brecht*, trans. Anna Bostock (London: New Left Books, 1973), p. 94.

2. In this history of dime novels, I synthesize information from Albert Johannsen, *The House of Beadle and Adams and its Dime and Nickel Novels*, 2 vols. and supplement (Norman: University of Oklahoma Press, 1950, 1962); Quentin Reynolds, *The Fiction Factory* (New York: Random House, 1955); Madeleine B. Stern, ed., *Publishers for Mass Entertainment in Nineteenth Century America* (Boston: G.K. Hall, 1980); and various articles in *Reckless Ralph's Dime Novel Round-Up* (first published in 1931 and renamed *Dime Novel Round-Up* in 1953).

3. Johannsen, *Beadle and Adams*, vol. 1, p. 9.

4. Ibid., pp. 5, 8.

5. Ibid., vol. 2, pp. 295–96; supplement, p. 40.

6. Ibid., vol. 1, p. 4.

7. Ibid., vol. 1, p. 32.

8. *Frank Merriwell's "Father"*, ed. Harriet Hinsdale (Norman: University of Oklahoma Press, 1964), p. 104. This authorial freedom contrasts with Patten's later experience of dime publishers: Norman L. Munro supplied him with story outlines, and Street and Smith gave him specific instructions on plots and characters (see below).

9. John Milton Edwards [William Wallace Cook], *The Fiction Factory* (Ridgewood, N.J.: The Editor Company, 1912), p. 82.

10. Reynolds, *Fiction Factory*, p. 114. Street and Smith also paid their authors less than Beadle and Adams: William Wallace Cook records that in 1910 they paid him $60 for 35,000 words; by dint of great output he could still live on this (Edwards, *Fiction Factory*, p. 118).

11. Reynolds, *Fiction Factory*, pp. 66–67.

12. Ibid., pp. 88–89.

13. Patten, *Frank Merriwell's "Father*," pp. 238, 242–43.

14. Ralph P. Smith, "Barred by the Post Office," *Reckless Ralph's Dime Novel Round-Up*, vol. 13 (October 1944), pp. 1–3.

15. Tony Goodstone, ed., *The Pulps* (New York: Chelsea House, 1970), p. ix; Ron Goulart, *Cheap Thrills* (New Rochelle, N.Y.: Arlington House, 1972), p. 10.

16. Harold Brainerd Hersey, *Pulpwood Editor* (1937; reprint ed., Westport, Conn.: Greenwood Press, 1974), pp. 23–29.

17. Theodore Peterson, *Magazines in the Twentieth Century* (Urbana: The University of Illinois Press, 1956), p. 22; James Playsted Wood, *The Story of Advertising* (New York: The Ronald Press Co., 1958), p. 243.

18. John A. Dinan, *The Pulp Western* (San Bernardino, Calif.: The Borgo Press, 1983), pp. 68–69.

19. Payment rates are provided by Hersey, *Pulpwood Editor*, p. 29; and Frank Gruber, *The Pulp Jungle* (Los Angeles: Sherbourne Press, 1967), pp. 23, 73. Gruber adds that in thirties' America, pulp writing was considered lucrative employment. The comments by the pulp contributor and artist appear in Dinan, pp. 21, 110.

20. Gruber, *Pulp Jungle*, p. 137.

21. Personal interview with Henry Steeger, 4 June 1981; letter to the author from Alden H. Norton, 11 September 1981.

22. Hersey, *Pulpwood Editor*, p. 122.

23. "The Golden Age of the Iron Maiden," *The Roundup*, April 1975, pp. 7–9.

24. *Seth Jones; or, The Captives of the Frontier*, Beadle's American Library, No. 1 (1860; reprint ed., London: Beadle, 1861), p. 94.

25. *Buffalo Bill, the King of Border Men!* in *Street & Smith's New York Weekly*, 17 February 1870, p. 5.

26. *Deadwood Dick, the Prince of the Road; or, The Black Rider of the Black Hills*, The Deadwood Dick Library, vol. 1, no. 1 (1877; reprint ed., Cleveland: Arthur Westbrook, 1899), pp. 4, 7.

27. For example, J. Edward Leithead, "John H. Whitson, Street & Smith Author," *Reckless Ralph's*, vol. 6 (December 1937), p. 1; "The Creator of Diamond Dick," *Dime Novel Round-Up*, vol. 29 (August 1960), pp. 66–68; W.C. Miller, "The First Diamond Dick Story," *Reckless Ralph's*, vol. 6 (June 1937), pp. 2–3.

28. A Old Scout, *Young Wild West; The Prince of the Saddle*, Wild West Weekly, no. 1 (New York: Frank Tousey, 1902), p. 5.

29. Ned Taylor, *The Young Rough Riders in the Rockies; or, A Fight in Midair*, Young Rough Riders Weekly, no. 38 (New York: Street & Smith, 1905), p. 1.

30. *Ted Strong's Rough Riders; or, The Boys of Black Mountain*, The Young Rough Riders Weekly, no. 1 (New York: Street & Smith, 1904), p. 13.

31. Cawelti, *Six-Gun*, p. 32.

32. "Dime-Novel Writers: An Hour's Chat with One of Them," *Republican*, 21 April 1884, n. pg.

33. *Dime Novels: A Defense by a Writer of Them* (1884; reprint ed., Philadelphia: Chas. H. Austin, 1938), n. pg.

34. *T.C. Harbaugh, Popular and Prolific Beadle Writer, Corrects Wrong Impression of Dime Novels and their Authors* (1894; reprint ed., Philadelphia: Chas. H. Austin, 1938), n. pg.

35. Edwards, *Fiction Factory*, p. 26.

36. William Wallace Cook, "Reference Book," in *Plotto* (Battle Creek, Mich.: Ellis Publishing Company, 1928), n. pg.

37. Cook, "Sixth Lesson" and "Seventh Lesson," in *Plotto*, n. pg.

38. Edwards, *Fiction Factory*, p. 164.

39. "Panic in the Pulps Launched WWA," *The Roundup*, May 1977, p. 1.

40. *War-Eagle; or, Issiniwa the Indian Brave*, De Witt's Ten Cent Romances, no. 42 (New York: Robert M. De Witt, 1869), p. 59.

41. *Saul Sabberday, the Idiot Spy; or, Luliona, the Seminole*, Beadle's Dime Library, vol. 10, no. 122 (1858; reprint ed., New York: Beadle & Adams, 1881), p. 24.

42. *The White Wizard; or, The Great Prophet of the Seminoles*, Beadle's Dime Library, vol. 2, no. 16 (1858; reprint ed., New York: Beadle & Adams, 1879), p. 16.

43. *The Red Revenger; or, The Pirate King of the Floridas*, The Novelette, no. 5 (Boston: Ballou, n.d.), pp. 31, 37, 38.

44. *Buffalo Bill, the King of Border Men!* in *Street & Smiths' New York Weekly*, 10 March 1870, p. 2.

45. *Buffalo Bill's Last Victory; or, Dove Eye, the Lodge Queen*, Sea and Shore Series, no. 24 (1883; reprint ed., New York: Street & Smith, 1890), p. 7.

46. *The Phantom Horseman; or, The Mad Hunter of the Mohawk*, Beadle's New Dime Novels, no. 390 (New York: Beadle & Adams, 1869), p. 23.

47. *The Rangers of the Mohawk*, Beadle's Dime Novels, no. 64 (New York: Beadle & Co., 1864), p. 69.

48. *The Mystic Canoe*, Beadle's Dime Novels, no. 82 (New York: Beadle, 1865), p. 94.

49. *The Lost Trail*, Beadle's Dime Novels, no. 71 (New York: Beadle, 1864), pp. 51–52.

50. *Oregon Sol; or, Nick Whiffle's Boy Spy*, Beadle's Pocket Library, vol. 2, no. 17 (1873; reprint ed., New York: Beadle & Adams, 1884), p. 28.

51. *Old Zip; or, The Cabin in the Air*, Beadle's New Dime Novels, no. 152 (New York: Beadle & Adams, 1871), p. 52.

52. *Oonomoo, the Huron*, Beadle's American Library, no. 25 (1862; reprint ed., London: Beadle, 1863), p. 19. This was twenty years before Mark Twain opened *The Adventures of Huckleberry Finn* with "You don't know about me, without you have read a book by the name of 'The Adventures of Tom Sawyer'. . . ." (Johannsen, Beadle and Adams, vol. 1, pp. 9–11, shows that Twain read Beadle dime novels.)

53. *Nathan Todd; or, The Fate of the Sioux Captive*, Beadle's American Library, no. 9 (1861; reprint ed., London: Beadle, 1861), p. 64.

54. *The Riflemen of the Miami*, Beadle's American Library, no. 18 (1862; reprint ed., London: Beadle, 1862), p. 92.

55. *Captain Crimson, the Man of the Iron Face; or, The Nemesis of the Plains*, Beadle's Dime Library, vol. 11, no. 142 (New York: Beadle & Adams, 1881), p. 17; *Wild Bill, the Pistol Dead Shot; or, Dagger Don's Double*, Beadle's Dime Library, vol. 13, no. 168 (New York: Beadle & Adams, 1882), p. 11.

56. *The Cowboy Clan; or, The Tigress of Texas*, Beadle's Dime Library, vol. 51, no. 658 (New York: Beadle & Adams, 1891), p. 17.

57. *Grit, the Bravo Sport; or, The Woman Trailer*, Beadle's Half Dime Library, vol. 9, no. 222 (New York: Beadle & Adams, 1881), p. 11. Bill Cody adopted this diagrammatic image in his own writing: when he wrote to Orville J. Victor, editor at Beadle and Adams, he said, "I wish to offer my expressions of sincere regret that you are now leaving the Literary Trails over which you have been the able Guide. . . . In every respect your advice has been valuable over the Pen Trails I have followed in my claim to authorship" (Letter to Victor, 27 April 1897, folder 11, Erastus F. Beadle Papers, New York Public Library).

58. *Buffalo Bill's Redskin Ruse; or, Texas Jack's Death-Shot*, Beadle's Dime Library, vol. 65, no. 845 (New York: Beadle & Adams, 1895), p. 10.

59. *Buck Taylor, King of the Cowboys; or, The Raiders and the Rangers*, Beadle's Half Dime Library, vol. 20, no. 497 (New York: Beadle & Adams, 1887), pp. 9, 13, 14.

60. After Beadle and Adams folded, Street and Smith took over Buffalo Bill fiction in 1901 and managed, after much persuasion, to hire Ingraham—see J. Edward Leithead, "Colonel Prentiss Ingraham," *Dime Novel Round-Up*, vol. 32 (January 1964), pp. 2–6. They liked best the dime novelist who most obviously presented adventure as a type of play. This firm, of course, created the most famous sports heroes of cheap fiction and turned many of their Rough Rider Westerns into stories about competitive games.

61. *Deadwood Dick, the Prince of the Road*, p. 6; *Buffalo Ben, the Prince of the Pistol; or, Deadwood Dick in Disguise*, The Deadwood Dick Library, vol. 1, no. 4 (1877; reprint ed., Cleveland: Arthur Westbrook, 1899), p. 4; *Omaha Oll, the Masked Terror; or, Deadwood Dick in Danger*, The Deadwood Dick Library, vol. 1, no. 10 (1878; reprint ed., Cleveland: Arthur Westbrook, 1899), p. 5.

62. *Deadwood Dick as Detective*, The Deadwood Dick Library, vol. 2, no. 24 (1879; reprint ed., Cleveland: Arthur Westbrook, 1899), p. 26.

63. *Deadwood Dick's Dream; or, The Rivals of the Road*, Beadle's Half Dime Library, vol. 8, no. 195 (New York: Beadle & Adams, 1881), p. 14.

64. *Corduroy Charlie, the Boy Bravo; or, Deadwood Dick's Last Act*, The Deadwood Dick Library, vol. 2, no. 16 (1879; reprint ed., Cleveland; Arthur Westbrook, 1899), p. 13.

65. *The Phantom Miner; or, Deadwood Dick's Bonanza*, The Deadwood Dick Library, vol. 1, no. 7 (1878; reprint ed., Cleveland: Arthur Westbrook, 1899), p. 17.

66. *The Young Rough Rider's Girl Guide; or, The Maid of the Mountains*, Young Rough Riders Weekly, no. 38 (New York: Street & Smith, 1905), p. 1.

67. *Ted Strong, King of the Wild West; or, Winning a Town by a Ride*, Rough Rider Weekly, no. 79 (New York: Street & Smith, 1905), pp. 2, 12.

68. The authors of the Rough Riders stories are listed in J. Edward Leithead, "Rough Rider Weekly and the Ted Strong Saga," *Dime Novel Round-Up*, vol. 40 (July 1972), pp. 1–28.

69. *The Young Rough Rider's Indian Trail; or, Okanaga the Cheyenne*, Young Rough Riders Weekly, no. 41 (New York: Street & Smith, 1905), p. 3.

70. *King of the Wild West's Wild Goose Band; or, Stella's Long Flight on Skees*, Rough Rider Weekly, no. 119 (New York: Street & Smith, 1906), p. 25.

71. *The Young Rough Riders in Kansas; or, The Trail of the Outlaw*, Young Rough Riders Weekly, no. 37 (New York: Street & Smith, 1904), p. 28.

72. Rough Rider Weekly, no. 94 (New York: Street & Smith, 1906), n. pg.

73. "A Chat with You," Rough Rider Weekly, no. 146 (New York: Street & Smith, 1907), p. 31.

74. "A Chat with You," Rough Rider Weekly, no. 106 (New York: Street & Smith, 1906), p. 28.

75. The stages of Rough Rider's decline and its battle with Wild West are discussed in J. Edward Leithead, "Ted Strong and his Rough Riders," *Dime Novel Round-Up*, vol. 29 (June 1961), pp. 66–71 and (July 1961), pp. 76–81. Rough Rider was never copied; its assertions about second-class imitations were strategic attacks on its competitor.

76. It is impossible to ascertain the authenticity of all the readers' letters. Certainly, Street and Smith did not concoct them all: the authors of some letters in another Street and Smith series have been identified in J.P. Guinon, "The Applause Column in Tip Top Weekly," *Dime Novel Round-Up*, vol. 28 (January 1960), pp. 2–5. There are many letters which give opinions on the contents of Rough Rider, all of them identified with a reader's name, a town, and a state. Quite a few elicit clear responses in terms of changes in the story. Whether or not these specific letters are authentic, the important point is that the publishers felt they had to be seen to be ordering their authors to follow the dictates of their readers.

77. *King of the Wild West Underground; or, Stella to the Rescue*, Rough Rider Weekly, no. 106 (New York: Street & Smith, 1906), p. 17.

78. *King of the Wild West's Buckskin Guide; or, Stella at the Grand Round-Up*, Rough Rider Weekly, no. 125 (New York: Street & Smith, 1906), p. 10.

79. "A Chat with You," Rough Rider Weekly, no. 130 (New York: Street & Smith, 1906), p. 30.

80. "A Chat with You," Rough Rider Weekly, no. 132 (New York: Street & Smith, 1906), p. 29.

81. "A Chat with You," Rough Rider Weekly, no. 140 (New York: Street & Smith, 1906), p. 30.

82. "The Wranglers' Corner," *Wild West Weekly*, 13 August 1927, p. 95.

83. Some pulps, such as *Western Story Magazine*, did promote certain best-selling writers, like Max Brand, as stars of the pulp magazines. However, these cases were relatively rare and they concerned authors for whom pulp publication was only the preliminary to book publication, not the sole market for their writing. I discuss this category of pulp author in chapter three.

84. "A Chat with You," *The Popular Magazine*, February 1905, n. pg.

85. "Western Story Announces the Winners of the November 3rd Advertising Prize Contest," *Western Story Magazine*, 2 February 1924, p. 144.

86. "Notice," *Far West*, September 1978, n. pg.

87. The editor was Charles Agnew MacLean, who also edited *The Popular Magazine*. He is quoted in Mabel Cooper Skjelver, "William Wallace Cook—The Marshall Years," *Dime Novel Round-Up*, vol. 45 (April, 1976), p. 52.

TWO: THE WESTERN FORMULA AND THE DISAPPEARING FRONTIER

1. I have culled my biographical information on Wister and Remington from Richard W. Etulain, *Owen Wister*, Western Writers Series, no. 7 (Boise: Boise State College, 1973); Peggy and Harold Samuels, *Frederic Remington* (Garden City, N.Y.: Doubleday, 1982); Ben Merchant Vorpahl, *My Dear Wister* (Palo Alto: American West Publishing Co., 1972); and G. Edward White, *The Eastern Establishment and the Western Experience* (New Haven: Yale University Press, 1968).

2. "A Few Words from Mr. Remington," *Collier's*, 18 March 1905, p. 16.

3. Owen Wister, *Roosevelt* (New York: Macmillan, 1930), p. 29.

4. Frank Luther Mott, *A History of American Magazines*, vol. 2 (Cambridge: Harvard University Press, 1938), p. 391. My information on these magazines comes from Mott and from James Playsted Wood, *Magazines in the United States*, 2nd ed. (New York: The Ronald Press, 1956).

5. Samuels, *Remington*, p. 158.

6. Ibid., pp. 331, 345.

7. For example, Cawelti, *Six-Gun*, p. 80; Wallace Stegner, "Foreword," *My Dear Wister*, pp. ix–xii.

8. Owen Wister's notebook, 8 July 1885, TS, pp. 5–6. Wister's journals are in box 3 of the Owen Wister Collection, Western History Research Center, University of Wyoming.

9. Owen Wister's notebook, 21 July 1885, p. 8.

10. Wister, *Roosevelt*, p. 29.

11. "Hank's Woman," *Harper's Weekly*, 27 August 1892, p. 822.

12. *The Virginian* (New York: Macmillan, 1902), p. 3.

13. "At the Sign of the Last Chance," in *When West Was West* (London: MacMillan, 1928), p. 413.

14. Quoted in Vorpahl, *My Dear Wister*, p. 287.

15. Vorpahl, *My Dear Wister*, pp. 155–81, 288–322.

16. *John Ermine of the Yellowstone* (New York: Macmillan, 1902), p. 246.

17. *Sundown Leflare* (New York: Harper, 1899), p. 3.

18. Peggy and Harold Samuels, eds., "Notes," *The Collected Writings of Frederic Remington* (Garden City, N.Y.: Doubleday, 1979), pp. 625–26 suggests that the dating of *The Way of an Indian* is problematical. However, the Samuelses never definitely prove that this work precedes *John Ermine*.

19. *The Way of an Indian* (London: Gay & Bird, 1906), pp. 222–23.

20. Smith, *Virgin Land*, p. 61.

21. Samuels, *Remington*, p. 349.

22. Wister wrote this verse in his diary just as he was ending a hunting trip in Wyoming (Owen Wister's journal, 19 November 1889, p. 6).

23. Samuels, *Remington*, p. 395.

24. Estelle Jussim, *Frederic Remington, The Camera and the Old West* (Fort Worth: Amon Carter Museum, 1983).

25. Samuels, *Remington*, p. 232.

26. Datings for Remington's works vary. I follow those established by museums holding Remington works.

27. These configurations are much less pronounced in Remington's paintings of Indians than in his depiction of white men; presumably the difference says something about his perception of the Indians' place in the Western landscape.

28. It is suggestive of a more general artistic response to the West that Daniel Peck traces the same patterns in Cooper's verbal descriptions of landscape (*A World by Itself*, New Haven: Yale University Press, 1977, pp. 57, 60).

29. *Pony Tracks* (Norman: University of Oklahoma Press, 1961), pp. 109–10.

30. *Crooked Trails* (New York: Harper, 1898), p. 52.

31. *The Jimmyjohn Boss and Other Stories* (New York: Harper, 1900), p. 88.

32. *Red Men and White* (New York: Grosset & Dunlap, 1895), p. 220.

33. "In the Back," in *Members of the Family* (New York: Macmillan, 1911), p. 89.

34. "The Evolution of the Cow-Puncher," *Harper's Monthly Magazine*, September 1895, p. 614.

35. "The Significance of the Frontier in American History," in *Annual Report of the American Historical Association for the Year 1893* (Washington, D.C.: GPO, 1894), p. 207.

36. *Lin McLean* (New York: A.L. Burt, 1897), p. 20.

37. The Samuelses identify the main members of this "school" as Charles Schreyvogel and Charles Marion Russell (*Remington*, pp. ix, 35, 300). Just one example of a film director imitating Remington is Howard Hawks's attempt to recreate Remington's visual effects in *El Dorado* (Richard Roud, review of *El Dorado*, *The Guardian*, 20 July 1967, p. 10).

38. The first remark is quoted in Samuels, *Remington*, p. 258; the second appears in Roosevelt's contribution to the Pamphlet for the Frederic Remington Monument Fund, 12 September 1910, n. pg., reel 94, Theodore Roosevelt Presidential Papers, Library of Congress; and the third appears in Theodore Roosevelt, letter to Owen Wister, 20 July 1901, reel 326, Presidential Papers.

39. Frank Atherton Ross, letter to Owen Wister, 3 May 1902, Owen Wister Papers, Library of Congress.

40. My biographical information on Hough comes from Delbert E. Wylder, *Emerson Hough*, Southwest Writers Series, no. 19 (Austin: Steck-Vaughan, 1969); and *Emerson Hough*, Twayne's United States Authors Series, No. 397 (Boston: Twayne, 1981).

41. Wylder, *Hough*, 1981, pp. 33, 35, 68.

42. *The Story of the Cowboy* (New York: Appleton, 1897), p. 8.

43. *Heart's Desire* (New York: Macmillan, 1905), p. 320.

44. *The Girl at the Halfway House* (New York: Appleton, 1900), p. 369.

45. *North of 36* (New York: Appleton, 1923), p. 77.

46. *The Covered Wagon* (New York: Appleton, 1922), pp. 376–77.

47. Cawelti, *Adventure*, p. 13; Robert Warshow, *The Immediate Experience* (Garden City, N.Y.: Doubleday, 1962), p. 130.

THREE: ESCAPING FROM THE PULPS

1. The figures for Faust's output vary. I follow those in Robert Easton, *Max Brand* (Norman: University of Oklahoma Press, 1970), p. 268. The figures for Grey's output were supplied by his son, Loren Grey, in a letter to the author, 6 April 1981. Haycox's works are enumerated in Richard Wayne Etulain, "The Literary Career of a Western Writer: Ernest Haycox, 1899–1950," dissertation, University of Oregon 1966, pp. 214–66. The information about Haycox's payment rates appears in Robert L. Gale, "Ernest Haycox," in *Fifty Western Writers*, ed. Richard W. Etulain and Fred Erisman (Westport, Conn.: Greenwood Press, 1982), p. 185.

2. Hersey, *Pulpwood Editor*, p. 23.

3. Ibid., p. 2.

4. My information on slick magazines comes mainly from Mott, *A History of American Magazines*, vol. 4 (Cambridge: Harvard University Press, 1957); Peterson, *Magazines in the Twentieth Century*; and Wood, *Magazines in the United States*.

5. Mott, *American Magazines*, vol.4, pp. 614, 586, 473, 549, 715; Peterson, *Magazines*, p. 59.

6. Mott, *American Magazines*, vol. 4; pp. 585–86; Peterson, *Magazines*, p. 18.; Wood, *Story of Advertising*, p. 413.

7. George Britt, *Forty Years—Forty Millions* (New York: Farrar & Rinehart, 1935), p. 100.

8. Frank Gruber, *Zane Grey* (New York: The World Publishing Co., 1970), p. 164.

9. This and other details of Grey's life and career are recorded in Frank Gruber, *Zane Grey*; Carlton Jackson, *Zane Grey*, Twayne's United States Authors Series, no. 218 (Boston: Twayne, 1973); and Jean Karr, *Zane Grey* (Surrey; The World's Work, 1951). Dates in the text for Grey's fiction refer to book publication, unless otherwise indicated.

10. Zane Grey, letter to Robert Davis, 19 March 1912, box 3, Robert Hobart Davis Papers, New York Public Library.

11. "The Log-Book," *The Argosy*, April 1915, p. 218; July 1915, p. 869; April 1915, p. 219; April 1915, p. 220.

12. "Contents," *McCall's Magazine*, November 1925, p. 1; *The Ladies' Home Journal*, December 1922, p. 196.

13. Joel Porte, *The Romance in America* (Middletown, Conn.: Wesleyan University Press, 1969), p. 39.

14. "The Western and the Contemporary," *Journal of American Studies*, vol. 6 (1972), pp. 97–108.

15. Joseph Campbell, *The Hero with a Thousand Faces* (New York: Pantheon, 1949), p. 30.

16. The phrases in capitals are Campbell's terms for the stages in the mythic journey.

17. *The Heritage of the Desert* (Roslyn, N. Y.: Walter J. Black, n.d.), p. 230.

18. *Wanderer of the Wasteland* (New York: Harper, 1923), p. 58.

19. *Horse Heaven Hill* (New York: Harper, 1959), p. 1.

20. Quoted in Jackson, *Zane Grey*, pp. 136–37.

21. E. M. Forster, *Aspects of the Novel* (London: Edward Arnold, 1927), p. 43.

22. *Wildfire* (New York: Harper, 1917), pp. 54–58.

23. Forster, *Aspects of the Novel*, pp. 116–17.

24. Grey's attempts to move from a simple to a more complex narrative brought a direct response from at least one of his readers. A letter in *The Saturday Review of Literature*, 28 February 1925, complains that "In 'Riders of the Purple Sage,' . . . there are more than fourteen instances where scenes of varying importance are related after the event. The characters are continually saying, 'Let's talk a while. . . . Tell me what happened. . . . Wal, now, jest let me talk. . . . You see it was this way. . . . ' That's not narrative power; that's easy writing" (p. 570).

25. This ending is in the manuscript version of the novel, published in "No-phaie's Redemption," in *Zane Grey's Indian Tales*, ed. Loren Grey (London: NEL, 1977), pp. 123–24.

26. *The Ladies' Home Journal*, April 1923, p. 235.

27. *The Vanishing American* (New York: Harper, 1925), p. 308.

28. By Edward H. Dodd, Jr., in "Twenty-five Million Words," *Publishers' Weekly*, 26 March 1938, p. 1359, according to Easton, *Max Brand*, pp. 203–4.

29. This and other details of Faust's career are recorded in Easton, *Max Brand*; and in William Bloodworth, "Max Brand," in *Fifty Western Writers*, pp. 32–41.

30. S. Allen McElfresh and Darrell C. Richardson, "Max Brand and the Western Story," in *Max Brand*, ed. Darrell C. Richardson (Los Angeles: Fantasy Publishing Co., 1952), p. 83.

31. "October 11, 1918—Camp Humphreys, Virginia," *The Notebooks and Poems of Max Brand*, ed. John Schoolcraft (New York: Dodd, Mead, 1957), p. 31.

32. "August 3, 1936, Florence," *Notebooks*, p. 82.

33. Letter to Bob Davis, 14 November 1927, box 11, Robert Hobart Davis Papers.

34. Easton, *Max Brand*, pp. 99, 222.

35. "The Round-Up," *Western Story Magazine*, 27 October 1927, p. 135.

36. Letters to Bob Davis, 1 April 1919, 21 April 1919, and 17 May 1919, box 8, Davis Papers.

37. Letter to Bob Davis, 22 December 1919, box 8, Davis Papers.

38. "The Round-Up," *Western Story*, 14 January 1922, p. 126.

39. "The Round-Up," *Western Story*, 10 March 1923, p. 132.

40. "The Round-Up," *Western Story*, 25 February 1922, p. 127.

41. The Round-Up," *Western Story*, 15 September 1923, pp. 129–30.

42. *The Night Horseman* (New York: Pocket Books, 1954), p. 189; *Destry Rides Again* (New York: Dodd, Mead, 1930), p. 285. Because the book publication of Faust's fiction sometimes occurred many years after its magazine serialization, the dates in the text are those of the works' first appearance.

43. *The Untamed* (New York: Putnam's, 1919), p. 2.

44. See, for example, *Torture Trail* (London: Hodder & Stoughton, 1966).

45. See Northrop Frye, *Anatomy of Criticism* (Princeton: Princeton University Press, 1957), p. 187.

46. *The Stolen Stallion* (London: Hodder & Stoughton, 1949), p. 25.

47. *Silvertip* (London: Hodder & Stoughton, 1942), p. 55.

48. *The Song of the Whip* (New York: Harper, 1936), p. 141.

49. "October 11, 1918—Camp Humphreys, Virginia," *Notebooks*, p. 31.

50. Faust suggested the first sequel in a letter to Davis, 15 May 1918, box 7, Davis Papers.

51. *Dan Barry's Daughter* (New York: Putnam's, 1924), p. 5.

52. *Fire-Brain* (New York: Putnam's, 1926), p. 390; *The Blue Jay* (New York: Dodd, Mead, 1927), p. 81; *Trouble Trail* (New York: Dodd, Mead, 1937), p. 291.

53. "April 29, 1921," *Notebooks*, p. 39.

54. *Happy Jack* (New York: Dodd, Mead, 1936), p. 41.

55. *Silvertip's Search* (London: Hodder & Stoughton, 1948), pp. 52, 55.

56. "Wine on the Desert," *This Week Magazine*, 7 June 1936; reprinted in *Wine on the Desert and Other Stories* (New York: Dodd, Mead, 1940), pp. 1–12.

57. Easton, *Max Brand*, p. 177.

58. Quoted in James Fargo, "The Western and Ernest Haycox," *The Prairie Schooner*, vol. 26 (1952), p. 181.

59. James Stevens and H.L. Davis, *Status Rerum* (The Dalles, Ore.: n.p., [1927]) is a diatribe against literary practitioners in Oregon and Washington. In it, Thacher is treated with particular sarcasm: "Professor Thacher has, nevertheless, certain individual claims to fame. He has been awarded honorable mention in the list of winners in a Chicago tire-naming contest, in which more than two and one-half million names were submitted. Professor Thacher has offered the fruits of his intellect in other national name and slogan contests, and has won distinction in practically all of them, for the winsomeness and *chic* of his titles" (pp. 4–5).

60. Etulain, "Literary Career," p. 74. I am heavily indebted to Etulain's dissertation for information about Haycox's life and career.

61. Haycox's words on the commercial value of his fiction are quoted in Etulain, "Literary Career," pp. 87–88; this material is not yet available for published quotation.

62. *West*, 7 January 1928, n. pg.

63. "Come An' Get It!" *West*, 28 November 1928, p. 124; 12 December 1928, pp. 125–26.

64. *Free Grass* (Garden City, N.Y.: Doubleday, 1929), pp. 8–9. Dates in the text for Haycox's fiction refer to book publication, unless otherwise indicated.

65. *Dead Man Range* (New York: Signet-NAL, 1975), p. 62.

66. *Riders West* (Garden City, N.Y.: Doubleday, 1934), pp. 46, 87.

67. "The Story Tellers' Circle," *Short Stories*, 10 March 1934, p. 163.

68. Ibid.

69. Etulain, "Literary Career," pp. 98, 109, 162, quotes from Haycox's correspondence; this material is not available for published quotation.

70. "Next Week," *Collier's*, 13 June 1936, p. 4; "Contents," *Collier's*, 25 January 1936, p. 4; 28 May 1938, p. 4; 1 July 1939, p. 4.

71. "A Watchmaker 'Times' His Market," *Collier's*, 25 August 1928, p. 37.

72. *Collier's*, 18 July 1936, pp. 34–35.

73. *Trail Smoke* (Garden City, N.Y.: Doubleday, 1936), p. 10.

74. Haycox's comments are quoted by Etulain, "Literary Career," p. 110, but are not available for published quotation.

75. *The Novel of the American West* (Lincoln: University of Nebraska, 1980), p. 21.

76. *Rim of the Desert* (London: Hodder & Stoughton, 1941), p. 13.

77. *The Wild Bunch* (London: Hodder & Stoughton, 1944), p. 10.

78. *Alder Gulch* (New York: Signet–NAL, 1978), p. 88.

79. *Saddle and Ride* (London: Hodder & Stoughton, 1940), p. 148.

80. *Bugles in the Afternoon* (London: Hodder & Stoughton, 1944), p. 124.

81. Quoted in Fargo, "The Western and Ernest Haycox," p. 182.

82. *Long Storm* (London: Hodder & Stoughton, 1947), p. 196.

83. *The Adventurers* was published posthumously, but was written in 1947, before *The Earthbreakers*.

84. *The Adventurers* (New York: Bantam, 1960), p. 255.

85. *The Earthbreakers* (London: Corgi-Transworld, 1960), p. 328.

86. Mody C. Boatright, "The American Myth Rides the Range: Owen Wister's Man on Horseback," *Southwest Review*, vol. 36 (1951), pp. 160–63, points out the echoes from Herbert Spencer and William Graham Sumner in *The Virginian*. Sometimes there are specific similarities between Westerns and naturalist fictions: for example, the relationship between hero and dog in Brand's *Torture Trail* is reminiscent of that in Jack London's "Bâtard" (1904).

FOUR: THE LAST FEW SPACES

1. Michael T. Marsden, "The Concept of the Family in the Fiction of Louis L'Amour," *North Dakota Quarterly*, vol. 46 (Summer 1978), p. 12, reports that L'Amour's novels average sales of over 6,000,000 per year.

2. I have culled my information about Le May's career from "LeMay, Alan," in *Encyclopedia of Frontier and Western Fiction*, ed. Jon Tuska and Vicki Piekarski (New York: McGraw-Hill, 1983), pp. 215–17; and William T. Pilkington, "LeMay, Alan," in *Contemporary Western Writers*, ed. James Vinson and Daniel Kilpatrick (London: St. James, 1982), pp. 486–89.

3. *Cattle Kingdom* (New York: Farrar & Rinehart, [1933]), pp. 293–94. The reference is to the Virginian's famous threat, "When you call me that, *smile!*" (*The Virginian*, p. 29).

4. *Gunsight Trail* (New York: Farrar & Rinehart, [1931]), p. 84.

5. *Painted Ponies* (London: Cassell, 1927), p. 33.

6. *Bug Eye* (New York: Farrar & Rinehart, [1931]), p. 17.

7. *Winter Range* (New York: Farrar & Rinehart, [1932]), p. 44.

8. Pilkington, "Lemay, Alan," p. 488.

9. Arthur Miller, "Author's Note," *The Misfits* (London: Secker & Warburg, 1961), p. 7.

10. *Useless Cowboy* (London: Collins, 1944), p. 6.

11. *The Searchers* (London: Collins, 1955), p. 144.

12. *The Unforgiven* (London: Collins, 1958), p. 23.

13. Gerald Haslam, *Jack Schaefer*, Western Writers Series, no. 20 (Boise: Boise State University, 1975), p. 22. This work is my main source of information on Schaefer's career.

14. *Shane* (London: Deutsch, 1954), pp. 31–32.

15. *Company of Cowards* (London: Deutsch, 1958), p. 27.

16. "The Kean Land," in *The Kean Land and Other Stories* (London: Deutsch, 1960), p. 3.

17. "Enos Carr," in *The Kean Land*, p. 225.

18. "Editor's Note to First Volume," *Out West* (London: Mayflower-Dell, 1965), p. 12.

19. *Monte Walsh* (London: Deutsch, 1965), p. 416.

20. "Author's Note," *The Big Range* (London: Deutsch, 1955), p. 7.

21. "The Canyon," in *The Canyon and Other Stories* (London: Deutsch, 1955), p. 8.

22. *First Blood* (London: Deutsch, 1954), p. 102.

23. "The Fifth Man," in *The Kean Land*, p. 191.

24. *Mavericks* (London: Deutsch, 1968), pp. 169–70.

25. Schaefer has made this comment explicit, outside his fiction. In Henry J. Nuwer, "An Interview with Jack Schaefer," *South Dakota Review*, vol. 2 (Spring 1973), Schaefer declared that he would write no more Westerns. Talking of *Mavericks*, he said: "I was sort of signing off with that book though I didn't know it at the time. It has Old Jake as a character in it who has helped destroy what he most liked and loved. You might say that is sort of an epitaph for me too" (p. 58).

26. This fictional immortality does have a correlative in the outside world: witness the differing fates of *Shane* and *Monte Walsh* in their film versions. The first is world famous as a cinema classic, the second little known by the general audience. This surely relates to the fact that *Shane* uses all the cyclical formulas, while *Monte* is a less neatly structured work about endings of different kinds.

27. *Beginnings* (New York: Basic Books, 1975), p. 21.

28. My major sources on L'Amour's career are Harold Keith, "Louis L'Amour: Man of the West," *The Roundup*, December 1975, pp. 1, 2, 4, 12; January 1976, pp. 8, 9, 11; February 1976, pp. 4, 5; Candace Klaschus, "Louis L'Amour: The Writer as Teacher," dissertation, University of New Mexico, 1982; and Michael T. Marsden, "Louis L'Amour," in *Fifty Western Writers*, pp. 257–67. L'Amour's status as a millionaire is recorded in Earl C. Gottschalk, Jr., "Eggheads May Shun Novels by L'Amour; Millions Love Them," *The Wall Street Journal*, 19 January 1978, p. 1, col. 3. While most of L'Amour's income still comes from paperback sales, Bantam has recently recognized his stature by publishing his work in hardcover editions; these publications are appearing high on *The New York Times* hardcover bestseller lists.

29. John Sutherland, *Fiction and the Fiction Industry* (London: Athlone Press, 1978), pp. 181, 174.

30. Marsden, "Louis L'Amour," p. 259.

31. Keith, "Louis L'Amour," January 1976, p. 11; Gottschalk, "Eggheads," p. 10, col. 3.

32. Nye, *Unembarrassed Muse*, p. 304; Petersen, *Bantam Story*, p. 33; Sutherland, *Fiction and the Fiction Industry*, p. 174.

33. Keith, "Louis L'Amour," January 1976, p. 9.

34. *Lonely on the Mountain* (London: Corgi-Transworld, 1981), back cover.

35. Stephen Fender, *"The Faerie Queene,"* in *English Renaissance Literature,* Frank Kermode, Stephen Fender, Kenneth Palmer (London: Gray-Mills, 1974), pp. 12–29.

36. James Fenimore Cooper, *The Last of the Mohicans* (London: John Miller, 1826), vol. 1, p. 150.

37. *Mojave Crossing* (London: Corgi-Transworld, 1964), p. 117.

38. *The Sackett Brand* (New York: Bantam, 1965), n. pg.

39. Quoted in J.D. Reed, "The Homer of the Oater," *Time,* 1 December 1980, n. pg.

40. *Galloway* (New York: Bantam, 1970), pp. 52, 71.

41. *Westward the Tide* (Kingswood, Surrey: The World's Work, 1950), p. 8.

42. *Shalako* (London: Corgi-Transworld, 1962), p. 26.

43. "Preface," *Sackett's Land* (New York: Bantam, 1975), p. v.

44. This is a feature of romance in general, but it constitutes a special problem for the blatantly commercial writer.

45. *Mustang Man* (London: Corgi-Transworld, 1966), p. 74.

46. *Heller with a Gun* ([London]: Fawcett, [1956]), pp. 59–60.

47. *The First Fast Draw* (New York: Bantam, 1959), pp. 67–68.

48. It is not unknown for fiction to delete preceding fictions, by supplanting information or correcting misconceptions: *Don Quixote* and *Northanger Abbey* are two of the best-known examples to do this, in the course of their burlesques of literary forms. L'Amour's references are, of course, much less elaborate and much less highly crafted than those of Cervantes or Austen. However, his use of the literary device does carry a new emphasis since, in his case, the contradiction between making space and making tradition is specifically played out in the marketplace.

49. *Hopalong Cassidy and the Riders of High Rock* (London: Hodder & Stoughton, 1952), p. 10.

50. *Hopalong Cassidy and the Rustlers of West Fork* (London: Hodder & Stoughton, 1951), p. 67.

51. *Hopalong Cassidy and the Trail to Seven Pines* (London: Hodder & Stoughton, 1952), p. 190.

52. *Hopalong Cassidy, Trouble-Shooter* (London: Hodder & Stoughton, 1953), p. 48.

53. *Hondo* ([London]: Gold Medal-Fawcett, 1953), p. 20.

54. *Last Stand at Papago Wells* ([London]: Gold Medal-Fawcett, 1958), p. 45.

55. *The Lonely Men* (London: Hale, 1981), p. 2.

56. *How the West Was Won* (London: Hale, 1976), p. 10.

57. *Lando* (London: Corgi-Transworld, 1963), p. 105; *The Key-Lock Man* (London: Corgi-Transworld, 1966), p. 1; *Galloway,* p. 7; *The Ferguson Rifle* (London: Corgi-Transworld, 1973), p. 1.

58. *Flint* (London: Corgi-Transworld, 1961), p. 11.

FIVE: ANTI-WESTERN WESTERNS

1. *Out West,* editor's note to first volume, p. 15.

2. *Out West,* editor's note to second volume, p. 18.

3. Telephone interview with Damarus Rowland, Westerns editor at Berkley Books, who now publish Playboy Westerns, 20 April 1983.

4. *The Return of the Vanishing American* (London: Cape, 1968), pp. 146–47.

5. *The Day of the Locust* (London: The Grey Walls Press, 1951), p. 86.

6. *Yellow Back Radio Broke-Down* (London: Allison & Busby, 1971), p. 39.

7. *The Kid* (London: Chatto & Windus, 1972), n. pg.

8. "E.L. Doctorow," *The Writer's World*, PBS, 19 May 1985.

9. *Welcome to Hard Times* (New York: Simon & Schuster, 1960), p. 170.

10. Cawelti, *Adventure*, p. 13.

11. *Midnight Cowboy* (London: Cape, 1966), p. 103.

12. *Cattle Annie and Little Britches* (London: Corgi-Transworld, 1979), p. 16.

13. *Beyond the Waste Land* (New Haven: Yale University Press, 1972), p. 17.

CONCLUSION

1. Nye, *Unembarrassed Muse*, p. 289; Michael T. Marsden, "The Making of *Shane*: A Story for All Media" in *Shane*, ed. James C. Work (Lincoln: University of Nebraska Press, 1984), p. 340.

2. Of dime novels, Charles Bragin says, "Publishers never revealed their sales, but we estimate that the Tip Top Weekly Merriwell stories had a circulation up to a million copies weekly, with Buffalo Bill, Nick Carter, and Diamond Dick series not far behind" (*Bibliography*, Dime Novel Club Issue 63, Brooklyn, N.Y.: Charles Bragin, 1964, p. 2); Kenneth Scott, *Zane Grey* (Boston: G. K. Hall, 1979), p. i, puts the total sales of Grey's novels at about 40 million; and in 1978, Bantam claimed that L'Amour's books were selling over 6 million copies per year (Gott-schalk, "Eggheads," p. 1). The comparison With Wister and Schaefer can be seen in the case of individual novels: while it took 18 years for *The Virginian* to sell 1 million copies and 35 years for *Shane* to sell 4 million, Grey's *Man of the Forest* sold over 700,000 copies in one year (Gruber, *Zane Grey*, p. 2) and 65 of L'A-mour's books have sold over 1 million copies each (Marsden, "Louis L'Amour," p. 257).

3. Specific figures are rare, but Frank Luther Mott's best-selling lists in *Golden Multitudes* (1947; reprint ed., New York: Bowker, 1960) show that Grey's *The Vanishing American* sold less than a million copies in the 1920s, while its seriali-zation in *The Ladies' Home Journal* sold 2.5 million copies per week; and Haycox's *Bugles in the Afternoon* sold less than 1.3 million copies as a book in the 1940s, but reached approximately 3.5 million readers through *The Saturday Evening Post.* Dodd, "Twenty-Five Million Words," p. 1360, says that in the 1920s and 1930s most of Faust's books sold about 20,000 copies each, whereas the pulps pub-lishing his fiction sold about a quarter million copies weekly.

4. Warshow, *Immediate Experience*, p. 87.

Selected Bibliography

Because much of the research for this book was done in England, I have often had to rely on British reprints of Western American novels. Wherever the year of American publication differs from that of the British reprint, I have included both dates in the entry.

I. GENERAL SECONDARY SOURCES

Agnew, Seth. "Destry Goes on Riding—or—Working the Six-Gun Lode." *Publishers' Weekly*, 23 August 1952, pp. 746–51.
———. "God's Country and the Publisher." *The Saturday Review of Literature*, 14 March 1953, pp. 26–27.
Arbuckle, Donald Redmond. "Popular Western: The History of a Commercial Literary Formula." Dissertation, University of Pennsylvania 1977.
Beer, Gillian. *The Romance.* The Critical Idiom, no. 10. London: Methuen, 1970.
Benjamin, Walter. *Understanding Brecht.* Translated by Anna Bostock. London: NLB, 1973.
Billington, Ray Allen, ed. *The Frontier Thesis: Valid Interpretation of American History?* New York: Holt, Rinehart, 1966.
Bloodworth, William. "Literary Extensions of the Formula Western." *Western American Literature*, 14 (1980): 287–96.
———. "Max Brand's West." *Western American Literature*, 16 (1981): 177–91.
Boatright, Mody C. "The Beginnings of Cowboy Fiction." *Southwest Review*, 5 (1966): 11–28.
———. "The Formula in Cowboy Fiction and Drama." *Western Folklore*, 28 (1969): 136–45.
Boorstin, Daniel J. *The Image: or, What Happened to the American Dream.* 1962. Reprint. Harmondsworth: Penguin, 1963.
Branch, Douglas. *The Cowboy and his Interpreters.* New York: Appleton, 1926.
Britt, George. *Forty Years—Forty Millions: The Career of Frank A. Munsey.* New York: Farrar & Rinehart, 1935.
Browne, Ray B., et al. *Frontiers of American Culture.* Lafayette, Ind.: Purdue University Studies, 1968.
Calder, Jenni. *There Must Be a Lone Ranger: The Myth and Reality of the American Wild West.* London: Hamish Hamilton 1974.
Campbell, Joseph. *The Hero with a Thousand Faces.* New York: Pantheon, 1949.
Cawelti, John G. *Adventure, Mystery, and Romance: Formula Stories as Art and Popular Culture.* Chicago: University of Chicago Press, 1976.
———. *The Six-Gun Mystique.* Bowling Green, Ohio: Bowling Green University Popular Press, 1971.
———. "Trends in Recent American Genre Fiction." *Kansas Quarterly*, 10 (Fall 1978): 5–18.
Chernow, Ron. "John Ford: The Last Frontiersman." *Ramparts*, 12 (April 1974): 45–48.
DeVoto, Bernard. "Phaëthon on Gunsmoke Trail." *Harper's Magazine*, December 1954, pp. 10–16.
Durham, Phillip, and Jones, Everett L. *The Frontier in American Literature.* New York: Odyssey Press, 1969.
———. *The Western Story: Fact, Fiction and Myth.* New York: Harcourt, 1975.

Etulain, Richard W. *Western American Literature: A Bibliography of Interpretive Books and Articles.* Vermillion, S.D.: Dakota Press, 1972.

———, ed. "The American Literary West." *Journal of the West,* 19 (January 1980).

———, and Erisman, Fred, eds. *Fifty Western Writers: A Bio-Bibliographical Sourcebook.* Westport, Conn.: Greenwood Press, 1982.

———, and Marsden, Michael T., eds. *The Popular Western: Essays toward a Definition.* Bowling Green, Ohio: Bowling Green University Popular Press, 1974.

Exman, Eugene. *The House of Harper: One Hundred and Fifty Years of Publishing.* New York: Harper, 1967.

Fender, Stephen. *"The Faerie Queene."* In *English Renaissance Literature: Introductory Lectures.* By Frank Kermode et al. London: Gray-Mills, 1974, pp. 12–29.

———. *Plotting the Golden West: American Literature and the Rhetoric of the California Trail.* Cambridge: Cambridge University Press, 1981.

———. "The Western and the Contemporary." *Journal of American Studies,* 6 (1972): 97–108.

Fenin, George N., and Everson, William K. *The Western: From Silents to Seventies.* Rev. ed. 1973; reprint ed., Harmondsworth: Penguin, 1977.

Fiedler, Leslie A. *Love and Death in the American Novel.* New York: Criterion Books, [1960].

———. *The Return of the Vanishing American.* London: Cape, 1968.

Fife, Jim L. "Two Views of the American West." *Western American Literature,* 1 (1966): 34–43.

Folsom, James K. *The American Western Novel.* New Haven: College & University Press, [1966].

———, ed. *The Western: A Collection of Critical Essays.* Twentieth Century Views. Englewood Cliffs, N.J.: Prentice Hall, 1979.

Forster, E.M. *Aspects of the Novel.* London: Edward Arnold, 1927.

Franklin, Wayne. *Discoverers, Explorers, Settlers: The Diligent Writers of Early America.* Chicago: University of Chicago Press, 1979.

Frantz, Joe B., and Choate, Julian Ernest, Jr. *The American Cowboy: The Myth and the Reality.* Norman: University of Oklahoma Press, 1955.

French, Warren. "West as Myth: Status Report and Call for Action." *Western American Literature,* 1 (1966): 55–57.

Frye, Northrop. *Anatomy of Criticism: Four Essays.* Princeton: Princeton University Press, 1957.

———. *The Secular Scripture: A Study of the Structure of Romance.* Cambridge: Harvard University Press, 1976.

Fussell, Edwin. *Frontier: American Literature and the American West.* Princeton: Princeton University Press, 1965.

Gedin, Per. *Literature in the Marketplace.* Translated by George Bisset. 1977. Reprint. London: Faber & Faber, 1982.

Glanz, Dawn. *How the West Was Drawn: American Art and the Settling of the Frontier.* Studies in the Fine Arts: Iconography, no. 6. Ann Arbor: UMI Research Press, 1982.

Graham, Don. "Old and New Cowboy Classics." *Southwest Review,* 65 (1980): 293–303.

Gurian, Jay. *Western American Writing: Tradition and Promise.* Deland, Fla.: Everett/Edwards, 1975.

Hackett, Alice Payne. *70 Years of Best Sellers, 1895–1965.* New York: Bowker, 1967.

Hart, James D. *The Popular Book: A History of America's Literary Taste.* New York: Oxford University Press, 1950.

Haslam, Gerald W., ed. *Western Writing*. Albuquerque: University of New Mexico Press, 1974.

Hazard, Lucy Lockwood. *The Frontier in American Literature*. New York: Thomas Y. Crowell, 1927.

Heilman, Robert B. "The Western Theme: Exploiters and Explorers." Partisan Review, 28 (1961): 286–97.

Hofstadter, Richard. *Social Darwinism in American Thought*. Rev. ed. New York: Braziller, 1959.

Inge, M. Thomas, ed. *Handbook of American Popular Culture*. vol. 1. Westport, Conn.: Greenwood Press, 1978.

Jones, Howard Mumford. *The Frontier in American Fiction: Four Lectures on the Relation of Landscape to Literature*. Jerusalem: Hebrew University, 1956.

Lamar, Howard R., ed. *The Reader's Encyclopedia of the American West*. New York: Thomas Y. Crowell, 1977.

Lavender, David. "The Petrified West and the Writer." *The American Scholar*, 37 (1968): 293–306.

Lewis, Freeman. *Paper-bound Books in America*. The Sixteenth R. R. Bowker Memorial Lecture. New York: The New York Public Library, 1953.

Lewis, R. W. B. *The American Adam: Innocence, Tragedy and Tradition in the Nineteenth Century*. Chicago: University of Chicago Press, 1955.

Macherey, Pierre. *A Theory of Literary Production*. Translated by Geoffrey Wall. London: Routledge & Kegan Paul, 1978.

Marovitz, Sanford E. "Myth and Realism in Recent Criticism of the American Literary West." *Journal of American Studies*, 15 (1981): 95–114.

Marx, Leo. *The Machine in the Garden: Technology and the Pastoral Ideal in America*. New York: Oxford University Press, 1964.

Milton, John R. *The Novel of the American West*. Lincoln: University of Nebraska Press, 1980.

Moore, Arthur K. *The Frontier Mind*. 1957. Reprint. New York: McGraw-Hill, 1963.

Mott, Frank Luther. *Golden Multitudes: The Story of Best Sellers in the United States*. 1947. Reprint. New York: Bowker, [1960].

———. *A History of American Magazines*. vols. 2–5. Cambridge: Harvard University Press, 1938, 1957, 1968.

Mottram, Eric. " 'The Persuasive Lips': Men and Guns in America, the West." *Journal of American Studies*, 10 (1976): 53–84.

Nash, Roderick. *Wilderness and the American Mind*. Rev. ed. New Haven: Yale University Press, 1973.

———, ed. *The Call of the Wild: 1900–1916*. New York: Braziller, 1970.

Nathan, Paul S. "Books into Films." *Publishers' Weekly*, 19 April 1947, p. 2130.

Neuburg, Victor E. *Popular Literature: A History and Guide from the Beginning of Printing to the Year 1897*. Harmondsworth: Penguin, 1977.

Nye, Russel B. *The Unembarrassed Muse: The Popular Arts in America*. New York: The Dial Press, 1970.

———, ed. *New Dimensions in Popular Culture*. Bowling Green, Ohio: Bowling Green University Popular Press, 1972.

Pember, Don R. *Mass Media in America*. 2nd ed. Chicago: Science Research Assocs., 1977.

Percy, Walker. "Decline of the Western." *The Commonweal*, 16 May 1958, pp. 181–83.

Petersen, Clarence. *The Bantam Story: Thirty Years of Paperback Publishing*. 2nd ed. New York: Bantam, 1975.

Peterson, Levi S. "The Primitive and the Civilized in Western Fiction." *Western American Literature*, 1 (1966): 197–207.

Peterson, Theodore. *Magazines in the Twentieth Century*. Urbana: University of Illinois Press, 1956.

Pilkington, William T. *Critical Essays on the Western American Novel*. Boston: G. K. Hall, 1980.

Pizer, Donald. *Realism and Naturalism in Nineteenth-Century American Literature*. Carbondale: Southern Illinois University Press, 1966.

Poirier, Richard. *A World Elsewhere: The Place of Style in American Literature*. London: Chatto & Windus, 1967.

Pomeroy, Earl. *In Search of the Golden West: The Tourist in Western America*. New York: Knopf, 1957.

Porte, Joel. *The Romance in America: Studies in Cooper, Poe, Hawthorne, Melville, and James*. Middletown, Conn.: Wesleyan University Press, 1969.

Pound, Robert T. "Western Formu-less." *The Writer's Monthly*, March 1925, pp. 204–7.

Rogers, Roy. "Don't Shoot, Ma!" *The American Magazine*, August 1949, pp. 28–29, 131–33.

Rosenberg, Bernard, and David Manning White, eds. *Mass Culture: The Popular Arts in America*. New York: Macmillan, 1957.

Said, Edward. *Beginnings: Intention and Method*. New York: Basic Books, 1975.

Savage, William W., Jr. *The Cowboy Hero: His Image in American History and Culture*. Norman: University of Oklahoma Press, 1979.

Sellars, Richard West. "The Interrelationship of Literature, History, and Geography in Western Writing." *The Western Historical Quarterly*, 4 (1973): 171–85.

Slotkin, Richard. *Regeneration through Violence: The Mythology of the American Frontier, 1600–1860*. Middletown, Conn.: Wesleyan University Press, 1973.

Smith, Henry Nash. *Virgin Land: The American West as Symbol and Myth*. Cambridge: Harvard University Press, 1950.

Sonnischen, C. L. *From Hopalong to Hud: Thoughts on Western Fiction*. College Station: Texas A & M University Press, 1978.

Sutherland, John A. *Fiction and the Fiction Industry*. London: Athlone Press, 1978.

Tebbel, John. *A History of Book Publishing in the United States*. 4 vols. New York: R.R. Bowker, [1972]–1981.

Trachtenberg, Alan. *The Incorporation of America: Culture and Society in the Gilded Age*. New York: Hill & Wang, 1982.

Turner, Frederick Jackson. "The Significance of the Frontier in American History." In *Annual Report of the American Historical Association for the Year 1893*. Washington, D.C.: GPO, 1894.

Tuska, Jon, and Piekarski, Vicki, eds. *Encyclopedia of Frontier and Western Fiction*. New York: McGraw-Hill, 1983.

Van Nostrand, Albert. *The Denatured Novel*. New York: Bobbs-Merrill, [1960].

Vinson, James, and Kilpatrick, Daniel, eds. *Contemporary Western Writers*. London: St. James, 1982.

Walcutt, Charles C. *Seven Novelists in the American Naturalist Tradition*. Minneapolis: University of Minnesota, 1963.

Waldmeir, Joseph. "The Cowboy, the Knight, and Popular Taste." *Southern Folklore Quarterly*, 22 (1958): 113–20.

Walle, Alf Howard, III. "The Frontier Hero: A Static Figure in an Evolving World." Dissertation, State University of New York at Buffalo 1976.

Warshow, Robert. *The Immediate Experience: Movies, Comics, Theatre, and Other Aspects of Popular Culture*. Garden City, N.Y.: Doubleday, 1962.

Webb, Walter Prescott. *The Great Plains*. Boston: Ginn, 1931.

Wecter, Dixon. *The Hero in America: A Chronicle of Hero-Worship*. 1941. Reprint. New York: Scribner's, 1972.

Westbrook, Max. "The Authentic Western." *Western American Literature*, 13 (1978): 214–25.

———. "The Themes of Western Fiction." *Southwest Review*, 43 (1958): 232–38.

Wilson, Daniel J. "Nature in Western Popular Literature from the Dime Novel to Zane Grey." *North Dakota Quarterly*, 44 (Spring 1976): 41–50.

Wood, James Playsted. *Magazines in the United States*. 2nd ed. New York: The Ronald Press Co., 1956.

———. *The Story of Advertising*. New York: The Ronald Press Co., 1958.

Zweig, Paul. *The Adventurer*. London: Dent, 1974.

II. COOPER AND BIRD

Primary Sources

Bird, Robert Montgomery. *Nick of the Woods: A Story of Kentucky*. Edited by W. Harrison Ainsworth. 3 vols. London: Richard Bentley, 1837.

Cooper, James Fenimore. *The Deerslayer: A Tale*. 3 vols. London: Richard Bentley, 1841.

———. *The Last of the Mohicans: A Narrative of 1757*. 3 vols. London: John Miller, 1826.

———. *The Pathfinder*. 1840. Reprint. London: Richard Bentley, 1843.

———. *The Pioneers*. 1823. Reprint. London: W. Simpkin & R. Marshall, 1827.

———. *The Prairie*. 1827. Reprint. London: Henry Colburn & Richard Bentley, 1832.

Secondary Sources

Bewley, Marius. *The Eccentric Design: Form in the Classic American Novel*. London: Chatto & Windus, 1959.

Cowie, Alexander. *The Rise of the American Novel*. New York: American Book Co., 1948.

Dahl, Curtis. *Robert Montgomery Bird*. Twayne's United States Authors Series. New Haven: College & University Press, 1963.

Dekker, George. *James Fenimore Cooper the Novelist*. London: Routledge & Kegan Paul, 1967.

———, and McWilliams, John P., eds. *Fenimore Cooper: The Critical Heritage*. London: Routledge & Kegan Paul, 1973.

Franklin, Wayne. *The New World of James Fenimore Cooper*. Chicago: University of Chicago Press, 1982.

Grossman, James. *James Fenimore Cooper*. 1949. Reprint. Palo Alto: Stanford University Press, 1967.

Lawrence, D.H. *Studies in Classic American Literature*. London: Secker, 1924.

Nevius, Blake. *Cooper's Landscapes: An Essay on the Picturesque Vision*. Berkeley: University of California Press, 1976.

Peck, H. Daniel. *A World by Itself: The Pastoral Moment in Cooper's Fiction*. New Haven: Yale University Press, 1977.

Ringe, Donald A. *James Fenimore Cooper*. Twayne's United States Authors Series, no. 11. Boston: Twayne, 1962.

Spiller, Robert E. *James Fenimore Cooper*. Pamphlets on American Writers, no. 48. Minneapolis: University of Minnesota Press, 1965.

Winters, Yvor. *In Defense of Reason.* 1947. Reprint. Denver: University of Denver Press, [1950].

III. DIME AND PULP WESTERNS

PRIMARY SOURCES

Selected Western Dime Novels

Adams, Capt. "Bruin" [Edward S. Ellis]. *The Wild Huntress; or, Grizzly,Old Grizzly, the Bear-Tamer.* Beadle's Pocket Library, 38, no. 483. N.Y.: Beadle & Adams, 1893.

Adams, Capt. J. F. C. [Edward S. Ellis]. *The Black Spy; or, The Yellowstone Trail.* Beadle's New Dime Novels, no. 120. N.Y.:. Beadle & Adams, 1873.

———. *Light-House Lige; or, Osceola, the Firebrand of the Everglades: A Tale of the Haunted Lake.* New and Old Friends, no. 5. New York: Beadle & Adams, 1873.

An Old Scout [Cornelius Shea]. *On the Plains with Buffalo Bill; or, Two Years in the Wild West and Other Stories.* Pluck and Luck, no. 725. New York: Frank Tousey, 1912.

———. *Young Wild West and the Cowboys; or, A Hot Time on the Prairie.* Wild West Weekly, no. 38. New York: Frank Tousey, 1903.

———. *Young Wild West and Little Moccasin; or, Arietta's Pawnee Peril.* Wild West Weekly, no. 451. New York: Frank Tousey, 1911.

———. *Young Wild West and the Stranded Show; or, Waking the Prairie Pilgrims.* Wild West Weekly, no. 79. New York: Frank Tousey, 1904.

———. *Young Wild West's Big Day; or, The Double Wedding at Weston.* Wild West Weekly, no. 16. New York: Frank Tousey, 1903.

———. *Young Wild West's Cowboy Carnival; or, The Round Up at Roaring Ranch.* Wild West Weekly, no. 76. New York: Frank Tousey, 1904.

———. *Young Wild West's Election; or, A Mayor at Twenty.* Wild West Weekly, no. 29. New York: Frank Tousey, 1903.

———. *Young Wild West's Game of Chance; or, Saved by Arietta.* Wild West Weekly, no. 72. New York: Frank Tousey, 1904.

———. *Young Wild West's Great Scheme; or, The Building of a Railroad.* Wild West Weekly, no. 17. New York: Frank Tousey, 1903.

———. *Young Wild West's Lightning Leap.* Wild West Weekly, no. 410. New York: Frank Tousey, 1910.

———. *Young Wild West's Luck; or, Striking it Rich at the Hills.* Wild West Weekly, no. 2. New York: Frank Tousey, 1902.

———. *Young Wild West: The Prince of the Saddle.* Wild West Weekly, no. 1. New York: Frank Tousey, 1902.

———. *Young Wild West's Rough Riders; or, The Rose Bud of the Rockies.* Wild West Weekly, no. 39. New York: Frank Tousey, 1903.

———. *Young Wild West's Victory; or, The Road Agents' Last Hold Up.* Wild West Weekly, no. 3. New York: Frank Tousey, 1902.

The Author of "Buffalo Bill" [W. Bert Foster]. *Buffalo Bill and the Trouble-Hunter; or, The Lure of the Mission Gold.* The Buffalo Bill Stories, no. 404. New York: Street & Smith, 1909.

———. *Buffalo Bill at Cañon Diablo; or, Pawnee Bill's Railroad Mutiny.* Buffalo Bill Stories, no. 493. New York: Street & Smith, 1910.

———. *Buffalo Bill's Crow Scouts; or, Pawnee Bill and the Absarokes.* New Buffalo Bill Weekly, no. 259. New York: Street & Smith, 1917.

The Author of "Buffalo Bill" [Prentiss Ingraham]. *Buffalo Bill and the Affair of Honor; or, Pawnee Bill's Mexican Comrades.* New Buffalo Bill Weekly, no. 315. New York: Street & Smith, 1918.

The Author of "Buffalo Bill" [Harry St. George Rathborne]. *Buffalo Bill's Escape; or, Pawnee Bill and the Running Fight.* New Buffalo Bill Weekly, no. 351. New York: Street & Smith, 1919.

The Author of "Diamond Dick." *Diamond Dick at Craven Creek; or, A Still Hunt in the Land of the Sky.* Diamond Dick Jr., no. 666. New York: Street & Smith, 1909.

———. *Diamond Dick's Ready Resource; or, A Mysterious Shooting.* Diamond Dick Jr., no. 762. New York: Street & Smith, 1911.

Belknap, Boynton H. [Edward S. Ellis]. *Peleg Smith; or, Adventures in the Tropics.* Beadle's Pocket Novels, no. 216. New York: Beadle & Adams, 1882.

Buntline, Ned [E. Z. C. Judson]. *Buffalo Bill, the King of Border Men!: The Wildest and Truest Story I Ever Wrote.* In *Street & Smith's New York Weekly,* 23 December 1869 to 10 March 1870.

———. *Buffalo Bill's Last Victory; or, Dove Eye, the Lodge Queen.* Sea and Shore Series, no. 24. 1883. Reprint. New York: Street & Smith, 1890.

———. *Ethelbert, the Shell-Hunter; or, The Ocean Chase.* Beadle's Boy's Library of Sport, Story and Adventure, 5, no. 111. 1860. Reprint. New York: Beadle & Adams, 1889.

———. *The Red Privateer; or, The Midshipman Rover: A Romance of 1812.* Beadle's Dime Library, 48, no. 621. 1885. Reprint. New York: Beadle & Adams, 1890.

———. *Red Ralph, the River Rover; or, The Brother's Revenge.* Beadle's Half Dime Library, 14, no. 350. 1870. Reprint. New York: Beadle & Adams, 1884.

———. *The Red Revenger; or, The Pirate King of the Floridas: A Tale of the Gulf and its Islands.* The Novelette, no. 5. Boston: Ballou, n.d.

———. *Saul Sabberday, the Idiot Spy; or, Luliona, the Seminole.* Beadle's Dime Library, 10, no. 122. 1858. Reprint. New York: Beadle & Adams, 1881.

———. *The Sea Bandit; or, The Queen of the Isle.* Frank Starr's American Novels, no. 188. New York: Frank Starr, 1870.

———. *The Smuggler; or, The Skipper's Crime: A Tale of Ship and Shore.* Frank Starr's American Novels, no. 183. 1862. Reprint. New York: Frank Starr, 1871.

———. *Tombstone Dick, the Train Pilot; or, The Traitor's Trail: A Story of the Arizonian Wilds.* Beadle's Dime Library, 28, no. 361. New York: Beadle & Adams, 1885.

———. *War-Eagle; or, Issiniwa the Indian Brave.* De Witt's Ten Cent Romances, no. 42. New York: Robert M. De Witt, 1869.

———. *The White Wizard; or, The Great Prophet of the Seminoles.* Beadle's Dime Library, 2, no. 16. 1858. Reprint. New York: Beadle & Adams, 1879.

Burr, Major Dangerfield [Prentiss Ingraham]. *Buffalo Bill's Secret Service Trail; or, The Mysterious Foe: A Romance of Redskins, Renegades and Army Rencounters.* Beadle's Dime Library, 53, no. 682. 1887. Reprint. New York: Beadle & Adams, 1891.

———. *Velvet Face, the Border Bravo; or, Muriel, the Danite's Bride: The Romance of a Border Mystery.* Beadle's Dime Library, 12, no. 156. New York: Beadle & Adams, 1881.

The Cowboys' Secret League: A Story of Daring Rescues and Heroic Deeds. The Original Buffalo Bill Library (Aldine Series), no. 434. London: The Aldine Publishing Co., n.d.

Dair, Colonel Spencer. *Red Hand of the North West.* American Indian, 1, no. 25. Ohio: Arthur Westbrook, 1911.

Ellis, Edward S. *Bill Biddon, Trapper; or, Life in the North-West.* Beadle's American Library, no. 7. London: Beadle & Co., [1861].

———. *The Boy Miners; or, The Enchanted Island: A Tale of the Yellowstone Country.* Beadle's Pocket Novels, no. 3. New York: Beadle & Adams, 1874.

———. *The Boy Pioneer.* Beadle's New Dime Novels, no. 264. New York: Beadle & Adams, 1868.

———. *Chinga the Cheyenne: A Sequel to Westward Bound!* Frank Starr's American Novels, no. 9. New York: Frank Starr, 1869.

———. *The Fighting Trapper; or, Kit Carson to the Rescue: A Tale of Wild Life on the Plains.* Frank Starr's Ten Cent American Novels, no. 139. New York: Frank Starr, 1874.

———. *The Forest Spy: A Tale of the War of 1812.* Beadle's American Library, no. 16. London: Beadle & Co., [1862].

———. *The Frontier Angel: A Romance of Kentucky Ranger's Life.* Beadle's American Library, no. 111. London: Beadle & Co., [1861].

———. *The Fugitives; or, The Quaker Scouts of Wyoming.* Beadle's American Library, no. 74. London: George Routledge, [1867].

———. *The Huge Hunter; or, The Steam Man of the Prairies.* Beadle's New Dime Novels, no. 276. New York: Beadle & Adams, 1870.

———. *The Hunters Cabin: An Episode of the Early Settlements of Southern Ohio.* Beadle's American Library, no. 20. London: Beadle & Co., [1862].

———. *The Hunter's Escape: A Tale of the North West in 1862.* Beadle's Dime Novels, no. 75. New York: Beadle & Co., 1864.

———. *Indian Jim: A Tale of the Minnesota Massacre.* Beadle's Dime Novels, no. 67. New York: Beadle & Co., 1864.

———. *Irona; or, Life on the Southwest Border.* Beadle's American Library. London: Beadle & Co., [1864].

———. *Kent, the Ranger; or, The Fugitives of the Border.* Beadle's Dime Novels, no. 59. New York: Beadle & Co., 1863.

———. *The Lost Trail: A Legend of the Far West.* Beadle's Dime Novels, no. 71. New York: Beadle & Co., 1864.

———. *The Mystic Canoe: A Romance of One Hundred Years Ago.* Beadle's Dime Novels, no. 82. New York: Beadle & Co., 1865.

———. *Nathan Todd; or, The Fate of the Sioux Captive.* Beadle's American Library, no. 9. London: Beadle & Co., 1861.

———. *Old Zip; or, The Cabin in the Air: A Story of the Sioux Country.* Beadle's New Dime Novels, no. 152. New York: Beadle & Adams, 1871.

———. *Oonomoo, the Huron.* Beadle's American Library, no. 25. 1862. Reprint. London: Beadle & Co., 1863.

———. *Oregon Sol; or, Nick Whiffle's Boy Spy.* Beadle's Pocket Library, 2, no. 17. 1873. Reprint. New York: Beadle & Adams, 1884.

———. *The Phantom Horseman; or, The Mad Hunter of the Mohawk.* Beadle's New Dime Novels, no. 390. New York: Beadle & Adams, 1869.

———. *The Rangers of the Mohawk: A Tale of Cherry Valley.* Beadle's Dime Novels, no. 64. New York: Beadle & Co., 1864.

———. *The Riflemen of the Miami.* Beadle's American Library, no. 18. London: Beadle & Co., 1862.

———. *The Rival Scouts; or, The Forest Garrison: A Story of the Siege and Fall of Fort Presqu'isle.* Beadle's Dime Novels, no. 78. New York: Beadle & Co., 1865.

———. *Seth Jones; or, The Captives of the Frontier.* Beadle's American Library, no. 1. 1860. Reprint. London: Beadle & Co., 1861.

———. *The Trail-Hunters; or, Monowano, the Shawnee Spy.* New and Old Friends, no. 9. New York: Beadle & Co., 1861.

Harbaugh, T. C. *Nick o' the Night; or, The Boy Spy of '76.* Beadle's Half Dime Library, 45, no. 1124. 1877. Reprint. New York: M. J. Ivers, 1902.

Ingraham, Prentiss. *Arizona Joe, the Boy Pard of Texas Jack.* Beadle's Half Dime Library, 20, no. 495. New York: Beadle & Adams, 1887.

————. *Bison Bill, the Prince of the Reins; or, The Red Riders of the Overland.* Beadle's Half Dime Library, 9, no. 216. New York: Beadle & Adams, 1881.

————. *Buck Taylor the Comanche Captive; or, Buckskin Sam to the Rescue: A Romance of Lone Star Heroes.* Beadle's Half Dime Library, 29, no. 737. New York: Beadle & Adams, 1891.

————. *Buck Taylor, King of the Cowboys; or, The Raiders and the Rangers: A Story of the Wild and Thrilling Life of William L. Taylor.* Beadle's Half Dime Library, 20, no. 497. New York: Beadle & Adams, 1887.

————. *Buffalo Bill's Bodyguard; or, The Still Hunt of the Hills: The Story of the "Robber of the Ranges."* Beadle's Dime Library, 41, no. 727. New York: Beadle & Adams, 1892.

————. *Buffalo Bill's Crack-Shot Pard; or, The Tenderfoot in the Wild West.* Beadle's Half Dime Library, 36, no. 929. New York: Beadle & Adams, 1895.

————. *Buffalo Bill's Flush Hand; or, Texas Jack's Bravos.* Beadle's Dime Library, 43, no. 743. New York: Beadle & Adams, 1893.

————. *Buffalo Bill's Redskin Ruse; or, Texas Jack's Death-Shot: A Romance of the Overland Desperado Giant.* Beadle's Dime Library, 65, no. 845. New York: Beadle & Adams, 1895.

————. *Buffalo Bill's Snap-Shot; or, Wild Kid's Texan Tally.* Beadle's Half Dime Library, 37, No. 948. N.Y.: Beadle & Adams, 1895.

————. *Buffalo Bill's Tough Tussle; or, The Buckskin Boss Boy.* Beadle's Half Dime Library, 37, no. 942. New York: Beadle & Adams, 1895.

————. *Captain Crimson, the Man of the Iron Face; or, The Nemesis of the Plains: A Romance of Love and Adventure in the "Land of the Setting Sun."* Beadle's Dime Library, 11, no. 142. New York: Beadle & Adams, 1881.

————. *The Cowboy Clan; or, The Tigress of Texas: A Romance of Buck Taylor and his Boys in Buckskin, and Companion Story to the "Lasso King."* Beadle's Dime Library, 51, no. 658. New York: Beadle & Adams, 1891.

————. *The Dead Shot Dandy; or, Benito, the Boy Bugler: A Romance of a Boy Waif on the Texas Prairies.* Beadle's Half Dime Library, 12, no. 304. New York: Beadle & Adams, 1883.

————. *Diamond Dirk; or, The Mystery of the Yellowstone.* Beadle's Pocket Library, 2, no. 15. 1878. Reprint. New York: Beadle & Adams, 1884.

————. *Gold Plume, the Boy Bandit; or, The Kid-Glove Sport.* Beadle's Half Dime Library, 8, no. 204. New York: Beadle & Adams, 1881.

————. *Grit, the Bravo Sport; or, The Woman Trailer.* Beadle's Half Dime Library, 9, no. 222. New York: Beadle & Adams, 1881.

————. *Keno Kit, the Boy Bugler's Pard; or, Dead Shot Dandy's Double.* Beadle's Half Dime Library, 12, no. 308. New York: Beadle & Adams, 1883.

————. *The Lasso King's League; or, The Tigers of Texas: A Romance of Heroes in Buckskin and a Companion Story to "Buck Taylor, the Saddle King."* Beadle's Dime Library, 51, no. 653. New York: Beadle & Adams, 1891.

————. *The Mysterious Marauder; or, The Boy Bugler's Long Trail.* Beadle's Half Dime Library, 13, no. 314. New York: Beadle & Adams, 1883.

————. *The Pony-Express Rider; or, Buffalo Bill's Frontier Feats: Deeds of Daring, Scenes of Thrilling Peril, and Romantic Incidents in the Early Life of W. F. Cody, the Monarch of Bordermen.* Beadle's Pocket Library, 30, no. 388. 1881. Reprint. New York: Beadle & Adams, 1891.

————. *Queen Helen, the Amazon of the Overland; or, The Ghouls of the Gold Mines.*

Beadle's Dime Library, 19, no. 246. New York: Beadle & Adams, 1883.
———. *Texas Jack: The Mustang King.* Beadle's Boy's Library of Sport, Story and Adventure, 1, no. 10. 1891. Reprint. New York: M. J. Ivers, 1899.
———. *The Vagabond of the Mines: A Romance of Detective Work on the Frontier.* Beadle's Half Dime Library, 24, no. 602. New York: Beadle & Adams, 1889.
———. *Wild Bill, the Pistol Dead Shot; or, Dagger Don's Double.* Beadle's Dime Library, 13, no. 168. New York: Beadle & Adams, 1882.
———. *The Wild Steer Riders; or, Texas Jack's Terrors.* Beadle's Dime Library, 45, no. 834. 1889. Reprint. New York: Beadle & Adams, 1894.
———. *The Young Cowboy; or, The Girl Trailer's Triumph.* Beadle's Pocket Library, 16, no. 204. 1881. Reprint. New York: Beadle & Adams, 1887.
Keen-Knife, the Prairie Prince. Buffalo Bill Novels, no. 141. London: Aldine Publishing, n.d.
Lasalle, Chas. E. [Edward S. Ellis]. *The Texan Trailer; or, Davy Crockett's Last Bear-Hunt.* Beadle's Dime Novels, no. 231. New York: Beadle & Co., 1871.
Lawson, W. B. *Dashing Diamond Dick; or, The Tigers of Tombstone.* New York Five Cent Library, no. 88. New York: Street & Smith, 1894.
———. *Diamond Dick's Deal; or, The Man-Bear of the Hornitas.* Diamond Dick Jr., no. 125. New York: Street & Smith, 1899.
———. *Diamond Dick's Death Trail; or, Cyclone Sam of "Shi-an."* New York Five Cent Library, no. 89. New York: Street & Smith, 1894.
———. *Diamond Dick's Discard; or, Diamond Dick, Jr.'s Dig-Out.* New York Five Cent Library, no. 112. New York: Street & Smith, 1894.
———. *Diamond Dick, Jr.'s Aerial Tussle; or, A Desperate Chance to Save a Life.* Diamond Dick Jr., no. 102. New York: Street & Smith, 1898.
———. *Diamond Dick, Jr.'s Darkest Hour; or, The Jaguar's [sic] of Jalisco.* New York Five Cent Library, no. 115. New York: Street & Smith, 1895.
———. *Diamond Dick, Jr.'s Drawn Game; or, The Fair Captive of the Mesas.* New York Five Cent Library, no. 113. New York: Street & Smith, 1894.
———. *Diamond Dick's Own Brand.* Great Western Library, no. 1. New York: Street & Smith, 1927.
———. *The Hawkins Gang's Last Exploit; or, The Terrors of Indiana.* The Old Log Cabin, no. 452. New York: Street & Smith, 1897.
Muller, Billex [Edward S. Ellis]. *Joe Napyank; or, The River Rifles.* Beadle's New Dime Novels, no. 302. New York: Beadle & Adams, 1870.
Powell, Dr. Frank [Prentiss Ingraham]. *The Doomed Dozen; or, Dolores, the Danite's Daughter: A Romance of Border Trails and Mormon Mysteries.* Beadle's Dime Library, 13, no. 158. New York: Beadle & Adams, 1881.
Randolph, Lieut. J. H. [Edward S. Ellis]. *Carson, the Guide; or, Perils of the Frontier.* Beadle's Pocket Novels, no. 37. New York: Beadle & Adams, 1870.
Robbins, Seelin [Edward S. Ellis]. *The Specter Chief; or, The Indians' Revenge.* Beadle's New Dime Novels, no. 246. New York: Beadle & Adams, 1871.
———. *Westward Bound: A Story of To-day.* Beadle's New Dime Novels, no. 219. New York: Beadle & Adams, 1866.
Rodman, Emerson [Edward S. Ellis]. *The Wood Rangers: A Tale of the Ohio.* American Novels, no. 2. New York: Irwin P. Beadle, 1865.
Stephens, Mrs. Ann S. *Malaeska; The Indian Wife of the White Hunter.* Beadle's Dime Novels, no. 1. New York: Irwin P. Beadle & Co., 1860.
Stoddard, Maj. Henry B. [Prentiss Ingraham]. *The Boy Vigilantes; or King Cole and his Band.* Beadle's Boy's Library of Sport, Story and Adventure, 5, no. 121. New York: Beadle & Adams, 1884.
———. *Kid Glove Kit and Pard; or, The Gold King of the Weird Canyon.* Beadle's Half Dime Library, 16, no. 398. New York: Beadle & Adams, n.d.

————. *Kid Glove Kit; or, Dainty Danford's Vow.* Beadle's Half Dime Library, 16, no. 391. New York: Beadle & Adams, 1885.

————. *Neck-Tie Ned, the Lariat-Thrower; or, The Dug-Out Pards: A Romance of the Alkali Country.* Beadle's Half Dime Library, 12, no. 306. New York: Beadle & Adams, 1883.

Taylor, Capt. Alfred B. [Prentiss Ingraham]. *Buffalo Bill's Bet; or, The Gambler Guide: A Romance of Western Trails.* Beadle's Half Dime Library, 8, no. 194. New York: Beadle & Adams, 1881.

————. *Buffalo Billy, the Boy Bullwhacker; or, The Doomed Thirteen: A Strange Story of the Silver Trail.* Beadle's Half Dime Library, 8, no. 191. New York: Beadle & Adams, 1881.

Taylor, Ned [William Wallace Cook]. *King of the Wild West and the "Bad Men"; or, Putting a Lid on the Territory.* Rough Rider Weekly, no. 81. New York: Street & Smith, 1905.

————. *King of the Wild West's Desert Trail; or, Stella's Fight for the Hoard of the Cocopahs.* Rough Rider Weekly, no. 168. New York: Street & Smith, 1907.

————. *King of the Wild West's Gulch Diggings; or Stella's Star Role.* Rough Rider Weekly, no. 116. New York: Street & Smith, 1906.

————. *King of the Wild West's Haunt; or, Stella's Escape from Sacrifice.* Rough Rider Weekly, no. 102. New York: Street & Smith, 1906.

————. *King of the Wild West's Posse; or, Stella's Own Vigilance Committee.* Rough Rider Weekly, no. 105. New York: Street & Smith, 1906.

————. *King of the Wild West's Saint; or, The End of Polygamy in Utah.* Rough Rider Weekly, no. 92. New York: Street & Smith, 1906.

————. *King of the Wild West's Stolen Pinto Pony; or, Stella's Night of Terror.* Rough Rider Weekly, no. 157. New York: Street & Smith, 1907.

————. *Ted Strong, King of the Wild West; or, Winning a Town by a Ride.* Rough Rider Weekly, no. 79. New York: Street & Smith, 1905.

————. *Ted Strong's Wild West Show; or, The Making of an Indian Chief.* Young Rough Riders Weekly, no. 77. New York: Street & Smith, 1905.

————. *The Young Rough Rider's Double; or, Unmasking a Sham.* Young Rough Riders Weekly, no. 42. New York: Street & Smith, 1905.

————. *The Young Rough Rider's Fight to the Death; or, The Mad Hermit of Bear's Hole.* Young Rough Riders Weekly, no. 40. New York: Street & Smith, 1905.

————. *The Young Rough Rider's Foray; or, The Mad Horse of Raven Hill.* Young Rough Rider's Weekly, no. 39. New York: Street & Smith, 1905.

————. *The Young Rough Rider's Girl Guide; or, The Maid of the Mountains.* Young Rough Riders Weekly, no. 38. New York: Street & Smith, 1905.

————. *The Young Rough Rider's Indian Trail; or, Okanaga the Cheyenne.* Young Rough Riders Weekly, no. 41. New York: Street & Smith, 1905.

————. *The Young Rough Riders in the Rockies; or, A Fight in Midair.* Young Rough Riders Weekly, no. 38. New York: Street & Smith, 1905.

Taylor, Ned [W. Bert Foster]. *King of the Wild West's Buckskin Guide; or, Stella at the Grand Round-up.* Rough Riders Weekly, no. 125. New York: Street & Smith, 1906.

————. *King of the Wild West's Helping Hand; or, Stella, the Girl Range Rider.* Rough Rider Weekly, no. 124. New York: Street & Smith, 1906.

————. *King of the Wild West's Wild Goose Band; or, Stella's Long Flight on Skees.* Rough Riders Weekly, no. 119. New York: Street & Smith, 1906.

Taylor, Ned [St. George Rathborne]. *King of the Wild West's Drag-Net; or, Stella Shows Her Colors.* Rough Riders Weekly, no. 175. New York: Street & Smith, 1907.

————. *King of the Wild West's Shadow on the Wall; or, Stella and the "Masked Men."* Rough Rider Weekly, no. 158. New York: Street & Smith, 1907.

————. *King of the Wild West's Winged Witch; or, Stella in a New Role.* Rough Rider Weekly, no. 172. New York: Street & Smith, 1907.

————. *King of the Wild West Underground; or, Stella to the Rescue.* Rough Rider Weekly, no. 106. New York: Street & Smith, 1906.

————. *Ted Strong's Friends; or, The Trial of Ben Tremont.* The Young Rough Riders Weekly, no. 2. New York: Street & Smith, 1904.

————. *Ted Strong's Peril; or, Saved by a Girl.* The Young Rough Riders Weekly, no. 10. New York: Street & Smith, 1904.

————. *Ted Strong's Ride for Life; or, Caught in the Circle.* The Young Rough Riders Weekly, no. 5. New York: Street & Smith, 1904.

————. *Ted Strong's Rival; or, The Cowboys of Sunset Ranch.* The Young Rough Riders Weekly, no. 9. New York: Street & Smith, 1904.

————. *Ted Strong's Rough Riders; or, The Boys of Black Mountain.* The Young Rough Riders Weekly, no. 1. New York: Street & Smith, 1904.

————. *Ted Strong's Strategem; or, Saving a Boy's Honor.* The Young Rough Riders Weekly, no. 4. New York: Street & Smith, 1904.

————. *Ted Strong's Triumph; or, The End of the Contest.* The Young Rough Riders Weekly, no. 30. New York: Street & Smith, 1904.

————. *Ted Strong's War-Path; or, The Secret of the Red Cliffs.* The Young Rough Riders Weekly, no. 3. New York: Street & Smith, 1904.

————. *Ted Strong's Water-Sign; or, In Shoshonee Land.* The Young Rough Riders Weekly, no. 20. New York: Street & Smith, 1904.

————. *The Young Rough Riders in Kansas; or, The Trail of the Outlaw.* Young Rough Riders Weekly, no. 37. New York: Street & Smith, 1904.

Taylor, Ned [John A. Whitson]. *King of the Wild West's Bronco Ball Tossers; or, Stella Bluffs the Umpire.* Rough Riders Weekly, no. 159. New York: Street & Smith, 1907.

"Texas Jack" [Prentiss Ingraham]. *Ned Wylde, the Boy Scout.* Beadle's Pocket Library, no. 9. 1876. Reprint. N.Y.: Beadle & Adams, 1884.

Wheeler, Edward L. *Blonde Bill; or, Deadwood Dick's Home Base.* The Deadwood Dick Library, 3, no. 31. 1880. Reprint. Cleveland, Ohio: Arthur Westbrook, 1899.

————. *Bob Woolf, the Border Ruffian; or, The Girl Dead-Shot.* Beadle's Half Dime Library, 2, no. 32. New York: Beadle & Adams, 1878.

————. *Buckhorn Bill; or, The Red Rifle Team: A Tale of the Dakota Moonshiners.* Beadle's Half Dime Library, 3, no. 61. New York: Beadle & Adams, 1878.

————. *Buffalo Ben, the Prince of the Pistol; or, Deadwood Dick in Disguise.* The Deadwood Dick Library, 1, no. 4. 1877. Reprint. Cleveland, Ohio: Arthur Westbrook, 1899.

————. *The Buffalo Demon; or, The Border Vultures: A Tale of the Southwest.* The Deadwood Dick Library, 1, no. 3. 1878. Reprint. Cleveland, Ohio; Arthur Westbrook, 1899.

————. *Corduroy Charlie, the Boy Bravo; or, Deadwood Dick's Last Act.* The Deadwood Dick Library, 2, no. 16. 1879. Reprint. Cleveland, Ohio: Arthur Westbrook, 1899.

————. *Deadwood Dick as Detective.* The Deadwood Dick Library, 2, no. 24. 1879. Reprint. Cleveland, Ohio: Arthur Westbrook, 1899.

————. *Deadwood Dick of Deadwood.* The Deadwood Dick Library, 2, no. 17. 1879. Reprint. Cleveland, Ohio: Arthur Westbrook, 1899.

————. *Deadwood Dick on Deck; or, Calamity Jane, the Heroine of Whoop-Up.* The

Deadwood Dick Library, 2, no. 15. 1878. Reprint. Cleveland, Ohio: Arthur Westbrook, 1899.

———. *Deadwood Dick's Device.* The Deadwood Dick Library, 2, no. 21. 1879. Reprint. Cleveland, Ohio: Arthur Westbrook, 1899.

———. *Deadwood Dick's Doom.* The Deadwood Dick Library, 3, no. 39. 1881. Reprint. Cleveland, Ohio: Arthur Westbrook, 1899.

———. *Deadwood Dick's Dream; or, The Rivals of the Road.* Beadle's Half Dime Library, 8, no. 195. New York: Beadle & Adams, 1881.

———. *Deadwood Dick's Eagles; or, The Pards of Flood Bar.* The Deadwood Dick Library, 1, no. 12. 1878. Reprint. Cleveland, Ohio: Arthur Westbrook, 1899.

———. *Deadwood Dick's Mission.* The Deadwood Dick Library, 5, no. 61. 1882. Reprint. Cleveland, Ohio: Arthur Westbrook, 1899.

———. *Deadwood Dick, the Prince of the Road; or, The Black Rider of the Black Hills.* The Deadwood Dick Library, 1, no. 1. 1877. Reprint. Cleveland, Ohio: Arthur Westbrook, 1899.

———. *Deadwood Dick, Jr.'s Drop; or, The Sojourn at Satan's Spring.* Beadle's Half Dime Library, 27, no. 700. New York: Beadle & Adams, 1890.

———. *Deadwood Dick, Jr. in Texas; or, The Ghouls of Galveston.* Beadle's Half Dime Library, 21, no. 539. New York: Beadle & Adams, 1887.

———. *The Double Daggers; or, Deadwood Dick's Defiance.* The Deadwood Dick Library, 1, no. 2. 1879. Reprint. Cleveland, Ohio: Arthur Westbrook, 1899.

———. *Jim Bludsoe, Jr., the Boy Phoenix; or, Through to Death: A Story of City and Far Western Life.* Beadle's Half Dime Library, 3, no. 53. New York: Beadle & Adams, 1878.

———. *Old Avalanche, the Great Annihilator; or, Wild Edna, the Girl Brigand.* Beadle's Half Dime Library, 3, no. 45. New York: Beadle & Adams, 1878.

———. *Omaha Oll, the Masked Terror; or, Deadwood Dick in Danger.* The Deadwood Dick Library, 1, no. 10. 1878. Reprint. Cleveland, Ohio: Arthur Westbrook, 1899.

———. *The Phantom Miner; or, Deadwood Dick's Bonanza.* The Deadwood Dick Library, 1, no. 7. 1878. Reprint. Cleveland, Ohio: Arthur Westbrook, 1899.

———. *Wild Ivan, the Boy Claude Duval.* The Deadwood Dick Library, 1, no. 5. 1878. Reprint. Cleveland, Ohio: Arthur Westbrook, 1899.

Whittaker, Frederick. *The Mustang-Hunters; or, The Beautiful Amazon of the Hidden Valley: A Tale of the Staked Plains.* Beadle's Dime Novels, no. 226. New York: Beadle & Co., 1871.

Selected Pulp Magazines[1]

Ace-High Western Stories. Chicago: Fictioneers, 1933.

Far West. Costa Mesta, Calif.: Wright Publishing, 1978.

The Popular Magazine. New York: Street & Smith, 1903.

Ranch Romances. New York: The Clayton Magazines, 1924.

Smith's Magazine. New York: Street & Smith, 1905.

Star Western. Chicago: Popular Publications, 1943.

Super Western. Mass.: Periodical House, 1937.

Ten Cent Story Western Magazine. Chicago: Popular Publications, 1932.

Western Story Magazine. New York: Street & Smith, 1919.

Wild West Weekly. New York: Street & Smith, 1927.

Zane Grey's Western Magazine. New York: Dell, 1947.

[1]The dates are those of the magazines' first publication.

Letters

Erastus Flavel Beadle Papers. Rare Books and Manuscripts Division, The New York Public Library, Astor, Lenox, and Tilden Foundations.

Secondary Sources

Admari, Ralph. "The House that Beadle Built 1859-1869." *The American Book Collector,* 4 (1933): 221–26, 288–91; 5 (1934): 22–25, 60–63, 92–94.

Bacon, Daisy. "The Golden Age of the Iron Maiden." *The Roundup,* April 1975, pp. 1, 2, 7, 9, 16.

Beitz, Les. "Heyday of the Pulp Westerns." *True West,* February 1967, pp. 10–14, 58–59.

Berard, Ralph. "Confessions of a Pulpeteer." *The Writer,* May 1941, pp. 146–48.

Bishop, W. H. "Story-Paper Literature." *The Atlantic Monthly,* September 1879, pp. 383–93.

Bosworth, Allan R. "The Golden Age of Pulps." *The Atlantic Monthly,* July 1961, pp. 57–60.

Bragin, Charles. *Bibliography: Dime Novels 1860–1964.* Dime Novel Club, issue 63. Brooklyn, N.Y.: Charles Bragin, 1964.

Case, Robert Ormond. "The Difference Is Real People." *The Roundup,* October 1958, pp. 3–8.

Cook, William Wallace. *Plotto: A New Method of Plot Suggestion for Writers of Creative Fiction.* Battle Creek, Mich.: Ellis Publishing, 1928.

Curti, Merle. "Dime Novels and the American Tradition." *The Yale Review,* 26 (1937): 761–78.

Dinan, John A. *The Pulp Western: A Popular History of the Western Fiction Magazine in America.* I. O. Evans Studies in the Philosophy and Criticism of Literature, no. 2. San Bernardino, Calif.: The Borgo Press, 1983.

Dizer, John T., Jr. "Street and Smith Box M58." *Dime Novels Round-Up,* 46 (Aug. 1977): 78–84.

Durham, Philip. "Dime Novels: An American Heritage." *The Western Humanities Review,* 9 (1954–55): 33–43.

———. ed. *"Seth Jones," Edward Ellis and "Deadwood Dick on Deck," Edward L. Wheeler: Dime Novels.* New York: Odyssey, 1966.

Edwards, John Milton [William Wallace Cook]. *The Fiction Factory: "Being the Experience of a Writer who, for Twenty-two Years, Has Kept a Story-Mill Grinding Successfully. . . ."* Ridgewood, N.J.: The Editor Co., 1912.

Ellsworth, Fanny. "Trade Secrets." *The Writer,* May 1953, pp. 148–50.

French, Warren. "The Cowboy in the Dime Novel." *Studies in English,* 30 (1951): 219–34.

Goodstone, Tony, ed. *The Pulps: Fifty Years of American Popular Culture.* New York: Chelsea House, 1970.

Goulart, Ron. *The Adventurous Decade.* New Rochelle, N.Y.: Arlington House, 1975.

———. *Cheap Thrills: an Informal History of the Pulp Magazines.* New Rochelle, N.Y.: Arlington House, 1972.

The Greatest Publishing House in the World. New York: Street & Smith, n.d.

Gruber, Frank. *The Pulp Jungle.* Los Angeles: Sherbourne Press, 1967.

Guinon, J. P. "The Applause Column in Tip Top Weekly." *Dime Novel Round-Up,* 28 (January 1960): 2–5.

Harbaugh, T. C. *T. C. Harbaugh, Popular and Prolific Beadle Writer, Corrects Wrong Impression of Dime Novels and their Authors.* 1894. Reprint. Philadelphia: Chas. H. Austin, 1938.

Harvey, Charles M. "The Dime Novel in American Life." *The Atlantic Monthly*, July 1907, pp. 37–45.

Hersey, Harold Brainerd. *Pulpwood Editor: The Fabulous World of the Thriller Magazines Revealed by a Veteran Editor and Publisher*. 1937. Reprint. Westport, Conn.: Greenwood Press, 1974.

Ingraham, Prentiss. "Dime-Novel Writers: An Hour's Chat with One of Them." *Republican*, 21 April 1884, n.pg.

Jenks, George C. "Dime Novel Makers." *The Bookman*, 20 (1904): 108–14.

Johannsen, Albert. *The House of Beadle and Adams and its Dime and Nickel Novels: The Story of a Vanished Literature*. 2 vols. Norman: University of Oklahoma Press, 1950; supplement, 1962.

Jones, Daryl. *The Dime Novel Western*. Bowling Green, Ohio: Bowling Green University Popular Press, 1978.

Joscelyn, Archie. "The 'Dope Sheet' for Serials." *The Writer's Monthly*, August 1925, pp. 116–17.

———. "The Plot of the Serial Story." *The Writer's Monthly*, July 1925, pp. 3–7.

Knott, James E. "My Remembrances of Gilbert Patten." *Dime Novel Round-Up*, 24 (September 1956): 65–72.

Leithead, J. Edward. "Arietta: Heroine of Wild West Trails." *Dime Novel Round-Up*, 31 (April 1963): 32–37.

———. "Colonel Prentiss Ingraham." *Dime Novel Round-Up*, 32 (January 1964): 2–6.

———. "The Creator of Diamond Dick." *Dime Novel Round-Up*, 29 (August 1960): 66–68.

———. "John H. Whitson, Street and Smith Author." *Reckless Ralph's Dime Novel Round-Up*, 6 (December 1937): 1.

———. "Rough Rider Weekly and the Ted Strong Saga." *Dime Novel Round-Up*, 40 (July 1972): 1–28.

———. "Ted Strong and his Rough Riders." *Dime Novel Round-Up*, 29 (June 1961): 66–71; (July 1961): 76–81.

MacLean, Charles Agnew. *Charles Agnew MacLean "For Auld Lang Syne."* New York: Street & Smith, 1928.

Miller, W. C. "The First Diamond Dick Story." *Reckless Ralph's Dime Novel Round-Up*, 6 (June 1937): 1.

Newton, D. B. "Panic in the Pulps Launched WWA." *The Roundup*, May 1977, pp. 1–4.

Noel, Mary. *Villains Galore: The Heyday of the Popular Story Weekly*. New York: Macmillan, 1954.

Pachon, Stanley A. "William Wallace Cook." *Dime Novel Round-Up*, 25 (September 1957): 67–75.

Patten, Gilbert. *Frank Merriwell's "Father": An Autobiography*. Edited by Harriet Hinsdale. Norman: University of Oklahoma Press, 1964.

Pearson, Edmund. *Dime Novels; or, Following an Old Trail in Popular Literature*. 1929. Reprint. New York: Keinikat Press, 1968.

Reynolds, Quentin. *The Fiction Factory; or, From Pulp Row to Quality Street: The Story of 100 Years of Publishing at Street and Smith*. New York: Random House, 1955.

Robinson, Henry Morton. "Mr. Beadle's Books." *The Bookman*, 69 (1929): 18–24.

Skjelver, Mabel Cooper. "William Wallace Cook—The Marshall Years." *Dime Novel Round-Up*, 45 (April 1976): 34–45.

———. "William Wallace Cook: Dime Novelist." *Annals of Wyoming*, 49–50 (Spring 1977): 109–30.

Smith, Ralph P. "Barred by the Post Office." *Reckless Ralph's Dime Novel Round-Up*, 13 (October 1944): 1–3.

Stern, Madeleine B., ed. *Publishers for Mass Entertainment in Nineteenth Century America*. Boston: G. K. Hall, 1980.

Thompson, Thomas. "Strong, Silent and Stupid." *The Writer*, September 1953, pp. 305–06.

Turner, E. S. *Boys Will Be Boys: The Story of Sweeney Todd, Deadwood Dick, Sexton Blake, Billy Bunter, Dick Barton, et al.* Rev. ed. London: Michael Joseph, 1975.

Twain, Mark. *The Adventures of Huckleberry Finn*. London: Chatto & Windus, 1884.

White, Trentwell Mason. *How to Write for a Living*. 2nd ed. Boston: The Writer, 1947.

Whittaker, Frederick. *Dime Novels: A Defense by a Writer of Them*. 1884. Reprint. Philadelphia: Chas. H. Austin, 1938.

Young, Clint. "Reading for Westerns." *The Writer*, May 1953, pp. 157–58.

IV. WISTER, REMINGTON, AND HOUGH

PRIMARY SOURCES

Hough, Emerson. *The Covered Wagon*. New York: Appleton, 1922.

——. *54–40 or Fight*. 1909. Reprint. London: Hodder & Stoughton, [1924].

——. *The Girl at the Halfway House: A Story of the Plains*. New York: Appleton, 1900.

——. *Heart's Desire: The Story of a Contented Town, Certain Peculiar Citizens and Two Fortunate Lovers*. New York: Macmillan, 1905.

——. *North of 36*. New York: Appleton, 1923.

——. *The Passing of the Frontier: A Chronicle of the Old West*. New Haven: Yale University Press, 1918.

——. *The Story of the Cowboy*. The Story of the West Series. Edited by Ripley Hitchcock. New York: Appleton, 1897.

Remington, Frederic. *The Collected Writings of Frederic Remington*. Edited by Peggy and Harold Samuels. Garden City, N.Y.: Doubleday, 1979.

——. *Crooked Trails*. New York: Harper, 1898.

——. "A Few Words from Mr. Remington." *Collier's Weekly*, 18 March 1905, p. 16.

——. *Frederic Remington's Own West*. Edited by Harold McCracken. London: W. Failsham, 1960.

——. "Horses of the Plains." *The Century Magazine*, January 1889, pp. 332–43.

——. *The Illustrations of Frederic Remington*. Edited by Marta Jackson. New York: Crown, 1970.

——. *John Ermine of the Yellowstone*. New York: Macmillan, 1902.

——. *Pony Tracks*. 1895. Reprint. Norman: University of Oklahoma Press, 1961.

——. "A Scout with the Buffalo-Soldiers." *The Century Magazine*, April 1889, pp. 899–912.

——. *Sundown Leflare*. New York: Harper, 1899.

——. *The Way of an Indian*. London: Gay & Bird, 1906.

Wister, Owen. "The Evolution of the Cow-Puncher." *Harper's Monthly Magazine*, September 1895, pp. 602–17.

——. "Hank's Woman." *Harper's Weekly*, 27 August 1892, pp. 821–23.

——. *The Jimmyjohn Boss and Other Stories*. New York: Harper, 1900.

——. *Lin McLean*. New York: A. L. Burt, 1897.

——. *Members of the Family*. New York: Macmillan, 1911.

———. *Red Men and White*. New York: Grosset & Dunlap, 1895.

———. *Roosevelt: The Story of a Friendship, 1880–1919*. New York: Macmillan, 1930.

———. *The Virginian: A Horseman of the Plains*. New York: Macmillan, 1902.

———. *The West of Owen Wister: Selected Short Stories*. Edited by Robert L. Hough. Lincoln: University of Nebraska Press, 1972.

———. *When the West Was West*. London: Macmillan, 1928.

LETTERS AND DIARIES

Theodore Roosevelt Presidential Papers. Manuscript Division, The Library of Congress, Washington, D.C.

The Owen Wister Collection. Western History Research Center, The University of Wyoming.

Owen Wister Papers. Manuscript Division, Library of Congress, Washington, D.C.

SECONDARY SOURCES

Baigell, Matthew. *The Western Art of Frederic Remington*. New York: Ballantine, 1976.

Boatright, Mody C. "The American Myth Rides the Range: Owen Wister's Man on Horseback." *Southwest Review*, 36 (1951): 157–63.

Bode, Carl. "Henry James and Owen Wister." *American Literature*, 26 (1954–55): 250–52.

Card, H. L. *The Collector's Remington: A Series*, vol. 1. R.I.: n.p., 1946.

Erisman, Fred. *Frederick Remington*. Western Writers Series, no. 16. Boise: Boise State University, 1975.

Etulain, Richard W. *Owen Wister*. Western Writers Series, no. 7. Boise: Boise State College, 1973.

Guthrie, A. B., Jr. "Action, Sir, Action." Review of *Owen Wister Out West*, edited by Fanny Kemble Wister. *The Saturday Review of Literature*, 12 April 1958, pp. 56–57.

Hassrick, Peter H. *Frederic Remington: Paintings, Drawings, and Sculpture in the Amon Carter Museum and the Sid W. Richardson Foundation Collections*. New York: Harry N. Abrams, 1973.

Hollman, Clide. *Five Artists of the Old West*. New York: Hastings House, 1965.

Jussim, Estelle. *Frederic Remington, the Camera and the Old West*. Fort Worth: Amon Carter, 1983.

Lambert, Neal. "Owen Wister's 'Hank's Woman': The Writer and His Comment." *Western American Literature*, 4 (1969): 39–50.

———. "Owen Wister's Virginian: The Genesis of a Cultural Hero." *Western American Literature*, 6 (1971): 99–107.

McCracken, Harold, ed. *A Catalogue of the Frederic Remington Memorial Collection*. New York: The Knoedler Galleries, 1954.

———. *Frederic Remington: Artist of the Old West*. Philadelphia: J. B. Lippincott, 1947.

———. *The Frederic Remington Book: A Pictorial History of the West*. Garden City, N.Y.: Doubleday, 1966.

"Remington Number." *Collier's Weekly*, 18 March 1905.

Robinson, Forrester G. "The Roosevelt-Wister Connection: Some Notes on the West and the Uses of History." *Western American Literature*, 14 (1979): 95–114.

Samuels, Peggy and Harold. *Frederic Remington: A Biography*. Garden City, N.Y.: Doubleday, 1982.

Stokes, Frances K. W. *My Father Owen Wister—and—Ten Letters Written by Owen Wister to his Mother during his First Trip to Wyoming in 1885*. Laramie, Wyo.: n.p., 1952.

Taft, Robert. *Artists and Illustrators of the Old West, 1850–1900*. New York: Scribner's 1953.

Vorpahl, Ben Merchant. *Frederic Remington and the West: With the Eye of the Mind*. Austin: University of Texas Press, 1978.

———. *My Dear Wister: The Frederic Remington—Owen Wister Letters*. Palo Alto: American West Publishing Co., 1972.

White, G. Edward. *The Eastern Establishment and the Western Experience: The West of Frederic Remington, Theodore Roosevelt, and Owen Wister*. New Haven: Yale University Press, 1968.

Wister, Fanny Kemble, ed. *Owen Wister Out West: His Journals and Letters*. Chicago: University of Chicago Press, 1958.

Wylder, Delbert E. *Emerson Hough*. Southwest Writers Series, no. 19. Austin Tex.: Steck-Vaughan, 1969.

———. *Emerson Hough*. Twayne United States Authors Series, no. 397. Boston: Twayne, 1981.

V. GREY, FAUST, AND HAYCOX

Primary Sources

Selected Works by Grey, Faust, and Haycox

Brand, Max [Frederick Faust]. *Black Jack*. London: Hodder & Stoughton, [1926].

———. *The Blue Jay*. New York: Dodd, Mead, 1927.

———. *The Border Kid*. London: Hodder & Stoughton, 1941.

———. *Clung*. London: Hodder & Stoughton, [1924].

———. *Crooked Horn*. London: Hodder & Stoughton, 1934.

———. *Dan Barry's Daughter*. New York: Putnam's, 1924.

———. *Destry Rides Again*. New York: Dodd, Mead, 1930.

———. *Fightin' Fool*. New York: Dodd, Mead, 1939.

———. *Fire-Brain*. New York: Putnam's, 1926.

———. *The Garden of Eden*. London: Hodder & Stoughton, [1927].

———. *Gun Gentlemen*. 1928. Reprint. London: Hodder & Stoughton, n.d.

———. *The Gun Tamer*. New York: Dodd, Mead, 1929.

———. *Happy Jack*. New York: Dodd, Mead, 1936.

———. *The Happy Valley*. New York: Dodd, Mead, 1931.

———. *The Jackson Trail*. New York: Dodd, Mead, 1932.

———. *The Longhorn Feud*. New York: Dodd, Mead, 1933.

———. *Mystery Ranch*. New York: Dodd, Mead, 1930.

———. *The Night Horseman*. 1920. Reprint. New York: Pocket Books, 1954.

———. *The Notebooks and Poems of "Max Brand."* Edited by John Schoolcraft. New York: Dodd, Mead, 1957.

———. *The Rancher's Revenge*. New York: Dodd, Mead, 1934.

———. *Riders of the Plains*. New York: Dodd, Mead, 1940.

———. *Rustlers of Beacon Creek*. New York: Dodd, Mead, 1935.

———. *The Seventh Man*. New York: Putnam's, 1921.

————. *Silvertip*. London: Hodder & Stoughton, 1942.

————. *Silvertip's Roundup*. 1943. Reprint. London: Hodder & Stoughton, 1945.

————. *Silvertip's Search*. 1945. Reprint. London: Hodder & Stoughton, 1948.

————. *Silvertip's Strike*. 1942. Reprint. London: Hodder & Stoughton, 1944.

————. *Singing Guns*. New York: Dodd, Mead, 1938.

————. *Steve Train's Ordeal*. New York: Dodd, Mead, 1952.

————. *The Stolen Stallion*. 1945. Reprint. London: Hodder & Stoughton, 1949.

————. *Torture Trail*. 1965. Reprint. London: Hodder & Stoughton, 1966.

————. *Trailin'*. New York: Putnam's, 1920.

————. *Trouble Trail*. New York: Dodd, Mead, 1937.

————. *The Untamed*. New York: Putnam's, 1919.

————. "Wine on the Desert." In *Wine on the Desert and Other Stories*. New York: Dodd, Mead, 1940, pp. 1–12.

Evans, Evan [Frederick Faust]. *Montana Rides!* New York: Harper, 1933.

————. *Montana Rides Again*. New York: Harper, 1934.

————. *The Song of the Whip*. New York: Harper, 1936.

Grey, Zane. *Betty Zane*. 1903. Reprint. London: Hodder & Stoughton, n.d.

————. *The Border Legion*. New York: Harper, 1916.

————. "Breaking Through: the Story of my own Life." *The American Magazine*, July 1924, pp. 11–13, 76–80.

————. *The Call of the Canyon*. 1924. Reprint. London: Hodder & Stoughton, n.d.

————. *Code of the West*. London: Hodder & Stoughton, 1934.

————. *The Day of the Beast*. New York: Harper, 1922.

————. *The Desert Crucible*. *The Argosy*, May 1915, pp. 225–57; June 1915, pp. 557–84; July 1915, pp. 814–35; August 1915, pp. 115–31; September 1915, pp. 400–20.

————. *Desert Gold*. New York: Harper, 1913.

————. *The Desert of Wheat*. New York: Harper, 1919.

————. *The Drift Fence*. New York: Harper, 1933.

————. *The Dude Ranger*. New York: Harper, [1951].

————. *Fighting Caravans*. New York: Harper, 1929.

————. *Forlorn River*. New York: Harper, 1927.

————. *The Heritage of the Desert*. 1910. Reprint. Roslyn, N.Y.: Walter J. Black, n.d.

————. *Horse Heaven Hill*. New York: Harper, 1959.

————. *Knights of the Range*. New York: Harper, 1939.

————. *The Last of the Plainsmen*. London: Hodder & Stoughton, 1908.

————. *The Last Trail*. 1907. Reprint. London: T. Werner Laurie, 1920.

————. *The Light of Western Stars: A Romance*. New York: Harper, 1914.

————. *The Lone Star Ranger*. New York: Harper, 1915.

————. *Majesty's Rancho*. New York: Harper, [1942].

————. *The Man of the Forest*. New York: Harper, 1920.

————. "The Man who Influenced Me Most." *The American Magazine*, August 1926, pp. 52–55, 130–36.

————. *The Mysterious Rider*. 1921. Reprint. London: Hodder & Stoughton, n.d.

————. *"Nevada": A Romance of the West*. New York: Harper, 1928.

————. *The Rainbow Trail: A Romance*. New York: Harper, 1915.

————. *Riders of the Purple Sage: A Novel*. New York: Harper, 1912.

————. *The Shepherd of Guadaloupe*. London: Hodder & Stoughton, [1930].

————. *The Spirit of the Border: A Romance of the Early Settlers in the Ohio Valley*. 1906. Reprint. London: Hodder & Stoughton, n.d.

———. *Sunset Pass*. New York: Harper, 1931.

———. *The Thundering Herd*. New York: Harper, 1925.

———. *To the Last Man*. New York: Harper, [1922].

———. *Under the Tonto Rim*. New York: Harper, 1926.

———. *The Vanishing American*. *The Ladies' Home Journal*. November 1922, pp. 3–5, 204–13; December 1922, pp. 21–23, 190–99; January 1923, pp. 20–21, 139–45; February 1923, pp. 24–25, 163–73; March 1923, pp. 24–25, 94–104; April 1923, pp. 32–33, 222–35.

———. *The Vanishing American*. New York: Harper, 1925.

———. *Wanderer of the Wasteland*. New York: Harper, 1923.

———. *Western Union*. New York: Harper, 1939.

———. "What the Desert Means to Me." *The American Magazine*, November 1924, pp. 5–8, 72–78.

———. *Wildfire*. New York: Harper, 1917.

———. *Wyoming*. 1953. Reprint. London: Hodder & Stoughton, 1954.

———. *Zane Grey's Indian Tales*. Edited by Loren Grey. London: NEL, 1977.

Haycox, Ernest. *Action by Night*. London: Hodder & Stoughton, 1943.

———. *The Adventurers*. 1955. Reprint. New York: Bantam, 1960.

———. *Alder Gulch*. 1942. Reprint. New York: Signet-NAL, 1978.

———. *The Best Western Stories of Ernest Haycox*. New York: Signet-NAL, 1975.

———. *The Border Trumpet*. 1939. Reprint. London: Hodder & Stoughton, 1940.

———. *Bugles in the Afternoon*. London: Hodder & Stoughton, 1944.

———. *Canyon Passage*. London: Hodder & Stoughton, 1945.

———. *Chaffee of Roaring Horse*. Garden City, N.Y.: Doubleday, 1930.

———. *Dead Man Range*. 1930. Reprint. New York: Signet-NAL, 1975.

———. *Deep West*. London: Stanley Paul, [1937].

———. *The Earthbreakers*. 1952. Reprint. London: Corgi-Transworld, 1960.

———. *The Feudists*. New York: Signet-NAL, [1960].

———. *Free Grass*. Garden City, N.Y.: Doubleday, Doran, 1929.

———. *Head of the Mountain*. New York: Paperback Library, 1972.

———. "Is There a Northwest?" In *Northwest Harvest: A Regional Stock-Taking*. Edited by Victor Lowitt Oates Chittick. New York: Macmillan, 1948, pp. 39–51.

———. *Long Storm*. 1946. Reprint. London: Hodder & Stoughton, 1947.

———. *Man in the Saddle*. 1938. Reprint. London: Hodder & Stoughton, 1939.

———. "One of the Fish." *Top-Notch*, 1 February 1923, pp. 82–92.

———. *Riders West*. Garden City, N.Y.: Doubleday, 1934.

———. *Rim of the Desert*. London: Hodder & Stoughton, 1941.

———. *Saddle and Ride*. London: Hodder & Stoughton, 1940.

———. "Sir Walter, Excepting. . . ." *Writer's Digest*, February 1942, pp. 11–15.

———. *Stagecoach*. 1949. Reprint. New York: Signet-NAL, 1973.

———. *Starlight Rider*. Garden City, N.Y.: Doubleday, 1933.

———. *Sundown Jim*. London: Stanley Paul, [1938].

———. *Trail Smoke*. Garden City, N.Y.: Doubleday, 1936.

———. *Trouble Shooter*. London: Stanley Paul, [1937].

———. *Whispering Range*. Garden City, N.Y.: Doubleday, 1930.

———. *The Wild Bunch*. 1943. Reprint. London: Hodder & Stoughton, 1944.

———. "Wilderness Anchorage." *Western Story Magazine*, 22 March 1924, pp. 70–79.

———. "Writers: Dealers in Emotions." *Library Journal*, 15 February 1946, pp. 248–51.

Selected Magazines Publishing Grey, Faust, and Haycox[2]

Adventure. New York: Butterick, 1933.
All-Story Weekly. New York: Frank A. Munsey, 1916, 1918–20.
All-Story Cavalier Weekly. New York: Frank A. Munsey, 1914.
The Argosy. New York: Frank A. Munsey, 1915, 1932, 1934, 1936.
Argosy–All Story Weekly. New York: Frank A. Munsey, 1920–23.
Collier's Weekly. New York: Crowell-Collier, 1928, 1933–43.
The Country Gentleman. Philadelphia: Curtis Publishing, 1916–19, 1921–23, 1928.
Esquire. Chicago: Esquire, 1950–51.
The Ladies' Home Journal. Philadelphia: Curtis Publishing, 1921–26.
McCall's Magazine. New York: McCall, 1925, 1930.
McClure's Magazine. New York: McClure, 1920.
Munsey's Magazine. New York: Frank A. Munsey, 1913.
Pictorial Review. New York: Pictorial Review, 1932.
The Popular Magazine. New York: Street & Smith, 1910, 1913.
The Saturday Evening Post. Philadelphia: Curtis Publishing, 1943, 1945.
Short Stories. Garden City, N.Y.: Doubleday, 1934.
Top-Notch. New York: Street & Smith, 1923.
West. Garden City, N.Y.: Doubleday, 1928–30.
Western Story Magazine. New York: Street & Smith, 1922–33.

LETTERS AND MANUSCRIPTS

Robert Hobart Davis Papers. Rare Books and Manuscripts Division, The New York Public Library, Astor, Lenox, and Tilden Foundations.
Zane Grey Papers. Manuscripts Division, The Library of Congress, Washington, D.C.

SECONDARY SOURCES

Bacon, Leonard. "Frederick Faust." Obituary, *The Saturday Review of Literature*, 27 May 1944, pp. 28–29.
Bacon, Martha. "Destry and Dionysus." *The Atlantic Monthly*, July 1955, pp. 72–74.
Bloodworth, William. "Max Brand." In *Fifty Western Writers: A Bio-Bibliographical Sourcebook*. Edited by Richard Etulain and Fred Erisman. Westport, Conn.: Greenwood Press, 1982, pp. 32–41.
Dodd, Edward H., Jr. "Twenty-Five Million Words." *Publishers' Weekly*, 26 March 1938, pp. 1358–60.
Easton, Robert. *Max Brand: The Big "Westerner."* Norman: University of Oklahoma Press, 1970.
"Ernest Haycox Memorial Number." *The Call Number*. vol. 25 (Fall 1963—Spring 1964).
Etulain, Richard W. "A Dedication to the Memory of Zane Grey, 1872–1939." *Arizona and the West*, 12 (1970): 217–20.
———. "The Literary Career of a Western Writer: Ernest Haycox, 1899–1950." Dissertation, University of Oregon, 1966.
Fargo, James. "The Western and Ernest Haycox." *The Prairie Schooner*, 26 (1952): 177–84.

[2]The dates are those of the issues which I have consulted.

Gale, Robert L. "Ernest Haycox." In *Fifty Western Writers: A Bio-Bibliographical Sourcebook.* Edited by Richard Etulain and Fred Erisman. Westport, Conn.: Greenwood Press, 1982, pp. 183–93

Gruber, Frank. *Zane Grey: A Biography.* New York: The World Publishing Co., 1970.

Hart, Harlow Irving. "The Most Popular Authors of Fiction in the Post-War Period, 1919–1926." *Publishers' Weekly,* 12 March 1927, pp. 1045–53.

Haycox, Jill Marie. "Introduction." *The Border Trumpet.* N.p.: Gregg Press, 1978.

————. "Introduction." *Canyon Passage.* N.p.: Gregg Press, 1979.

————. "Introduction." *The Earthbreakers.* N.p.: Gregg Press, 1979.

Jackson, Carlton. *Zane Grey.* Twayne's United States Authors Series, no. 218. Boston: Twayne, 1973.

Karr, Jean. *Zane Grey: Man of the West.* Surrey: The World's Work, 1951.

London, Jack. "Bâtard." In *The Faith of Men, and Other Stories.* London: Heinemann, 1904, pp. 171–79.

Marshall, Jim. "Books and Saddles." *Collier's Weekly,* 29 November 1941, pp. 13, 64.

Newton, D. B. "Letters to a Graduate Student." *The Roundup,* November 1965, pp. 5, 6, 17.

Nolan, William F. "The Phenomenon of Max Brand." *The Roundup,* 7 July 1976, pp. 6–11.

Richardson, Darrell C., ed. *Max Brand: The Man and his Work.* Los Angeles: Fantasy Publishing Co., 1952.

Ronald, Ann. *Zane Grey.* Western Writers Series, no. 17. Boise: Boise State University, 1975.

Scott, Kenneth W. *Zane Grey: Born to the West: A Reference Guide.* Boston: G. K. Hall, 1979.

Stevens, James, and Davis, H. L. *Status Rerum: A Manifesto, upon the Present Condition of Northwestern Literature, Containing Several Near-Libelous Utterances, upon Persons in the Public Eye.* The Dalles, Ore.: n.p., 1927.

Topping, Gary. "Zane Grey: A Literary Reassessment." *Western American Literature,* 13 (1978): 51–64.

Werner, W. L. Letter. *The Saturday Review of Literature,* 28 February 1925, p. 570.

Whipple, T. K. "American Sagas." *The Saturday Review of Literature,* 7 February 1925, pp. 505–6.

————. *Study Out the Land: Essays.* 1931. Reprint. Berkeley: University of California Press, 1943.

VI. LE MAY, SCHAEFER, AND L'AMOUR

PRIMARY SOURCES

Burns, Tex [Louis L'Amour]. *Hopalong Cassidy and the Riders of High Rock.* 1951. Reprint. London: Hodder & Stoughton, 1952.

————. *Hopalong Cassidy and the Rustlers of West Fork.* London: Hodder & Stoughton, 1951.

————. *Hopalong Cassidy and the Trail to Seven Pines.* 1951. Reprint. London: Hodder & Stoughton, 1952.

————. *Hopalong Cassidy, Trouble-Shooter.* 1952. Reprint. London: Hodder & Stoughton, 1953.

L'Amour, Louis. *The Burning Hills.* 1956. Reprint. London: Corgi-Transworld, 1957.

————. *The Daybreakers.* 1960. Reprint. London: Corgi-Transworld, 1972.

————. *The Ferguson Rifle.* London: Corgi-Transworld, 1973.

————. *The First Fast Draw.* New York: Bantam, 1959.

————. *Flint.* 1960. Reprint. London: Corgi-Transworld, 1961.

————. *Galloway.* New York: Bantam, 1970.

————. *Guns of the Timberlands.* 1955. Reprint. London: Hammond, 1965.

————. *Heller with a Gun.* 1955. Reprint. [London]: Fawcett, [1956].

————. *Hondo.* [London]: Gold Medal-Fawcett, 1953.

————. *How the West Was Won.* 1962. Reprint. London: Hale, 1976.

————. *Jubal Sackett.* New York: Bantam, 1985.

————. *The Key-Lock Man.* 1965. Reprint. London: Corgi-Transworld, 1966.

————. *Kilkenny.* New York: Ace Books, 1954.

————. *Lando.* 1962. Reprint. London: Corgi-Transworld, 1963.

————. *Last Stand at Papago Wells.* [London]: Gold Medal-Fawcett, 1958.

————. "Lit a Shuck for Texas." *Thrilling Western,* Spring 1949, pp. 32–39.

————. *The Lonely Men.* 1969. Reprint. London: Hale, 1981.

————. *Lonely on the Mountain.* 1980. Reprint. London: Corgi-Transworld, 1981.

————. *The Man from Broken Hills.* London: Corgi-Transworld, 1976.

————. *Mojave Crossing.* London: Corgi-Transworld, 1964.

————. *Mustang Man.* London: Corgi-Transworld, 1966.

————. *Ride the Dark Trail.* London: Corgi-Transworld, 1972.

————. *Sackett.* New York: Bantam, 1961.

————. *The Sackett Brand.* New York: Bantam, 1965.

————. *Sackett's Land.* 1974. Reprint. New York: Bantam, 1975.

————. *Shalako.* London: Corgi-Transworld, 1962.

————. *Sitka.* 1957. Reprint. New York: Bantam, 1958.

————. *The Sky-Liners.* 1967. Reprint. London: Hale, 1978.

————. *Taggart.* New York: Bantam, 1959.

————. *The Tall Stranger.* [London]: Gold Medal-Fawcett, [1959].

————. *To the Far Blue Mountains.* 1976. Reprint. London: Corgi-Transworld, 1977.

————. *To Tame a Land.* [London]: Gold Medal-Fawcett, [1956].

————. *Treasure Mountain.* 1972. Reprint. London: Corgi-Transworld, 1973.

————. *Westward the Tide.* Kingswood, Surrey: The World's Work, 1950.

————. *Yondering.* New York: Bantam, 1980.

Le May, Alan. *Bug Eye.* New York: Farrar & Rinehart, [1931].

————. *By Dim and Flaring Lamps.* 1962. Reprint. London: Collins, 1963.

————. *Cattle Kingdom.* New York: Farrar & Rinehart, [1933].

————. *Gunsight Trail.* New York: Farrar & Rinehart, [1931].

————. *Painted Ponies.* London: Cassell, 1927.

————. *The Searchers.* 1954. Reprint. London: Collins, 1955.

————. *The Smoky Years.* London: Collins, 1935.

————. *Thunder in the Dust.* New York: Farrar & Rinehart, [1934].

————. *The Unforgiven.* 1957. Reprint. London: Collins. 1958.

————. *Useless Cowboy.* 1943. Reprint. London: Collins, 1944.

————. *Winter Range.* New York: Farrar & Rinehart, [1932].

Mayo, Jim [Louis L'Amour]. "Fork Your Own Broncs." *Thrilling Ranch Stories,* October 1947, pp. 37–43.

————. "McQueen of the Tumbling K." *Thrilling Western,* Summer 1948, pp. 54–64.

————. "Roundup in Texas." *Thrilling Western,* Summer 1949, pp. 46–56.

————. *Showdown at Yellow Butte.* New York: Ace Books, 1953.

———. "Showdown on the Tumbling T." *Thrilling Western,* January 1952, pp. 2–21.

———. *Utah Blaine.* New York: Ace Books, 1954.

Mulford, Clarence Edward. *Bar–20.* London: Hodder & Stoughton, [1914].

———. *The Coming of Cassidy—and the Others.* Chicago: A. C. McClurg, 1913.

———. *Hopalong Cassidy Takes Cards.* Garden City, N.Y.: Doubleday, 1937.

Schaefer, Jack. *The Big Range.* 1953. Reprint. London: Deutsch, 1955.

———. *The Canyon and Other Stories.* 1953. Reprint. London: Deutsch, 1955.

———. *Company of Cowards.* 1957. Reprint. London: Deutsch, 1958.

———. *First Blood.* 1953. Reprint. London: Deutsch, 1954.

———. *Heroes without Glory: Some Goodmen of the Old West.* 1965. Reprint. London: Deutsch, 1966.

———. *The Kean Land and Other Stories.* 1959. Reprint. London: Deutsch, 1960.

———. *Mavericks.* 1967. Reprint. London: Deutsch, 1968.

———. *Monte Walsh.* 1963. Reprint. London: Deutsch, 1965.

———. "A New Direction." *Western American Literature,* 10 (1976): 265–72.

———. *Old Ramon.* 1960. Reprint. London: Deutsch, 1962.

———. *Shane.* 1949. Reprint. London: Deutsch, 1954.

———, ed. *Out West.* 2 vols. 1955, 1961. Reprint. London: Mayflower-Dell, 1965.

Secondary Sources

Bannon, Barbara A. "Louis L'Amour." *Publishers' Weekly,* 8 Oct. 1973, pp. 56–57.

Cleary, Michael. "Jack Schaefer: The Evolution of Pessimism." *Western American Literature,* 14 (1979): 33–47.

Erisman, Fred. "Jack Schaefer: The Writer as Ecologist." *Western American Literature,* 13 (1978), 3–13.

Folsom, James K. "*Shane* and *Hud*: Two Stories in Search of a Medium." *The Western Humanities Review,* 24 (1970): 359–72.

Gottschalk, Earl C. "Eggheads May Shun Novels by L'Amour; Millions Love Them." *The Wall Street Journal,* 19 January 1978, p. 10, col. 3.

Haslam, Gerald. *Jack Schaefer.* Western Writers Series, no. 20. Boise: Boise State University, 1975.

Keith, Harold. "Louis L'Amour: Man of the West." *The Roundup,* December 1975, pp. 1, 2, 4, 12; January 1976, pp. 8, 9, 11; February 1976, pp. 4, 5.

Klaschus, Candace. "Louis L'Amour: The Writer as Teacher." Dissertation, University of New Mexico, 1982.

Marsden, Michael T. "The Concept of the Family in the Fiction of Louis L'Amour." *North Dakota Quarterly,* 46 (Summer 1978): 12–21.

———. "Louis L'Amour." In *Fifty Western Writers: A Bio-Bibliographical Sourcebook.* Edited by Richard Etulain and Fred Erisman. Westport, Conn.: Greenwood Press, 1982, pp. 257–67.

———. "*Shane*: From Magazine Serial to American Classic." *South Dakota Review,* 15 (Winter 1977–78): 59–67.

Nesbitt, John D. "Change of Purpose in the Novels of Louis L'Amour." *Western American Literature,* 13 (1978): 65–81.

Nuwer, Henry J. "An Interview with Schaefer." *South Dakota Review,* 11 (Spring 1973): 48–58.

Pilkington, William T. "LeMay, Alan." In *Contemporary Western Writers.* Edited by James Vinson and Daniel Kilpatrick. London: St. James, 1982, pp. 486–89.

Reed, J. D. "The Homer of the Oater." *Time,* 1 December 1980, n.pg.

Work, James C., ed. *Shane: The Critical Edition*. Lincoln: University of Nebraska Press, 1984.

VII. ANTI-WESTERN WESTERNS

PRIMARY SOURCES

Abbey, Edward. *The Brave Cowboy*. 1956. Reprint. London: Eyre & Spottiswoode, 1957.
Clark, Walter Van Tilburg. *The Ox-Bow Incident*. 1940. Reprint. London: Gollancz, 1941.
Day, Robert. *The Last Cattle Drive*. 1977. Reprint. New York: Avon, 1978.
Doctorow, E. L. *Welcome to Hard Times*. New York: Simon & Schuster, 1960.
Edson, J. T. *The Trouble Busters*. 1965. Reprint. London: Hale, 1975.
———. *The Ysabel Kid*. London: Brown, Watson, [1964].
Flynn, Robert. *North to Yesterday*. London: Hutchinson, 1967.
Gilman, George G. *Edge: The Loner*. 1971. Reprint. London: NEL, 1976.
———. *Edge: Slaughter Road*. London: NEL, 1977.
Herlihy, James Leo. *Midnight Cowboy*. 1965. Reprint. London: Cape, 1966.
McMurtry, Larry. *Horseman, Pass By*. New York: Harper, 1961.
Markson, David. *The Ballad of Dingus Magee*. 1965. Reprint. London: Anthony Blond, 1967.
Miller, Arthur. *The Misfits*. London: Secker & Warburg, 1961.
Reed, Ishmael. *Yellow Back Radio Broke-Down*. 1969. Reprint. London: Allison & Busby, 1971.
Seelye, John. *The Kid*. London: Chatto & Windus, 1972.
Smith, H. Allen. *The Return of the Virginian*. Garden City, N.Y.: Doubleday, 1974.
Voss, George L. *The Man who Believed in the Code of the West*. New York: St. Martin's, 1975.
Ward, Robert. *Cattle Annie and Little Britches*. 1977. Reprint. London: Corgi-Transworld, 1979.
West, Nathanael. *The Day of the Locust*. 1939. Reprint. London: The Grey Walls Press, 1951.

SECONDARY SOURCES

Cleary, Michael. "John Seelye's *The Kid*: Western Satire and Literary Reassessment." *South Dakota Review*, 17 (Winter 1979–80): 23–43.
"Conversations with Western American Novelists: Walter Van Tilburg Clark." *South Dakota Review*, 9 (Spring 1971): 27–38.
Emblidge, David. "Marching Backward into the Future: Progress as Illusion in Doctorow's Novels." *Southwest Review*, 62 (1977): 397–404.
Fiedler, Leslie A. "Malamud's Travesty Western." *Novel*, 10 (1977): 212–19.
Keyes, John. "Personality in the Land of Wish: Popular Motifs in Nathanael West's *The Day of the Locust*." *The University of Windsor Review*, 15 (1979–80): 38–50.
McMurtry, Larry. "Cowboys, Movies, Myths, and Cadillacs: Realism in the Western." In *Man and the Movies*. Edited by W. R. Robinson. Baton Rouge: Louisiana State University Press, 1967, pp. 46–52.
Mizener, Arthur. "The New Romance." *The Southern Review*, 8 (January 1972): 106–17.

Olderman, Raymond. *Beyond the Waste Land: A Study of the American Novel in the Nineteen-Sixties.* New Haven: Yale University Press, 1972.

Peavy, Charles D. "Songs of Innocence and Experience: Herlihy's Midnight Cowboy." *Forum (Houston),* 13 (Winter 1976): 62–67.

Woolf, Michael P. "The Madman as Hero in Contemporary American Fiction." *Journal of American Studies,* 10 (1976): 257–69.

Index

CHRISTINE BOLD received her M.A. from the University of Edinburgh and her Ph.D. from University College London, and is currently an assistant professor at the University of Alberta in Canada. Her articles on the Western have appeared in several scholarly journals.